Helping Students Graduate:

A Strategic Approach to Dropout Prevention

Jay Smink and Franklin P. Schargel

EYE ON EDUCATION
6 DEPOT WAY WEST, SUITE 106
LARCHMONT, NY 10538
(914) 833–0551
(914) 833–0761 fax
www.eyeoneducation.com

Library of Congress Cataloging-in-Publication Data

Helping students graduate: a strategic approach to dropout prevention/ [edited by] Jay Smink and Franklin P. Schargel.
　　　p. cm.
Includes bibliographical references.
ISBN 1-930556-75-6
1. Dropouts--United States--Prevention. 2. Motivation in education--United States. 3. School improvement programs--United States. 4. Educational change--United States. I. Smink, Jay. II. Schargel, Franklin P.

LC143.H42 2004
373.12'913'0973--dc22

2004040428

10 9 8 7 6 5 4 3 2

Editorial and production services provided by
Richard H. Adin Freelance Editorial Services
52 Oakwood Blvd., Poughkeepsie, NY 12603-4112
(845-471-3566)

Also Available from EYE ON EDUCATION

Dropout Prevention Tools
Franklin P. Schargel

Strategies to Help Solve Our School Dropout Problem
Franklin P. Schargel and Jay Smink

At-Risk Students:
Reaching and Teaching Them, 2nd Edition
Richard Sagor and Jonas Cox

Achievement Now!
How to Assure No Child is Left Behind
Dr. Donald J. Fielder

Student Transitions from Middle to High School:
Improving Achievement and Creating a Safer Environment
J. Allen Queen

The Directory of Programs for Students At Risk
Thomas Williams

Constructivist Strategies:
Meeting Standards and Engaging Adolescent Minds
Foote, Vermette, and Battaglia

Beyond Vocational Education: Career Majors, Tech Prep,
Schools Within Schools, Magnet Schools, and Academies
David Pucel

Dealing with Difficult Parents
(And with Parents in Difficult Situations)
Todd Whitaker and Douglas Fiore

101 "Answers" for New Teachers and Their Mentors:
Effective Teaching Tips for Daily Classroom Use
Annette Breaux

About the National Dropout Prevention Center and Network

The National Dropout Prevention Center/Network (NDPC/N) serves as a research center and resource network for practitioners, researchers, and policy makers to reshape school and community environments to meet the needs of youth in at-risk situations, including students with disabilities so they receive the quality education and services necessary to succeed academically and graduate from high school. NDPC/N is a well-established national resource for sharing solutions for student success. It does so through its clearinghouse function, active research projects, publications, and a variety of professional development activities. NDPC/N also conducts a variety of third-party evaluations and Program Assessment and Reviews (PAR). The PAR process helps schools develop the capacity for self-directed, continuous school improvement with an emphasis on improving student academic achievement and increasing the graduation rate. By promoting awareness of successful programs and policies related to dropout prevention, the work of NDPC/N and its members has made an impact on education from the local to the national level.

NDPC/N is the repository of the most current information on dropout prevention, providing the best information in the following ways:

- ◆ Research-based, yet practical, publications based on the successful work of practitioners and researchers from the field.
- ◆ Personal assistance with finding the answers you need, when you need them.

- Our Web site, www.dropoutprevention.org, contains the latest statistics, model programs, effective strategies information, and other useful links and articles.

NDPC/N is actively involved in improving programs and services provided to youth and families in at-risk situations by:

- Conducting third-party evaluations.
- Providing project leadership in local and multistate demonstration projects.
- Developing research-based tools to improve teaching and learning.

Membership in the National Dropout Prevention Network offers the following benefits:

- Quarterly thematic issues of the *National Dropout Prevention Newsletter* provide information about current programs and resources that can enhance and support dropout prevention efforts.
- *Dropout Prevention Update* is an electronic monthly newsletter containing links to the latest information on grants, policy, the 15 effective strategies, and resources related to at-risk youth.
- *The Journal of At-Risk Issues* provides an arena for scholars to share their research and application about issues related to youth from at-risk situations.
- *The International Journal on School Disaffection* is a forum for analyzing the roots of disaffection in the myriad contexts it is found and exploring the commonalities that exist in systems across the globe.
- A complimentary copy of each of the latest NDPC/N publications—whether a book, research report, or practical guidebook—each item offers professional insight into a variety of dropout prevention strategies.

Acknowledgments

While only the authors' names appear on the front cover (and the authors bear responsibility for any errors or omissions), this book is a collaborative effort.

Our first acknowledgment goes to the staff at the National Dropout Prevention Center, especially those senior staff who contributed to several sections about the fifteen strategies. Patricia "Pat" Cloud Duttweiler wrote about systemic renewal, professional development, and out-of-school experiences; Marilyn Madden, family involvement and violence prevention; Marty Duckenfield, service learning; Linda Shirley, diverse learning styles and multiple intelligences; Jan Wright, early childhood education; and Cheryl Lane, individualized learning. We also extend a special note of gratitude to Peg Chrestman for her tireless word processing assistance and for editing the initial drafts.

In addition to these professional leaders at the Center, hundreds of other educational, community, and business leaders across the nation have given vision and direction to successful dropout prevention programs in local schools. Although we cannot name them all, several appear as contact persons in the sections describing effective strategies. The involvement of these innovative schools in numerous National Dropout Prevention Center and Network activities afforded the Center's staff the opportunity to witness the success of different strategies with students in at-risk situations. As local school staff engaged in research, demonstration projects, and professional development activities, the Center's staff and the authors studied the strategies compiled here. On behalf of the school leaders and policy makers who we hope will use this book as a guide in developing their own school improvement plans, we thank them.

We are grateful to our editor, Celia Bohanon, who made our two voices sound more like one, and to our publisher, Robert Sickles, who understood the vision, supported it and made it a reality.

Franklin extends thanks to Sandy Schargel—Franklin's intellectual partner, first reader, inspiration and critic—for her faith and understanding.

Finally, our gratitude to David S. and Kelly G., who supplied the inspiration by explaining that being at risk need not be debilitating.

Caveats

In this book, we have focused on the problem of dropouts from primary and secondary schools. Although we believe this is far more critical to our nation than the post-secondary school dropout problem, the latter is also a serious concern. Colleges and universities accept the better graduates of our nation's public and private schools, yet they manage to retain only 45 to 50 percent of these students. In totality, only about 25 percent of our school-aged population now graduates from post-secondary schools. In an increasingly brain-dependent society, this should be of great concern.

Many of the programs described in this book cannot be duplicated exactly. Schools vary in so many factors (size, community, culture, location, staff, faculty, and administration, to name a few) that "copy cat" duplication will not work. Nevertheless, the programs can serve as models of effective strategies in action, to be adapted or customized to fit individual schools, teachers, educational leaders, and communities.

The fact that we list programs and schools using the fifteen most effective strategies for dropout prevention is not intended as an endorsement. We merely wish to identify some schools and programs that are putting these strategies to work. The schools and programs listed here have provided contact information for publication here. We gratefully acknowledge their support and cooperation.

About the Authors

Jay Smink
Editor and Author

Jay Smink has been the executive director of the National Dropout Prevention Center at Clemson University since 1988. He is a professor of education in the College of Health, Education, and Human Development. He also serves as the executive director of the National Dropout Prevention Network, a professional organization of 2,000 members representing education, business, and community leaders who are concerned with school dropout issues. He earned his M.Ed. in industrial education and D.Ed. in educational administration from Penn State. His B.S. is in industrial arts from Millersville State College in Pennsylvania. Dr. Smink is recognized as a national leader and authority on dropout prevention, school reform, mentoring, service learning, alternative schools, school-to-work, educational marketing, and program evaluation. Dr. Smink is interested in hearing from readers of this book at sjay@clemson.edu

Franklin P. Schargel
Editor and Author

Franklin P. Schargel spent thirty-three yeas as a teacher, counselor, and administrator in schools in the New York City School System. He has earned a Bachelor's Degree (CCNY) and two Masters (Brooklyn College (CCNY) and Pace University). In July 2002 he was elected Chair of the Education Division of the American Society for Quality. He is a well-known author of over 60 published articles and books (*Transforming Education Through Total Quality Management: A Practitioner's Guide, Strategies to Help Solve Our School Dropout Problem* (coauthor), and *Dropout Prevention Tools*). Mr. Schargel is an international speaker and consultant with expertise in continuous improvement in education, the Malcolm Baldrige Award in Education, Dropout Prevention and systemic educational improvement. His work has been described in the pages of the *New York Times, Business Week,* and *Fortune Magazine* and on National Public Radio and the Public Broadcasting System. He is currently Senior Managing Associate of the School Success Network whose mission is to improve the success of schools and school districts. Franklin would be interested in hearing from readers of this book at franklin@schargel.com

Table of Contents

Effective Strategies for Dropout Prevention

Since 1986, the National Dropout Prevention Center/Network (NDPC/N) has conducted and analyzed research, sponsored extensive workshops, and collaborated with a variety of practitioners to further the mission of reducing America's dropout rate by meeting the needs of youth in at-risk situations, including students with disabilities.

Students report a variety of reasons for dropping out of school; therefore, the solutions are multidimensional. The NDPC/N has identified 15 Effective Strategies that have the most positive impact on the high school graduation rate. These strategies, appear to be independent, but actually work well together and frequently overlap. Although they can be implemented as stand-alone programs (i.e., mentoring or family engagement projects) positive outcomes will result when school districts develop a program improvement plan that encompasses most or all of these strategies. These strategies have been successful in all school levels from K–12 and in rural, suburban, or urban centers.

A School and Community Perspective

Students who come to school reflect the wider community; when students leave school, either before or after graduation, they return to that community. It's impossible to isolate "school" within the walls of the school building. Effective strategies to keep students in school take advantage of these links with the wider community.

- ◆ **Systemic Renewal**

   Systemic renewal calls for a continuing process of evaluating goals and objectives related to school policies, practices, and organizational structures as they impact a diverse group of learners.

- ◆ **School-Community Collaboration**

   When all groups in a community provide collective support to the school, a strong infrastructure sustains a caring environment where youth can thrive and achieve.

- ◆ **Safe Learning Environments**

   A comprehensive violence prevention plan, including conflict resolution, must deal with potential violence as well as crisis management. A safe learning environment provides daily experiences, at all grade levels, that enhance positive social attitudes and effective interpersonal skills in all students.

Early Interventions

Evidence has shown that early identification of children at risk and effective interventions are vital components of ensuring a successful school experience. Attitudes and behaviors can often be changed before they are deeply entrenched. These three strategies begin at birth, but continue throughout a child's school years:

- ◆ **Family Engagement**

   Research consistently finds that family engagement has a direct, positive effect on children's achievement and is one of the most accurate predictors of a student's success in school.

- ◆ **Early Childhood Education**

   Birth-to-five interventions demonstrate that providing a child additional enrichment can enhance brain development. The most effective way to reduce the number of children who will ultimately drop out is to provide the best possible classroom instruction from the beginning of their school experience through the primary grades.

- ◆ **Early Literacy Development**

   Early interventions to help low-achieving students improve their reading and writing skills establish the necessary foundation for effective learning in all subjects.

Basic Core Strategies

These student-centered strategies engage potential dropouts in dynamic and meaningful learning opportunities in alternative, traditional, and community settings. Research and experience show that the following four strategies can make a significant impact on the school dropout problem.

- ◆ **Mentoring/Tutoring**

  Mentoring is a one-to-one caring, supportive relationship between a mentor and a mentee that is based on trust. Tutoring, also a one-to-one activity, focuses on academics and is an effective practice when addressing specific needs such as reading, writing, or math competencies.

- ◆ **Service-Learning**

  Service-learning connects meaningful community service experiences with academic learning. This teaching/learning method promotes personal and social growth, career development, and civic responsibility and can be a powerful vehicle for effective school reform at all grade levels.

- ◆ **Alternative Schooling**

  Alternative schooling provides potential dropouts a variety of options that can lead to graduation, with programs paying special attention to the student's individual social needs and academic requirements for a high school diploma.

- ◆ **After-School Opportunities**

  Many schools provide after-school and summer enhancement programs that eliminate information loss and inspire interest in a variety of areas. Such experiences are especially important for students at risk of school failure because they fill the afternoon "gap time" with constructive and engaging activities.

Making the Most of Instruction

No sustained and comprehensive effort to keep students in school can afford to ignore what happens in the classroom. Strategies that produce better teachers, expand teaching methods to accommodate a range of learning styles, take advantage of today's cornucopia of technological resources, and meet the individual needs of each student can yield substantial benefits.

♦ **Professional Development**

Teachers who work with youth at high risk of academic failure need to feel supported and have an avenue by which they can continue to develop skills, techniques, and learn about innovative strategies.

♦ **Active Learning**

Active learning embraces teaching and learning strategies that engage and involve students in the learning process. Students find new and creative ways to solve problems, achieve success, and become lifelong learners when educators show them that there are different ways to learn.

♦ **Educational Technology**

Technology offers some of the best opportunities for delivering instruction to engage students in authentic learning, addressing multiple intelligences, and adapting to students' learning styles.

♦ **Individualized Instruction**

Each student has unique interests and past learning experiences. An individualized instructional program for each student allows for flexibility in teaching methods and motivational strategies to consider these individual differences.

♦ **Career and Technical Education**

A quality CTE program and a related guidance program are essential for all students. School-to-work programs recognize that youth need specific skills to prepare them to measure up to the increased demands of today's workplace.

1

Coming to Terms with *At Risk*

Jay Smink

The Term *At-Risk Students*

Among the many uncertainties surrounding the school dropout issue is how to talk about schools with poor performance, teachers with inadequate preparation, or students with low achievement without falling back on stereotypes or giving offense. Two decades ago, for example, the report *A Nation at Risk: The Imperative for Educational Reform* (National Commission on Excellence in Education, 1983) never used the terms *at-risk youth* or *students at risk*. Nevertheless, they soon became common parlance. Today, the term *at-risk student* is much more controversial; many educators hesitate to attach a negative label to students already facing so many challenges.

For this book, we sought experts in the areas of each of the 15 strategies for dropout prevention. We asked them to describe the research base, offer best practices, and express their thoughts on helping students graduate. Clearly, this book focuses on the students most in danger of leaving high school without a diploma. Several of the contributing authors took great pains not to describe these students as *at risk*; others felt comfortable using the term. However, all share our deep concern about these students; all seek to offer constructive suggestions to improve their situation.

We believe that the best way to address this potential stumbling block is to face it openly and objectively. Therefore, in this chapter we will review the past use of the term *at risk,* summarize the research about factors that place students at risk, and present our ideas about how to define and use the term when discussing strategies for dropout prevention.

Early Use and Definitions

The precise origin of the term *at risk* is not known, although it appears in the fields of medicine, psychology, and education. In a paper entitled *Children and Youth at Risk: Some Conceptual Considerations* prepared for the Pan-Canadian Education Research Symposium, Kimberly Schonert-Reichl (2000) offers a comprehensive literature review. According to Schonert-Reichl, the concept in relationship to schools harks back to almost 200 years ago, when members of the New York Free School Society asked the state legislature to create a school for children from impoverished families.

An abundance of legislation in the 1960s clearly targeted children with low socioeconomic status (SES) and high need for additional academic assistance, but the term *at risk* appeared rarely, if ever. The 1983 *Nation at Risk* report shocked educators and policy makers throughout the 1980s, sparking wider use of the term.

In February 1989, for example, the prestigious journal *Educational Leadership,* published by the Association for Supervision and Curriculum Development (ASCD), focused on "Dealing with Diversity: At-Risk Students." Authors of 19 articles described efforts to address the needs of dropouts or special groups of students; five even included the term *at risk* in the title. Slavin and Madden (1989) described what works for students at risk, defining a student at risk as "one who is in danger of failing to complete his or her education with an adequate level of skills" (p. 4). They also identified risk factors: low achievement, retention in grade, behavior problems, poor attendance, low socioeconomic status, and attendance at schools with large numbers of poor students. In the same issue, Cuban (1989) linked the concept to schooling in urban settings—an association that endured for at least a decade.

In *Making Schools More Responsive to At-Risk Students* (Pallas, 1989), published by the ERIC Clearinghouse on Urban Education, the author aimed to clarify several shifts in thinking about approaches to educating at-risk students over the past 35 years and to present a "new way of defining at-risk students" (p. 1). This ERIC Digest discussed different definitions and varied perspectives used to identify these students, using phrases such as educational deprivation, cultural deprivation, failure of social institutions, minority children, and family issues. The report presented a new definition—"young people are at risk, or educationally disadvantaged, if they have been exposed to inadequate or inappropriate educational experiences in the family, school, or community" (p. 1)—and described a number of social factors associated with such exposure. Those indicators of risk included poverty, family composition, mother's education, and language background.

Risk Factors: The Research Base

The 1980s also brought the 1987 School Improvement Act, with amendments (1988) offering this definition:

> (1) the term "at-risk" means students who, because of learning deficiencies, lack of school readiness, limited English proficiency, poverty, educational or economic disadvantage, or physical or emotional handicapping conditions, face greater risk of low educational achievement and have greater potential of becoming school dropouts (sec. 3243).

In *A Practitioner's Guide: Strategies, Programs, and Resources for Youth Employability Development*, Public/Private Ventures (1988) presented a complete section on "Who Is At Risk?" Stating that in 1981 "unemployment among minority teenagers in metropolitan poverty areas was close to 44%, as compared to the national average for all teens at 20%," the authors reported that the youth most at risk are also likely to be school dropouts, have long periods of joblessness, perform poorly in school, and have special needs (p. 3)—a situation that persists today, as we will see in the next two chapters.

Over the last few decades, educators and officials in most states have varied widely in their use of the term *at risk*. Many are now shifting to other words to describe these students, or using phrases such as *students in high-risk environments* or *students with high risk factors*. Iowa has been one of the states using the term consistently. In fact, in 1996, the Iowa Department of Education defined the term with the following descriptors: (1) does not meet goals with ongoing education programs, (2) does not complete high school, and (3) does not become a productive worker upon leaving high school. A student who matches one or more of these descriptors is considered to be *at risk* (Iowa Department of Education, 1996).

Iowa proceeded to build a sound research-based student risk assessment program, developing a checklist of 30 specific factors that place students at risk. The assessment rubric describes three levels of student risk and clearly identifies students in need of assistance. The risk profile then permits local schools to identify and implement intervention strategies to increase student academic achievement levels and improve schools (Morley & Veale, 2003).

Much current research addresses how students in at-risk situations function, both in school and in society. For example, in "Creating a Sense of Place:

Anchoring At-Risk Students Within K–12 Classrooms," Bailey and Stegelin (2003) make the case that the term *at risk* describes approximately one-third of the total student population and represents those who are most at risk for school dropout. They list the categories of students typically described as at risk:

- students from low-SES homes, eligible for free lunches, and classified as "poor" according to the federal government's definition of poverty,
- children in African-American or Hispanic families,
- students whose first language is not English,
- children who are handicapped and have special needs,
- gifted students whose needs are not being met,
- capable students who are not succeeding in the classroom,
- students who disrupt the learning process for others, exhibiting behavior problems, aggression, or high levels of activity,
- students who challenge, demoralize, frustrate, and exasperate their teachers (p. 18).

Bailey and Stegelin (2003) also develop a strong rationale for five psychological needs of at-risk students: "(a) feelings of competence, (b) feelings of belonging, (c) feelings of usefulness, (d) feelings of potency, and (e) feelings of optimism" (p. 18). They write about how important it is for school leaders and teachers to understand these psychological needs, and specifically about how creating a sense of place can meet those needs.

A review of the terminology and definitions used in other countries affords a wider perspective. For example, the Australian National Equity Program for Schools (NEPS) has a 25-year history of funding programs for students at risk, identified as follows:

- Students up to 19 years of age who are at risk of leaving school, or who have already left school, before completing year 12 or equivalent, or whose level of achievement or behaviour at school is adversely affected by circumstances such as family dislocation, itinerance, violence or abuse, homelessness, truancy or substance abuse (Research on Students, 2003).

Though use of the term *students at risk* is spreading in Australia, an expanded term *students at educational risk*, is also gaining ground; those who prefer this more specific reference reason that it is less likely to carry negative connotations somehow linking the risk to the students themselves.

In the United Kingdom (UK), another term applied to school dropouts or troubled young people is *disaffected youth*. While *dropout* conjures up images of young people in trouble or at risk in many different arenas, *school disaffec-*

tion refers specifically to students' attitudes about school. According to Reva Klein (1999) in her book *Defying Disaffection*, the term's scope includes not only those who have left school, but those who remain physically present at school but otherwise have dropped out. Her research and book describe various programs in the UK that aim to reengage children in their education. In one chapter she discusses how young and disaffected students take one of four routes in the education system: "Either they are pushed out—excluded—or they truant persistently, fail their exams, or drop out before taking them" (p. 9). Whatever direction they pursue, they face lifelong problems very similar to those encountered by disaffected youth in American schools.

The school dropout issue—more commonly referred to as *school disaffection*—is rapidly gaining priority in the international community. In 2003, in collaboration with Trentham Books (a British educational publisher), the National Dropout Prevention Center/Network launched a new publication called *The International Journal on School Disaffection*. Featuring research and best practices from around the world, the journal reflects the growing interest of policy makers, researchers, and practitioners worldwide. In the inaugural issue, for example, an article entitled "School Disaffection—Africa's Growing Problem?" describes the continued decline in school enrollment and retention rates despite large-scale interventions by UNESCO (Smith, 2003).

Contemporary Use of the Term *At-Risk Students*

Educators, social workers, and other professionals who interact with children and families remain very guarded in their use of the term *at-risk student*. By contrast, the broadcast news media and the press use the term—and use it freely—to capture attention and make critical points. Policy makers, business leaders, and school and community leaders dealing with all kinds of students in at-risk situations hear the message.

In article after article, readers of *Education Week* see the term *at-risk students* accurately applied. For example, Ouchi (2003) makes the case that every school has a unique collection of students, with different proportions of gifted students, special education students, arts-oriented students, and at-risk students. Likewise, a newspaper article in the *Columbus Dispatch* carried the headline "More class time helps at-risk kids" (Bainbridge, 2003).

Even the legislation known as the No Child Left Behind Act of 2001 includes the term in the title of Part D: *Prevention and Intervention Programs for Children and Youth Who Are Neglected, Delinquent, or At-Risk*. The text goes on to describe one purpose of this part: to prevent at-risk youth from dropping out of school. Section 1424 also uses the term, and Section 1432 offers a definition:

(2) At-Risk—The term *at-risk*, when used with respect to a child, youth, or student, means a school aged individual who is at-risk of academic failure, has a drug or alcohol problem, is pregnant or is a parent, has come into contact with the juvenile justice system in the past, is at least 1 year behind the expected grade level for the age of the individual, has limited English proficiency, is a gang member, has dropped out of school in the past, or has a high absenteeism rate at school (No Child Left Behind, 2002).

Our Recommendation

We concur with the simple definition of at-risk students suggested by Sagor (2004), building on their review of the literature and their own experiences in education:

> An at-risk student is "someone who is unlikely to graduate on schedule with both the skills and the self-esteem necessary to exercise meaningful options in the areas of work, leisure, culture, civic affairs, and inter/intrapersonal relationships" (p. 1).

If policy makers, program planners, or others seek greater specificity, the definition in the No Child Left Behind Act of 2001 offers an alternative.

We understand the use of the term *at-risk students* in the context of a high-profile story; we accept its use in reports that refrain from attaching it as a negative label to specific individuals or groups of students. In this book, we endeavor to use the term *at-risk student* carefully, and never as the immutable description of any individual. Indeed, Schonert-Reichl (2000) suggests that the term *risk status* should be viewed in terms of steps along a continuum ranging from low risk to high risk. Furthermore, she suggests that risk status is not a fixed quality; it will vary across time, circumstances, and contexts. Following this approach, we recommend using the term *at-risk* to describe the *situation*, not the *student*. As a general rule, we prefer the phrase *students in at-risk situations*. Like our contributing authors, we care about these students. With the dropout prevention strategies examined here, we seek to change these situations—and to help all students graduate.

References

Bailey, B., & Stegelin, D. A. (2003). Creating a sense of place: Anchoring at-risk students within K–12 classrooms. *The Journal of At-Risk Issues, 9*(2), 17–26.

Bainbridge, W. (2003, July 11). More class time helps at-risk kids. *The Columbus Dispatch.* Retrieved July 14, 2003 from Chief Academic Officer by School Match, at chiefacademicofficer@schoolmatch.com.

Cuban, L. (1989). At-risk students: What teachers and principals can do. *Educational Leadership 46*(5), 29–32.

Iowa Department of Education. (1996). *Guidelines for serving at-risk students.* Des Moines, IA: Office of Education Services for Children, Families and Communities.

Klein, R. (1999). *Defying disaffection: How schools are winning the hearts and minds of reluctant students.* Stoke on Trent, England: Trentham Books Limited.

Morley, E. M., & Veale, J. R. (2003, October). *Student risk assessment for identifying needs and evaluation impacts.* Paper presented at the National Dropout Prevention Network Conference, Kansas City, MO.

National Commission on Excellence in Education. (1983). *A nation at risk: The imperative for educational reform* (Stock No. 065-000-00177-2). Washington, DC: U.S. Government Printing Office.

No Child Left Behind Act of 2001, 20 U.S.C. § 6301 (2002).

Ouchi, W. G. (2003, September 3). Making schools work. *Education Week.* Retrieved September 5, 2003, from http://www.edweek.org/ew/ew_printstory.cfm?slug=01ouchi.h23.

Pallas, A. M. (1989). Making schools more responsive to at-risk students. *ERIC/CUE Digest 60.* Retrieved September 3, 2003, from http://www.ericfacility.net/databases/ERIC_Digests/ed316617.html.

Public/Private Ventures. (1988). *A practitioner's guide: Strategies, programs, and resources for youth employability development.* Philadelphia: Author.

Research on students for educational risk. (n.d.). Retrieved September 3, 2003, from Department of Education and Training, Government of Western Australia Web site http://www.eddept.wa.edu.au/saer/resource/label.htm

Sagor, R., & Cox, J. (2004). *At-risk students: Reaching and teaching them.* Larchmont, NY: Eye On Education.

Schonert-Reichl, K. A. (2000, April 6–7). *Children and youth at-risk: Some conceptual considerations.* Paper presented at the 2000 Pan-Canadian Education Research Agenda Symposium on Children and Youth At Risk. Retrieved September 3, 2003, from http://www.cmec.ca/stats/pcera/symposium2000/schonert. empdf.

School Improvement Act of 1987. (1988). *Augustus F. Hawkins–Robert Stafford elementary and secondary school improvement amendments of 1988. Part B—Fund for the improvement and reform of schools and teaching. Subpart 4–General Provisions.* U.S. Statutes At Large 100th Congress 2nd Session. 1988 Vol. 102, pp 1–104b.

Slavin, R. E., & Madden, N. A. (1989). What works for students at risk: A research synthesis. *Educational Leadership 46*(5), 4–13.

Smith, R. L. (2003). School disaffection—Africa's growing problem. *The International Journal on School Disaffection, 1*(1).

2

School Dropouts: A National Issue

Franklin P. Schargel

In this chapter, we look at the school dropout problem in the context of American society today. We describe legislative measures and outline demographic and societal trends that influence the educational arena in the 21st century, we identify the need for a concerted effort to address the school dropout problem and set forth the fundamental components of a successful reform initiative.

Every September, approximately 3.5 million young people in America enter the eighth grade. Over the succeeding four years, more than 505,000 of them drop out[1] —an average of nearly more than 2805 per day of the school year. Picture it: Every single school day, more than 70 school buses drive out of America's schoolyard, filled with students who will not return.

---

1 Each year, hundreds of thousands of young adults leave school without successfully completing a high school program. As these numbers accumulate year by year, they mount into the millions. "In October 1998, there were 3.9 million 16- through 24-year-olds who were not enrolled in a high school program and had not completed high school"—a figure that represents 11.8 percent of the total population in this age group (U.S. Department of Education. *Dropout Rates in the United States: 1998*, "Status Dropout Rates").

Who are these students? Disproportionately, their ranks include students of color, students from low-income families, students whose first language is other than English, and students with disabilities. No community, no matter how affluent, is exempt.

Where are they headed? Dropouts today are more likely to be single parents, slip into poverty, be on welfare, commit crimes, and go to prison.

Who pays the price? We all do. Our economy needs workers who can compete against the best from around the world. Our communities need adults who can work together, identify obstacles, and solve problems. Our nation needs people who can think creatively, write clearly, and use technology effectively. Our world needs citizens who can speak different languages, understand different perspectives, and build bridges across cultures.

America today faces a crisis in education. If our nation is to compete globally, we must improve what our schools do. This means raising our standards, as most states have done in response to the No Child Left Behind legislation. But at the same time, our schools must serve the needs of students who already cannot meet our present standards—and the data show that this category includes one out of every five students, many of them from families where English is not the primary language.

Even those who would grapple with the school dropout issue find it hard to understand. School systems use different definitions for and different ways of counting dropouts. The problem has a multiplicity of causes, not all identified. Many believe dropouts are an inner-city problem affecting only minorities. Some think the issue has no impact on middle or elementary schools. Few clearly grasp the problem's vast scope and systemic effects.

Counting the Dropouts

How many dropouts are there? It depends on how you count. Trying to determine who drops out, why they drop out, and even the number of dropouts is a complicated process. And yet accurate information can help us recognize the severity of the problem and identify strategies to tackle it.

The federal government provides a definition, but only 36 states and the District of Columbia cooperate with the U.S. Department of Education (USDE) by reporting data. Noncooperating states include large states such as California, Florida, Michigan, New York, and North Carolina, most of which

Although it is hard to track dropouts accurately, the best available data show that in 1990, 26 percent of American young people failed to graduate from high school. By 2000, the figure had jumped to 30 percent. Dropout rates in New York and Texas have increased by about the national average, while those in Massachusetts and North Carolina have grown more than the national average (Rothstein, 2002).

are believed to have higher than average dropout rates. Although 46 states and the District of Columbia "usually report" dropout data through the Common Core of Data Survey to the USDE's National Center for Education Statistics (NCES), only 22 of them and the District of Columbia use the common definition adopted by NCES (National Education Goals Panel, 2000).

According to the federal definition, a dropout is an individual who

♦ was enrolled in school at some time during the previous school year and was not enrolled on October 1 of the current school year, or

♦ was not enrolled on October 1of the previous school year although expected to be (e.g., was not reported as a dropout the year before) and

♦ was not graduated from high school or completed state- or district-approved educational program and

♦ does not meet any of the following exclusionary conditions:

• transfer to another public school district, private school, or state- or district-approved educational program,

• temporary school-recognized absence due to suspension or illness, or death.

States differ in their definition of dropouts; they use different time periods during the school year when dropout data are collected, different data collection methods, different ways of tracking youth no longer in school, and different methods of calculating the dropout rate. Some states subtract students who return to school from the dropout total; others do not. Some districts count students enrolled in high school equivalency programs as dropouts; others do not. Some states count as dropouts those who register early for college without obtaining a high school diploma, enter the military, or enter correctional or mental institutions; others do not. States allow students to leave school at different ages. "Some states do not report students who receive a certificate of attendance or other alternative certificate, and some do not report the number of students age 19 or younger who are awarded a diploma on the basis of the Graduate Equivalency Degree (GED) exam. Students who completed high school with some credential other than a regular diploma can account for a sizable proportion of the high school completers. For example, in Florida, Louisiana, Oklahoma, and Tennessee, 19 percent or more of the completers received an alternative credential" (USDE. *Key Statistics on Public Elementary and Secondary Schools and Agencies: School Year 1995--1996*, p. 31).

Dropout statistics have implications beyond the schoolhouse. The success/failure rate of local schools (frequently measured by graduation rates and post-secondary school attendance rates) helps determine the resale value of homes and is used to influence businesses to move into an area. On the other hand, those who want to shock the public have a motivation to use the methods indicating a high dropout rate. The reality is that as a nation, we do not have a standardized operational definition of who is a dropout, nor do we have a standard method for counting and reporting dropouts.

Some school districts, seeking additional educational services, carry phantom students on the school records even after they have dropped out.[2] Some states now label districts with a "low performance rating" for having too many dropouts. Therefore, it is in administrators' best interest to embrace a calculation method that makes their rate appear low. In other cases, inflating the rate of dropouts attracts additional funding for at-risk students.

Two recent reports from the Business Roundtable and the Manhattan Institute, question the data collection and tallying method used by the U.S. Department of Education. The USDE puts the national dropout rate at 11 percent. The Business Roundtable places the figure as high as 30 percent, almost three times the government estimates. Using data gathered from the U.S. Census Bureau's 1999 Population Estimates and the USDE/NCES Digest of Educational Statistics for 2001, the Roundtable developed the graduation rates for the 18-year-old population for the 1998–1999 school year by dividing the total number of high school graduates in that school year by the total number of 18-year-olds in each state in the same year (Business Roundtable, 2003).

The Business Roundtable believes that the methods used by the government are "substantially biased downward," for the following reasons:

♦ The Department of Education must rely on less accurate data sources to generate the national dropout rate, because each year 14 or more states do not report their state dropout rates using common definitions and data collection standards. Many of the census numbers are based on self-reported information. In addition, individuals who are without a diploma might be hesitant to admit to it.

♦ Official dropout data pertain to students in grades 9 to 12, thus excluding students who drop out before grade 9. (State compulsory attendance laws keep most children in school at least until grade 9.) According to the Roundtable's analysis, 18 percent of all dropouts failed to complete any schooling above the 8th grade.

♦ Individuals with a GED certificate are counted as high school graduates, although they did not receive a regular high school diploma. But GED holders fare far worse in the labor market and are treated differently in post-secondary educational institutions than individuals who earn regular high school diplomas. A 1997 study found

---

2 In New York State, dead students were counted as present and even received report cards with passing grades. *New York Times,* December 16, 1999, p. A30.

that only 14 percent of male GED holders had completed one or more years of college, versus 49 percent of those with a regular high school diploma.

◆ Poor and minority teens are not always counted in household surveys because they may have transient living conditions and/or employment status.

◆ Department of Education data exclude many immigrants who never attended school in the United States. During March 2001, approximately 30 percent of all foreign-born 18- to 24-year-olds held neither a regular high school diploma nor a GED certificate.

◆ Official state dropout figures typically do not collect data from private schools. While it is presumed that private schools have a lower dropout rate than public schools, a complete count is not available.

◆ No longitudinal studies exist about the accuracy of school transfer data. While these students are reported to have transferred, no data have been collected to verify that they have registered in other schools in their new neighborhood.

Another source of inaccuracy in the USDE dropout figures is that students who become incarcerated are not counted, although many are dropouts or have not finished high school.

◆ According to the Business Roundtable report, members of the institutionalized population have extraordinarily high dropout rates. A 1996 survey of jail inmates and 1997 surveys of federal and state prison inmates found 372,665 jail and prison inmates under the age of 25. Of this group, 298,700, or 80 percent, lacked a regular high school diploma.

◆ According to the 1990 census, nearly 327,000 18- to 24-year-olds were inmates of institutions. A recent study by Child Trends Data-Bank in Washington, DC indicates that the decline in the reported dropout rate of black students is due to the rise in their imprisonment. Bruce Western, professor of sociology at Princeton University in New Jersey, said, "About half the fall in the dropout rate is due to the rise in the imprisonment of young black males." Incarceration rates for black men aged 22 to 30 who haven't finished high school leaped to 40 percent in 1999 from only 14 percent in 1980 (Coeyman, 2003).

The Business Roundtable suggests that a more accurate way of counting high school graduation rates is to compare the annual number of diplomas awarded by public and private high schools to the number of 17- and 18-year-olds in America. Using this method, which has not been adopted by the U.S. Department of Education, the nation's high school graduation rate was only 70 to 71 percent in recent years. The Business Roundtable report concludes:

> During the past five years, the estimated national number (gathered by the U.S. Department of Education) of 16- to 24-year-old school dropouts has ranged from 502,000 to 524,000, with an average of 510,000. We believe that the...survey, which is based on self-reports and proxy responses by adult household members, substantially underestimates the true annual number of youth who leave the school system prior to receiving a regular high school diploma.

For the school calendar year 1997–1998, the Business Roundtable estimates that the total number of dropouts—at all grade levels, and in private and public schools—was 846,300, nearly 70 percent higher than the official estimate of 505,000 school dropouts.

Using a similar approach and data interpretation, Dr. Jay Greene, writing for the Manhattan Institute, estimates America's graduation rate for 1998 at 71 percent. The Manhattan Institute study concluded that 11 of the 46 large public school systems had dropout rates of 40 percent or higher. These districts included Cleveland (63 percent), Minneapolis (49.5 percent), Chicago (48.7 percent), New Orleans (45.4 percent), Portland, OR (42.7 percent), St. Louis (41.2 percent), and Baltimore (39.6 percent). Large school systems in California, Florida, Michigan, New York, and Texas were excluded from the list because their data are not reported using the U.S. Department of Education's definitions (Greene, 2002).

Counting the Cost

Yes, education is expensive. But the alternative is much more expensive.

Consider the direct cost to the individual. As the 21st century dawned, average yearly earnings in the United States (for all races and genders) were as follows:

$16,121	No high school diploma
$24,572	High school graduate
$26,958	Some college, no degree
$32,152	Associate degree
$45,678	Bachelor's degree
$55,641	Master's degree
$86,833	Doctorate

Multiply each figure by the average number of working years (40) to estimate mean earnings over a person's lifetime. A high school diploma alone adds $338,040 to lifetime earnings. An associate degree adds another $303,200; a bachelor's degree, another $541,040. A master's degree adds

$398,520 more; a doctorate, $1,247,680 more. The total difference in lifetime earnings between a high school dropout and a Ph.D. is $2,828,480—almost 3 million dollars (U.S. Bureau of the Census, 2002).

- Forty-five percent of all minimum-wage earners are high school dropouts, but only 3 percent of college graduates work for the minimum wage (Department of Labor, Bureau of Labor Statistics, reported in *Time Magazine*, November 22, 1999).

- In the past 25 years the median income for college graduates increased 13 percent, while the median income for high school dropouts decreased 30 percent (U.S. Census Bureau, 2000).

- Today, only 60 percent of dropouts have been able to find work one year after leaving school (OERI 1991), and if they can't work today, there is little likelihood that they will be working tomorrow. "In any given year, the likelihood of slipping into poverty is about three times higher for high school dropouts than for those who finished high school" (Annie E. Casey Foundation, *1998 Kids Count Data Book*, p. 22).

- According to Census Bureau estimates, jobs for high school graduates have been decreasing since 1999. The unemployment percentage rate for high school graduates in 2000 was 3.5 percent. The unemployment rate for individuals without a high school diploma was 6.5 percent. (U.S. Bureau of the Census, Bureau of Labor Statistics, March 2000).

High school dropouts trapped in low-income situations face a widening earnings gap. According to the Federal Reserve, the gap between the 10 percent of the families with the highest incomes and the 20 percent with the lowest incomes jumped 70 percent from 1998 through 2001. The gap between minorities and whites grew 21 percent. The median net worth for the lowest income group, whose pretax income in 1998 was $7,900, rose 25 percent to $10,300 in 2001. The median net worth of the top 10 percent rose 69 percent from $169,000 to $833,600. The median income for all families rose 10 percent to $39,900 in 2001. Median net worth for whites rose 17 percent to $120,900 but fell 4.5 percent to $17,000 for minorities (Hagenbaugh, 2003).

Next, consider the indirect costs.

- High school dropouts cost the nation about $944 billion in lost revenue while increasing welfare and crime-related spending by $24 billion (NMBEE).

- The national average per student expenditure in 1999–2000 dollars is $8,105 (U.S. Department of Education, NCES, 2000).

- In 1996, the national average cost of prisons was $20,142 per prisoner in federal prisons and $23,500 in state prisons. The cost per

U.S. resident was $103 (U.S. Bureau of Justice, 1999). The cost of incarcerating 2,166,260 people in federal, state, local and juvenile detention facilities is $47,269,959,460 *per year* in 1996 dollars.

◆ America holds 110,284 people in juvenile facilities (Butterfield, 2003).

◆ Eighty-two percent of America's prisoners are high school dropouts (USDJ, Juvenile Justice Bulletin, April, 1998).

◆ Every dollar put into quality preschool education produces $7 in economic benefit.

◆ Every dollar put into primary and secondary education produces a $3.40 to $7.40 return (New Mexico Business Roundtable for Educational Excellence).

The Educational Arena Is Changing

No Child Left Behind

The legislation known as No Child Left Behind (NCLB)—sponsored by the George W. Bush administration and endorsed by Democrats as well as Republicans—is more than a reauthorization of the Elementary and Secondary School Act. The NCLB legislation has vast implications, particularly for at-risk students. Its provisions affect every state and every school district in the country. While the legislation provides states, districts, and schools with additional federal funds (a increase of more than 20 percent from 2000 to 2002), it requires them to improve school quality and close the achievement gap. The main focus of NCLB is to have every student achieving at a state-defined proficient level by the 2013–2014 school year. No Child Left Behind state requirements include the following:

◆ Have in place by the 2002–2003 school year challenging academic content and achievement standards for all students in reading/language arts and mathematics.

◆ Have in place by the 2005–2006 school year a state assessment system for annual tests in reading/language arts and mathematics in grades 3 to 8, and for a single test in grades 10 to 12.

◆ Align state standards with assessments.

◆ Have all students attain a level of proficiency, as defined by state assessments, by the 2013–2014 school year.

◆ Provide school districts assistance in developing parental involvement programs for the district and the schools.

◆ Identify the number of limited English proficient (LEP) students and help develop an English proficiency test if local districts are unable to do so.

◆ Require all teachers of core academic subjects to be "highly qualified" by the end of the 2005–2006 school year.

◆ Require all teachers and paraprofessionals in Title I programs to meet the "highly qualified" standards set by the states, starting with the 2002–2003 school year.

◆ Identify all Title I schools that fall into the categories labeled as *needing improvement*, *corrective action*, or *restructured*; notify parents what those terms mean and what options they have (No Child Left Behind Act, 2002).

High-Stakes Testing

One of the more controversial aspects of the NCLB legislation is its mandate that all children in schools nationwide take standardized tests from the fourth through the twelfth grade. In many instances, a child who fails the test cannot move on to the next grade. In several states, students must pass such a "gateway" exam to earn a high school diploma. Proponents claim that the tests will motivate students and educators to work harder, ultimately improving student achievement. Opponents express concern that the tests will heighten the dropout problem, in particular, causing more poor and minority students to drop out. Higher achievement for some will come at the cost of failure and disaffection for others. However, the research on the impact of exit examinations on dropout rates is both limited and inconclusive.

For example, in Texas some 12,000 children were retaking the third grade in the 2003–2004 school year because they failed the Texas Assessment of Knowledge and Skills (TAKS). In the Houston Independent School District, 803 students failed the test for the third time. The year before, diagnostic tests had identified more than 23,000 Houston kindergartners and first- and second-grade students last year as being at-risk for reading difficulties (Zuniga, 2003).

The testing structure has identified a widening of the achievement gap between whites and black students. In the 19 states using exit examinations, 12 reported data showing passing rates for minority students and students living in poverty, 20 points or more lower than those of white students. According to the Center on Educational Policy, Minnesota had the largest gap between the passing rates of white and black students among states that require high school exit examinations in math. Just 33 percent of black students passed the state's basic-skills math test on their first attempt—a 45-point difference behind the passing rate for white students. And black students' passing rate was 38 points behind on the reading test. By 2008, exit tests will affect over 70 percent of public school students (Walsh, 2003).

"Highly Qualified Teachers"

The NCLB legislation calls for a "highly qualified teacher" in each of the nation's classrooms by 2005. Certainly, America's schools need teachers who are well versed in subject matter content as well as how to teach it. In a survey conducted by the Educational Testing Service, nine out of ten teachers stated that they need more professional development to help them motivate their students, and more than eight in ten said they need professional development to help them diagnose and address the learning needs of their students (Langraf, 2003).

According to a *Newsweek* survey, half of all teachers will retire by 2010; according to the National Education Association, the American Federation of Teachers and the U.S. Department of Education, we will need 2.6 million new teachers in the next few years; yet half of all those trained in the field never enter the classroom (Kantrowitz & Wingert, 2000). Currently more than half—56 percent—of high school students taking physical science do so from a teacher not trained in the field. Only about 40 percent of eighth-grade math teachers majored in mathematics, as opposed to about 70 percent internationally. Most of the most experienced, most qualified math teachers are concentrated in the lower primary grades, where they give students a good foundation and love of mathematics. Children are then taught by less qualified fifth- and sixth-grade teachers who may not be preparing them for the in-depth mathematics demanded in the upper grades ("Middle School Malaise," 2003). The problem is much worse in schools that serve the poor, minorities, and those at-risk.

A qualified teacher is the greatest stimulus to student learning. Yet we send our least qualified, least trained teachers into schools where the students need just the opposite. Education Week found "a dearth of well-qualified teachers in high-poverty, high-minority, and low-achieving schools." ("Quality Counts," 2003). A *Dallas Morning News* survey rated more than 7,000 schools in Texas according to a Teacher Preparation Index—a rating scale of 1 to 10, based on the percentage of teachers who were certified, the percentage certified and teaching in their specialty, and the percentage with at least two years experience. Schools whose student body was more than 90 percent white had a rating of 6.3. For schools with a largely Latino student body, the average was 4.6; for those with mostly black students, the figure was 3.4. Schools where less than 10 percent of the students were from economically disadvantaged families had an average Teacher Preparation Index of 6.2, compared with 4.3 where more than 90 percent of students were in this category. In schools where more than 50 percent of the students were proficient in English, the rating was 5.7; in the rest, it was only 3.6 (Navarette, 2003).

Nearly half of all new teachers leave the profession after five years. According to the Harvard University Graduate School of Education *Project on the Next Generation of Teachers*, 56 percent of new teachers report that no assistance was available to help them manage their new responsibilities effectively. Because 33 percent of districts' new hires are hired after the start of the school year, professional development offered in August or early September provides little assistance to those who need it most (*Education Week*, 2003). Given the normal attrition for retirement and other reasons, schools lose 23 percent more teachers each year than they gain through recruitment and hiring. The National Commission on Teaching and America's Future (NCTAF) believes that the teacher shortage problem is not one of shortage but rather of retention. The teaching profession suffers from a near-chronic rate of attrition. Without a more systemic approach to retaining educators, our nation's schools will never meet the federally mandated goal of highly qualified educators in every classroom in America. (NCTAF, 2003).

While America's students have become more diverse, the teaching pool has remained predominantly white and female. Male teachers constituted about one-third of the teaching force from 1970 to 1999 but only 21 percent in 2001—the lowest percentage in 40 years (National Education Association, 2003). In 2001, according to the same source, 90 percent of teachers and 61 percent of students were white; 8 percent of teachers and 17 percent of students were black; 16 percent of all students and less than 6 percent of teachers were Hispanic. Just about one in 10 teachers is a minority ("Face of the American Teacher," 2003). While students benefit from highly qualified teachers, whatever their race or gender, male and minority teachers can also offer role models for male and minority students.

Men, women, and minorities can earn more money in other fields, with less stress. Industry offers higher pay and a better work environment to individuals educated in mathematics, science, and other highly competitive fields. To address the shortage of teachers and school administrators, we must improve the salaries and working conditions in our educational system.

Nationwide Trends

Data furnished by the Bureau of the Census, the Bureau of Labor Statistics, the Departments of Labor, Education, and Correction, and a variety of not-for-profit foundations and for-profit agencies show several trends in the United States that will have a dramatic effect on education in the 21st century.[3] These include demographic changes (an aging population, new immi-

---

3 The U.S. Bureau of the Census collects data and issues 43 reports during the course of the ten years between censuses. A number of them have been used

gration patterns, movement within the country, a changing family structure) and societal changes (increased poverty, teenage sex and pregnancy, drug use, crime and violence).[4]

An Aging Population

As America's demographics shift, the proportion of children is declining and that of the elderly is expanding. In the year 2000, there were 35 million people 65 and older in the United States; that figure is projected to rise to 39.7 million in 2010. Over the next 10 years, we can expect this group to dominate American politics and demand more government services—not only health and social services, but also other forms of public assistance (such as an expanded public transportation system). Local, state, and federal budgets will also feel the pressure ("Baby Boomers," 2003).

As our population ages, we will become more dependent on fewer younger workers (and on the schools that educate those workers). Further, as today's white, non-Latino workers age, they will be replaced in the workforce by minority groups—groups that traditionally have greater difficulty in school and a higher dropout rate.

New Patterns of Immigration

We are now quite visibly a nation of immigrants. Most of the "old immigrants" (1492–1965) came from Europe; the societies they left had well-established governments, defined infrastructures, and structured school systems, with trained teachers, organized curriculum, and a tradition of compulsory schooling.

Today, many immigrant students come from nations without compulsory education. Some have never attended school; some are illiterate in their native language as well as English; many have severe reading limitations. In the United States, school placement is based on age; a five-year-old enters kindergarten, a fourteen-year-old is in the seventh or eighth grade. But placing a student who has never been in school or who has limited school experience in a middle school because of their age puts the child in a vulnerable position. The added burden of having to learn English at the same time as learning subject material, increases the odds that the child will fail or be retained.

In addition, today's immigration patterns are leading to a more culturally and ethnically diverse population. More and more teachers are encountering the challenge of teaching classes containing students with a wide mix of native languages and cultural backgrounds.

---

in gathering information for this book, including Current Population Reports, Series P23-189, 1995; Statistical Abstracts, 1995; Day, 1993.

4 Readers will recognize that the demographic and social factors described here are not uniquely American. Such changes are occurring to a greater or lesser extent within most industrialized societies.

"While there is enormous variance, today's immigrant on average has less education, is more likely to drop out of high school, and has an income that does not seem to be catching up with those of native-born Americans" (U.S. Bureau of the Census, *Population Profile of the United States*, 1995). Helping these new immigrants, some of whom will become citizens, to catch up requires a sustained investment of both time and energy.

Student Diversity

In the ten years between 1990 and 2000, the percentage of minority groups in the U.S. population increased from 21.9 percent (54.5 million) to 26.3 percent (72.5 million), with the Hispanic population increasing by more than 50 percent. By 2015, one-third of Americans will be members of minority groups. Minority students presently constitute almost 40 percent of public K through 12 enrollment (McBay, 2003).

High school completion rates improved for 18- to 24-year-old minorities between 1990 and 2000, increasing to 84 percent for African-Americans and 64 percent for Hispanics. However, these rates remained below the 88 percent completion rate for whites in this age group (McBay, 2003).

Movement Within the Country

Not only are people moving into the United States, they are moving within the country as well. One in six Americans moves each year; the average American makes 11.7 moves in a lifetime (U.S. Bureau of the Census, *Current Population Reports*, 1993). While most moves are local—from one residence to another within the same county—almost eight million people annually move between counties, and almost seven million people move to another state (Roberts, 1995).

The United States Constitution places public education in the hands of the states. Curricula, standards, and the quality of public education vary dramatically from state to state, and even from district to district within a state. A student who moves from a school with high educational standards to a less demanding school loses in one way. But a student who moves to a more challenging school may fall far behind, become disengaged, and possibly even drop out.

Changing Family Structures

In the past century, families have changed radically. Large households are becoming less common, as are households headed by a married couple, and the number of married childless couples is greater than the number of couples with children. The fastest-growing family group is the single-parent household. One third of all family groups are headed by one parent, including 23 percent of all-white, 61 percent of black and 33 percent of Hispanic family groups. Single mothers represent 86 percent of all single parents, and the number of single-parent homes grew from 3.8 million in 1970 to 11.4 million in 1994 (Day, 1993).

Divorce has become more common, and it affects the economic wellbeing of newly single mothers and their children. Half of the black single mothers and one third of the white single mothers who were not poor while they were married were likely to be living in poverty within a year after divorce (Day, 1993). Households with single mothers and children under 18 increased 165 percent between 1970 and 2000, and the "traditional married couple family now represents just 51% of households" (Metropolitan Life Foundation, 2000).

Men and women are marrying later than ever before; increasingly, women are choosing careers, delaying marriage and childbirth. Almost two-thirds of all families now have a mother in the workforce. Even in two-parent families, it is not unusual to have both parents working two or more jobs (Day, 1993).

These changes in family structures and lifestyles are changing schools as well. Schools now provide meals and extended-day childcare services; they also take a direct role in teaching skills that were traditionally within the domain of the family or church—from driver's education to sex education, from swimming to personal hygiene. Teachers act as supportive adults in order to help learning take place, but also—often uncomfortably—as surrogate parents dealing with matters beyond their traditional scope or formal training. For many youngsters, the primary adult they speak to during the week is a teacher.

Poverty

Contrary to popular belief, the largest group living in poverty is not the elderly but the young. Some 15,700,000 children are poor. There are more poor American children now than at any other time in the past three decades (U.S. Bureau of the Census, *Profile of the Nation*, 1995, p. 2). The Department of Labor estimates that one out of four children live in poverty. Approximately 7.6 million school-age children, more than 17 percent of the total student population, live in poverty (U.S. General Accounting Office, 1993).

Children bring their problems of poverty into the nation's schools and classrooms. Students who are hungry have difficulty concentrating in class; students who lack adequate medical care may fail to thrive academically; students who have been abused can't function as they should.

Teenage Sex and Pregnancy

Teenagers are having sex younger than ever before—according to one survey, as early as age 14 (Annie E. Casey Foundation, 1998). A Kaiser Family Foundation Study of more than 1,500 teens, ages 12 to 18, found that at least 73 percent of boys and 55 percent of girls are sexually active by 18 (*USA Today*,

June 25, 1996, p. D1). Even though there is an increased awareness and use of birth control devices, the pregnancy rate of sexually active teenagers is still above 20 percent (Annie E. Casey Foundation, 1998). More than two thirds of the teenagers who had babies in 1996 were unmarried; among black teenagers having babies, only 10 percent were married (Annie E. Casey Foundation, 1998).

Furthermore, almost 80 percent of the unmarried women who had a child before finishing high school are living in poverty (compared to 8 percent of those who finish high school, marry and have a baby after the age of 20) (*New York Times*, March 22, 1994, p. B6).

Drugs

The acceptance and the use of drugs have grown since the 1960s. "The number of teenagers using marijuana has nearly doubled, according to the Substance Abuse and Mental Health Services Administration, which conducted 22,181 interviews. Among teenagers 7.3 percent said they had smoked marijuana in the preceding month, up from 4 percent in 1992" (*New York Times*, September 13, 1995).

The use of drugs is not just an inner-city problem. For example: "Twenty-four percent of students in New York State have used marijuana at least once, compared with 19 percent in New York City. Four percent of those in New York State have tried crack as opposed to 2 percent in New York City. Twelve percent in New York State have tried cocaine as opposed to 9 percent nationally. White students used drugs more than Hispanic or blacks" (*New York Times*, December, 1993).

Students who use drugs not only lower the quality of their own learning, but also often disrupt the classroom and interfere with the learning of others.

Crime and Violence

Violence and crime play a large part in the lives of today's children. Children are both victims and perpetrators of violent crime. They face violence in the media, in their homes, and even at school. The American Psychological Association reports that the average child is exposed to 8,000 television murders and more than 100,000 other acts of violence before entering seventh grade (*New York Times*, March 3, 1992; Painter, 1996). The availability of guns and the glorification of violence in films and television have made the use of weapons to settle disputes acceptable. Children have come to see violence as a way to solve problems.

Jeffrey Grogger, an economist at the University of California at Los Angeles, found that minor levels of violence lowered the chance of students graduating from high school by about one percentage point and their chance of going to a four-year college by four percentage points. Moderate levels of violence reduced the likelihood of high school graduation by about five percentage points and of college attendance by seven percentage points (*Business Week*, August 11, 1997, p. 24).

Disaffected, frequently violent, youth or at-risk children have potentially negative effects on the attitudes, behavior, and achievement of other students. Many a school's accepted way to address the antagonistic, estranged, or indifferent youngster is retention in a grade. Studies show that this increases the chances of dropping out.

What Can We Do about Dropouts?

Schools are succeeding in what they have always done well—preparing highly motivated young people for post-secondary schools and careers. These students learn under almost any conditions. Schools continue to fail where they have always failed—with students with low expectations, students with otherwise committed parents, students with physical and mental handicaps, students who are not interested in the present educational environment. *And that number is growing.*

Seeking to be globally competitive, the federal government and the states have been raising standards and adding new assessments. Other voices call for national standards and national assessments. Yet as a nation, we frequently ignore the students who cannot meet *today's* standards. Some even say that a 1 percent or 2 percent dropout rate may be acceptable. But for a child who leaves school, the dropout rate is 100 percent. For the nation, the costs are frequently unknown and unknowable. Could a potential dropout, kept in school, become a skilled surgeon, a creative inventor, or a passionate high school teacher?

A great deal has been written on dropout prevention and at-risk children. Much of this literature has focused on placing the blame, rather than remedying the situation or preventing its occurrence. Some blame the dropout problem on the parents; others blame society; still others blame the children. Some choose a short-term, quick fix solution to this complex problem; when that fails, they try another. Many a proposed remedy addresses the symptoms rather than the causes. Few programs—far too few—focus on systemic reform.

A significant decrease in the number of dropouts cannot possibly come from placing blame, or from inspection-based activities such as tests or higher standards. Rather, it requires fundamental changes in curriculum design processes, workflow design, and staff training; it demands creative technology use and the development of partnerships with key stakeholders. We need to build dropout prevention into all existing and newly created programs. If we don't, our whole nation will be the loser.

The Need for Systemic Renewal

We are in the midst of a period of major educational reform. Most of these efforts will not succeed. They will fail for a variety of reasons. The three most prevalent are that the attempted reforms are episodic, that they address symptoms rather than causes, and that they are not systemic.

Reforms Are Episodic

First of all, many reform efforts follow a pattern of starts and stops, spurts, and pauses. A movement may begin with rapid growth, spurred by a champion or a group with a passion for its success. At some point, it reaches a plateau; its leaders pause, perhaps seeking new allies, perhaps—as they should—measuring and assessing their progress. Meanwhile, those who resist change (for whatever reason) muster their forces to oppose the reform. At this juncture, the movement will either gather strength, fade, or fail.

Schools believe that goals, once achieved, are stopping points. In reality, they are merely plateaus. Once a goal is reached, a new plan must be developed and deployed, actions taken and the results measured. The cycle is continual.

Reforms Address Symptoms Rather than Causes

Secondly, most organizations address symptoms rather than the causes of a problem. For one thing, it seems easier, because the symptoms are usually apparent and visible. In addition, as a society we are highly reactive. Rather than taking preventive measures, we wait for a problem to develop. Because we spend most of our time, energy, and resources putting out fires, we have little to devote to correcting the underlying causes.

Reforms Are Not Systemic

The third and most significant reason for failure is the absence of systemic renewal. Educational organizations—indeed, all organizations—are like jigsaw puzzles, composed of interrelated, interconnected pieces. Changing one piece changes and may well distort the entire puzzle. In an organization, changing just one element will not necessarily improve the whole. A district that introduces a new technology or science program without preparing the parents, staff, and teachers in earlier or subsequent grades and schools may be setting the program up for failure. (This is one of the primary reasons why "new math" failed.) Reformers who neglect to look at the whole picture are doomed to fail.

Those who seek a single cure for the complex ills of education—who believe that eliminating one problem will supply the needed remedy—are destined for disillusionment. By contrast, systemic renewal focuses on discovering the root causes, directing efforts to remove them, and preventing their recurrence.

Conclusion

Among the most enduring educational problems is that of the student dropout rate. Its ramifications are woven into the fabric of today's American society, an older society whose family structures differ from those of decades past. Elements such as poverty, new patterns of immigration, and other societal shifts make it imperative that our implementation of educational reform includes systemic redress of the dropout problem.

References

Annie E. Casey Foundation (1998). *Kids Count Data Book. (Baltimore, MD) www.aecf.org*.

Baby boomers transform an old bloc. (2003, June 15). *New York Times*.

Barkley, R. (1996). National Education Association National Center for Innovation. Conversation, August 21, 1996.

Business Roundtable. (2003). *The hidden crisis in the high school dropout problems of young adults in the U.S. Recent trends in overall school dropout rates and gender differences in dropout behavior*. Center for Labor Market Studies, Northeastern University, Boston, Massachusetts. Prepared for the Business Roundtable, Washington, D.C. Retrieved November 29, 2003, from http://www.businessroundtable.org/pdf/914.pdf).

Koretz, G. (1997, August 11). The class of boxcutter high: Violent schools mean fewer grads. *Business Week*, p. 24.

Butterfield, F. (2003, July 28). Study finds 2.6 percent increase in U.S. prison population. *New York Times*.

Coeyman, M. (2003, July 1). The story behind dropout rates. *The Christian Science Monitor*, p. 13. Accessed Online [1 August 2003], www.c5monitor.com2003/0701/p13s01-lcpr.htm.

Day, J. C. (1993). *Population projections of the United States, by age, sex, race, and Hispanic origin: 1993 to 2050*. U.S. Bureau of the Census, Current Population Reports, Series P25-1104. Washington, DC: U.S. Government Printing Office.

Greene, J. P., & Winters, M. A. (2002, November). *Public school graduation rates in the United States, civic report 31*. Center for Civic Innovation at the Manhattan Institute.

Hagenbaugh, B. (2003, January 23). Nation's wealth disparity widens. *USA Today*, p. A1.

High school dropout rates—Child trends. (n.d.). www.childtrendsdatabank.org/pdf/1_PDF.pdf.

Kantrowitz, B., & Wingert, P. (2000, October 2). Teachers wanted. *Newsweek*, pp. 37–41.

Langraf, K. M. (2003, April 2). Providing teachers the help they need…and want! *Education Week*, p. 34.

McBay, S. M. (2003, summer). Still underserved after all these years. *Issues in Science and Technology* online. Retrieved November 29, 2003, from http://www.nap.edu/issues/19.4/mcbay.html.

MetLife Foundation. (2000). *Survey of the American teacher, 2000: Are we preparing students for the 21st century?* Retrieved November 29, 2003, from http://www.metlife.

com/Applications/Corporate/WPS/CDA/PageGenerator/0,1674,P2321,00.
html.

Middle school malaise. (2003, May 28). *New York Times*, [accessed on line, http://groups.yahoo.com/group/smallschools/message/2441.

National Commission on Teaching and America's Future (NCTAF). (2003). *No dream denied: A pledge to America's children*. Washington, DC: Author.

National Education Association. (2003). *Status of the American public school teacher 2000–2001*. Washington, DC: Author.

National Educational Goals Panel. (2000, August). *National Educational Goals Panel Monthly*, 2(19), p. 2.

Navarette, R. (2003, August 19). Teacher key to student achievement. *Albuquerque Journal*, p. A5.

New Mexico Business Roundtable for Educational Excellence (NMBEE). (n.d.). www.nmbusinessround table.org. Thorstensen, B.I. *If you build it they will come: Investing in public education*. University of New Mexico. Retrieved Online from: http://abec.unm.edu/resources/gallery/present/invest_in_ed.pdf.

Goleman, D. (1992, March 3). Teaching emotional literacy in public sschool systems. *New York Times*.

Uchitelle, L. (1994, March 22). Job extinction evolving into a fact of life in U.S. *New York Times*, p. A1.

Myers, S. L. (1995, September 13). Two more quit as candidates for school job. *New York Times*, p. A1.

Seeye, K. Q. (1999, December 16). Gore proposal would set aside $115 billion for education fund. *New York Times*, p. A1.

No Child Left Behind Act of 2001, 20 U.S.C. § 6301 (2002).

Painter, K. (1996, July 10). *USA Today*.

Quality counts: If I can't learn from you… (2003, January 9). *Education Week*.

Roberts, S. (1995). *Who we are: A portrait of America based on the latest U.S. census*. Washington, DC: CSPAN.

Rothstein, R. (2002, October 9). Dropout rate is climbing and likely to go higher. *New York Times*. Retrieved 29 November 2003 from http://www.bridges4kids.org/articles/10-02/NYTimes10-9-02.html.

The face of the American teacher. (2003, July 2). *USA Today*, p. D1.

U.S. Bureau of the Census. (1993). Geographic mobility: March 1992 to March 1993. *Profile of the Nation*, Current Population Reports, pp. 20–481.

U.S. Bureau of the Census. (1995). *Statistical abstract, 1995*. 115th edition. Washington, DC: U.S. Government Printing Office.

U.S. Bureau of the Census. (1995). *Current population reports, Series P23-189: Population profile of the United States: 1995*. Washington, DC: U.S. Government Printing Office.

U.S. Bureau of the Census. (2000). *Historical income tables–households*. Retrieved from www.census.gov.

U.S. Bureau of the Census. (2002, July). *The big payoff: Educational attainment and synthetic estimates of work-life earnings*.

U.S. Department of Education. *Dropout rates in the United States: 1998*. "Status dropout rates."

U.S. Department of Education, Office of Educational Research and Improvement. (1996) (November, 1996). *Key statistics on public elementary and secondary schools and agencies: School year 1995–96.* Washington, DC: Author.

U.S. Department of Education, National Center of Educational Statistics. (2000). Common Core of Data, *Public School District Universe Survey, 1999–2000.* Available from the Education Finance Statistics Center: http://nces.ed.gov/edfin/.

U.S. Department of Education, National Center of Educational Statistics. (1999). *The condition of education.* Office of Educational Research and Improvement, NCES 1999-025.

U.S. Department of Education, Office of Educational Research and Improvement. (1991). *Youth indicators 1991: Trends in the well-being of American youth.* Washington, DC: Author.

U.S. Department of Justice, Bureau of Justice Statistics. (1999). *State Prison Expenditures, 1996.* Washington, DC: Author.

U.S. Department of Justice. (April, 1998). *Juvenile Justice Bulletin.* (source)

U.S. Department of Labor, Bureau of Labor Statistics (2000, March). *Unemployment rate, 2000 annual average.* (2000, December).

U.S. Department of Labor, Bureau of Labor Statistics. (1999, November 22). Reported in *Time Magazine.*

U.S. General Accounting Office. (2002, February). *School dropouts: Education could play a stronger role in identifying and disseminating prevention strategies.* Washington, DC: U.S. General Accounting Office, (GAO-02-240) www.gao/new.items/d02240.pdf.

Shapiro, J. P., with Wright, A. R. (1995, August 14). Sins of the fathers. *U.S. News,* p. 51.

Walsh, J. (2003, August 14). Minnesota's schools face an alarming racial gap. *Star Tribune.*

Zuniga, J. A. (2003, August 18). Prospect of TAKS delaying third grade for some kids. *Houston Chronicle.*

3

Who Drops Out and Why

Franklin P. Schargel

The first step to resolving our school dropout problem is to define the nature of the problem. In this chapter, we describe the various criteria by which dropout rates are measured. We take a closer look at the factors linked to high dropout rates and the characteristics of students who drop out of school. The statistics lead us to the conclusion that the dropout problem can be addressed effectively only by a systemic approach.

Defining the Dropout

Trying to determine who drops out, why they drop out, and even the number of dropouts is a complicated process.

"Some states do not report students who receive a certificate of attendance or other alternative certificate, and some do not report the number of students 19 or younger who are awarded a diploma on the basis of the Graduate Equivalency Degree test. Students who completed high school with some credential other than a regular diploma can account for a sizable proportion of the high school completers. For example, in Florida, Louisiana, Oklahoma, and Tennessee, 19 percent or more of the completers received an alternative credential" (Key Statistics on Public Elementary and Secondary

Schools and Agencies: School Year 1995–1996, U.S. Department of Education, Office of Educational Research and Improvement, 1997, p. 31).

Educators, school boards, and elected officials respond to different pressures in computing statistics on school attendance. Some school districts, seeking additional educational services, carry phantom students on the school records even after they have dropped out. Some states now label districts with a "low performance rating" for having too many dropouts. There, it is in administrators' best interest to embrace a calculation method that makes their rate appear low. In other cases, inflating the rate of dropouts attracts additional funding for at-risk students.

Forty-six states and the District of Columbia "usually report" (National Educational Goals Panel Monthly, Volume 2, No. 19, August 2000, p. 2) dropout data through the Common Core of Data Survey to the National Center for Education Statistics (NCES) but only twenty-two of them and the District of Columbia were using a common dropout definition adopted by the NCES.

Dropout statistics have implications beyond the schoolhouse. The success/failure rate of local schools (frequently measured by graduation rates and post-secondary school attendance rates) helps determine the resale value of homes and is frequently used to influence businesses to move into an area. On the other hand, those who want to shock the public have a motivation to use the methods indicating a high dropout rate. The reality is that as a nation, we do not have a standardized operational definition of who is a dropout, nor do we have a standard method for counting and reporting dropouts. Nevertheless, some useful statistics are available.

Types of Dropout Rates

The U.S. Department of Education uses a variety of ways of calculating dropout rates. Each type provides a different perspective of the student dropout population and reveals different ways of viewing the issue. Adding to the confusion is the debate about the best way to count dropouts. Results can vary enormously depending on the methods used. In Texas, for example, the high school dropout rate for the 1998–1999 school year ranged from a low of 2.2 percent to as high as 36.6 percent, depending on the counting method used (Viadero, 2001).

The NCES presents definitions and data for four types of dropout rates in order to provide a more complete profile of the dropout problem in the United States.

Event Dropout Rates

Event dropout rates describe the proportion of students who leave school each year without completing a high school program. For example, event dropout rates for the year 2000 describe the proportion of youths 15 through 24 years of age who dropped out of grades 10 to 12 during the previous 12 months. This annual measure of recent dropout occurrences provides important information about how effective educators are in keeping students enrolled in school. Demographic data collected in the Current Population Survey (CPS) permit event dropout rates to be calculated across a variety of individual characteristics, including race, sex, region of residence, and income level.

Five out of every hundred young adults enrolled in high school in October 1999 left school before October 2000 without successfully completing a high school program. The percentage of young adults who left school each year without successfully completing a high school program decreased from 1972 through 1987. Despite year-to-year fluctuations, the percentage of students dropping out of school each year has stayed relatively unchanged since 1987 (U.S. Department of Education, *Dropout Rates*, 2000).

Status Dropout Rates

Status rates provide cumulative data on dropouts among all young adults within a specified age range. Specifically, status dropout rates represent the proportion of young adults 16 through 24 years old who are out of school and who have not earned a high school credential. Status rates are higher than event rates because they include all dropouts, regardless of when they last attended school. Since status rates reveal the extent of the dropout problem in the population, this rate also can be used to estimate the need for further education and training designed to help dropouts participate fully in the economy and life of the nation.

Over the last decade, between 347,000 and 544,000 tenth- through twelfth-grade students left school each year without successfully completing a high school program. (Each year some of these young adults return to school or an alternative certification program, and others age out of this group.) (U.S. Department of Education, *Dropout Rates*, 2000).

- ◆ Each year between 1972 and 2001, the status dropout rate was lowest for whites and highest for Hispanics. Between 1972 and 2001, the status dropout rates for white and black young adults declined, while the rate for Hispanics remained relatively constant. The gap between blacks and whites narrowed during the 1970s and 1980s, but not in the period since then.

- ◆ In October 2000, some 3.8 million young adults were not enrolled in a high school program and had not completed high school. These youths accounted for 10.9 percent of the 34.6 million 16- through 24-year-olds in the United States in 2000. (U.S. Department of Education, *The Condition of Education 2003.* 2003).

- In 2000, 44.2 percent of Hispanic young adults born outside of the United States were high school dropouts. Hispanic young adults born within the United States were less likely to be dropouts than those born elsewhere, but still more likely to be dropouts than other youths born with the United States.

- Status rates declined from the early 1970s into the late 1980s but since then have remained stable.

- Status dropout rates of whites remain lower than for blacks, but over the past quarter century the difference between blacks and whites has narrowed. Hispanic young adults in the United States continue to have higher status dropout rates than either whites or blacks (U.S. Department of Education, *Dropout Rates,* 2000).

Cohort Dropout Rates

Cohort rates measure what happens to a group of students from a single age group or specific grade over a period of time. "If a group of students were followed over time, the annual event dropout rates would add up to a larger cohort dropout rate. For example, if 4 percent of students dropped out each year beginning with grade 9, by the end of grade 12 this would add up to a cohort rate of about 15 percent. A cohort rate gives an estimate of how many students eventually fail to complete high school" (U.S. Department of Education, *Key Statistics on Public Elementary and Secondary Schools and Agencies: School Year 1995–1996,* p. 32).

High School Completion Rates

The high school completion rate represents the proportion of 18- to 24-year-olds not currently enrolled in high school or below who have completed a high school diploma or an equivalent credential, including a Graduate Equivalency Degree (GED). An increasing number of non–high school graduates are using the GED to obtain high school certification. In 1998, half a million Americans obtained a GED degree, more than double the number who received it in 1971. One-seventh of all school graduates are actually GED recipients. The GED examinations cover mathematics, reading, social studies, science, and writing. Since 1988, they have included an open-ended writing component as well as multiple-choice questions (Murnane & Tyler, 2000).

- In 2000, 86.5 percent of all 18- through 24-year-olds not enrolled in high school had completed high school.

- Completion rates rose slightly from the early 1970s to the late 1980s but have remained fairly constant during the 1990s.

- By 2000, 91.8 percent of white and 83.7 percent of black 18- through 24-year-olds had completed high school.
  (U.S. Department of Education, *Dropout Rates,* 2000)

Graduate Equivalency Degree (GED)

The Census Bureau counts as high school completers those who dropped out but passed a high school equivalency test. Even though the GED examination has been made more difficult, it still requires less proficiency than getting a high school diploma. Furthermore, some employers value the social habits and discipline gained by young people staying in school and graduating. Holders of GED certificates are generally paid less than those with a high school diploma (NCES, The Condition of Education, 1999).

The majority of students complete a regular diploma and graduate from high school; others complete high school by an alternative route, such as passing the GED exam. During the 1990s, the percentage of young adults who were not enrolled in school but held a high school credential remained relatively unchanged. However, the percentage holding an alternative certification increased from 4.9 percent in 1990 to 9.1 percent in 1997 (and the percentage holding regular diplomas decreased by a similar amount) (NCES, *The Condition of Education*, 1999).

Why Students Drop Out

Would it be useful to draw a profile of the typical dropout? Those who favor such a profile believe that defining those predictors would facilitate early identification and intervention for those most likely to drop out. Those who oppose developing a profile argue that labeling students as likely dropouts would lead educators to expect less of those students. Although it is impossible to draw a definitive image of a "typical" dropout, certain features appear with greater frequency than others.

Factors Linked to High Dropout Rates

Student Retention

Poor academic performance linked to retention in one grade is the single strongest school-related predictor of dropping out. One report indicated that out of every ten dropouts, nine had been retained at least one year. Slavin and Madden (1989) noted that retention does not improve achievement: "[P]romoted students perform better than non-promoted students in the next year on measures of academic achievement, personal adjustment, self-concept and attitudes toward school… [Further, a] widely quoted finding from the Youth in Transition Study is that one grade retention increases the risk of dropping out by 40 to 50 percent, and more than one by 90 percent" (pp. 104–105).

In Massachusetts, overall retention rates for ninth-graders jumped from 6.3 percent in 1995 to 8.4 percent in 2001. Twelve districts held over 20 percent of their ninth-graders back. The three with the highest ninth-grade retention rates—between 27 and 38 percent—enroll a majority of nonwhite students. African-Americans and Hispanics are retained at over three times the rate of whites. Retaining a student without providing targeted and intensive support mechanisms and interventions leads to huge management problems for the school and dramatically increases the likelihood that students will drop out (Edley & Wald, 2002).

Poverty

Poverty poses a serious challenge to children's access to quality learning opportunities and their potential to succeed in school. Data indicate that children from low-income families are more likely to drop out and therefore more likely to remain poor themselves. High school dropouts have lower earnings, experience more unemployment, and are more likely to end up on welfare and in prison than their peers who complete high school and college.

◆ The probability of falling into poverty is three times higher for high school dropouts than for those who have finished high school. In 1997, high school graduates earned an average of $7,000 more than high school dropouts ($22,154 versus $15,011) (*Nevada KIDS COUNT Data Book*, 2000).

◆ As the economy changed between 1973 and 1995, the average hourly wage, adjusted for inflation, of high school dropouts fell by 23 percent (*Nevada KIDS COUNT Data Book*, 2000).

◆ An economic downturn causes a decrease in the number of poor children with working parents ("Poor Children," 2003). In 1999, 15 percent of 6- to 12-year-olds (3.3 million) were in self care; that is, the children either took care of themselves or were tended by a sibling age 12 or younger on a regular basis. "Children in self care may be at increased risk for accidents and injuries, for social and behavioral problems, and for academic and school adjustments" ("Left Unsupervised," 2003, p. 23).[CB]Need page number for quote.

◆ "Students from low-income families are three times as likely to drop out of school as those from more affluent homes" (Annie E. Casey Foundation, *Kids Count Data Book*, 1993). Female students from families in the lowest quartile of socioeconomic status (SES) drop out of school at five times the rate of females from the highest quartile. Male students in the lowest quartile drop out at two and a half times the rate of those in the highest quartile (Annie E. Casey Foundation, 1998).

Ethnicity

The data show that black and Hispanic students are more vulnerable to dropping out of school than white students (Kiagas, 2003):

- In 2000, the status dropout rate was 7 percent for whites, 13 percent for blacks, and 28 percent for Hispanics.

- In 2000, 92 percent of white 18- to 24-year-olds had completed secondary schooling; the completion rate was 84 percent for black 18- to 24-year-olds and just 64 percent for Hispanic 18- to 24-year-olds.

- In 1999, 18 percent of black students and 13 percent of Hispanic students in kindergarten through 12th grade had to repeat a grade (compared with 7 percent of white students).

- In 1999, 35 percent of blacks and 20 percent of Hispanics in grades 7 to 12 had been suspended or expelled (compared with 15 percent of whites).

- In 1998, about one-quarter of Hispanic and black students completed an advanced mathematics course, whereas about one-half of white students did so. Chemistry II, physics II, or advanced biology was the highest science course completed by about 10 percent of Hispanics, 11 percent of blacks, and 18 percent of whites.

- In 1998, minority students were half as likely as whites and one-third as likely as Asian students to have taken calculus. Among high-school graduates that year, minority students were less likely than white or Asian students to have taken physics (19 percent versus 31 percent of white, and 46 percent of Asian high school graduates) (McBay, 2003).

As we have seen, the dropouts pay a price. An analysis of employment trends from 1979 to 2000 for young less-educated black men (Offner & Holzer, 2002) found:

- Only 52 percent of young, less-educated black males are employed today, compared to 62 percent 20 years ago.

- The employment rate of young, less-educated black males is much lower in cities than in suburbs, and the gap has widened over the last decade.

- Young, less-educated blacks in older industrial metro areas, and in major cities like New York, Los Angeles, and San Francisco, are employed at lower rates than those in rural areas.

Although they are a diverse group, coming from Mexico, Central America, and South America, Hispanics in the United States are frequently treated as a homogeneous population; disaggregated data are limited. The following information about Hispanics is available:

Between 1990 and 2000, Hispanics became the largest minority group in the United States (El Nasser, 2003):

♦ From April 2000 to July 2002, the U.S. population grew by 2.5 percent; the Hispanic population grew by 9.8 percent. The Hispanic growth rate equaled one half of the national increase to 38.8 million people. Hispanics now comprise nearly 12 percent of the total population. Between 1990 and 2000, the Hispanic population increased by approximately 10 million people, accounting for 38 percent of the nation's overall population growth during the decade.

♦ Hispanics are expected to account for 51 percent of the population growth between 2000 and 2050; by mid-century, the number of Hispanics is expected to reach 98 million, representing about one-fourth of the total U.S. population and more than three times their present number. The 2000 census reports that the Hispanic population has grown by nearly 60 percent since 1990. The increase in Hispanic residents outpaces overall population growth rate. The Hispanic growth rate is in all 50 states (risk to Opportunity, p.1) (White House Initiative, 2003, March).

♦ Hispanics now outnumber the African-American population. The doubling of the Hispanic population in the 1990s has been caused by increases in immigration and a higher birth rate.

The Hispanic population is younger on average than the population overall (Kiagas, 2003).

♦ In 2000, the median age of Hispanics in the United States was 26.6 years, younger than the median age for any other racial or ethnic group (Hispanics: 26.6; American Indian, 28.5; black, non-Hispanic 30.6; Asian, 32.4; white, non-Hispanic 38.6).

♦ The number of Hispanic children as a proportion of all children has been increasing; projections indicate that by 2020, one in five children will be of Hispanic origin.

Hispanics continue to be over-represented in poverty. In 2000, Hispanics comprised just fewer than 12 percent of the U.S. population but comprised about 21 percent of those living in poverty; 28 percent of Hispanic children were living in poverty (Kiagas, 2003).

Hispanic children and students face more challenges than most of their peers (Kiagas, 2003):

♦ In 2000, one-fourth of Hispanics under the age of 18 had no public or private health insurance.

♦ Hispanic children are less likely than white or black children to be enrolled in center-based pre-primary education at the age of 3.

- In 1999, Hispanic children were less likely than white or black children to be read to or to visit a library.

- Most Hispanic students attend schools where minorities are the majority of the student body. (Data indicate that minority schools have less experienced teachers.)

- In 2000, minorities constituted 39 percent of public school students in kindergarten through 12th grade; of these, 44 percent were Hispanic. Between 1972 and 2000, the percentage of Hispanic students in public schools increased 11 percentage points and the overall percentage of minority students increased by 17 percentage points.

- The largest concentration of Hispanic students is in the West (America's fastest growing section) where they represented 32 percent of students in 2000 (doubling in the past 28 years).

- Sixty-five percent of all Hispanic students live in large cities or the urban fringe of large cities. Hispanic students comprised one-quarter or more of public school enrollment in five states (Arizona, California, Nevada, New Mexico, and Texas). Hispanics were the largest racial/ethnic group in four of the largest city school districts (New York City, Los Angeles Unified, Dade County (Florida), and Houston Independent).

- Fifty-nine percent of Hispanic 4th grade students were in public schools where more than 50 percent of the students were eligible to receive free or reduced-price lunch; 17 percent of Hispanic students were enrolled in schools with 100 percent of students eligible for free or reduced-price lunch.

- According to teacher reports, Hispanic kindergartners are less likely than white kindergartners to stay focused on tasks, to be eager to learn, and to pay attention. In 1998, 67 percent of Hispanic first-time kindergartners were reported to persist at the tasks, 70 percent to be eager to learn, and 62 percent to pay attention in class.

- Hispanic 8th and 12th graders have a higher absenteeism rate than whites. In 2000, 26 percent of Hispanic students in the 8th grade and 34 percent of Hispanics in the 12th grade reported that they had been absent three or more days in the preceding month.

The Census Bureau and the United States Department of Education report that Hispanics make up an increasingly disproportionate share of the nation's dropouts (*CNN Students' News*, 2002):

- "In 2000, approximately 1.56 million residents ages 16 to 19 were not high school graduates and not enrolled in school. Of the total, nearly 34 percent, or more than 528,000 children, were Hispanic. That number is up from 22 percent of the 1.59 million in 1990."

◆ The increase is due in part to the overall rise in the Hispanic population during the 1990s. Hispanics represent nearly 16 percent of all 16- to 19-year olds in 2000, up from 11 percent in 1990.

◆ The increase in Hispanic dropouts is also due to their migration from large urban centers to small-town and rural school districts that lack the money, staffing, and programs to help them adapt to schools and overcome language barriers.

◆ One half of all Hispanic immigrants never enrolled in a U.S. school. They are not included in the nation's dropout rate.

In a 2003 study of Hispanics (Fry, 2003), the Pew Hispanic Center found:

◆ Because of the enormous growth in the number of Hispanic youth due to immigration and high birth rates, the number of Latino 16- to 19-year-old dropouts grew dramatically, from 347,000 to 529,000, between 1990 and 2000. However, the dropout rate for native-born Latinos declined over that period from 15.2 percent to 14.0 percent. Of the 529,000 16- to 19-year-old Latino high school dropouts in 2000, one third (roughly 175,000) are immigrants who had little or no contact with U.S. schools.

◆ There is a staggering dropout problem plaguing Hispanic students. Today one out of every three Hispanic Americans has dropped out of high school. (White House Initiative on Educational Excellence, Risk to Opportunity, 2002, March, p. 3)

◆ The dropout rate for immigrant Central American youth is nearly 25 percent.

◆ Thirty-five percent of Latino youths are immigrants, compared to less than five percent of non-Latino youth.

◆ Mexican immigrants constitute 54 percent of Hispanic immigrants and the largest segment of all immigrants into the United States. Mexican immigrants experience nearly twice the dropout rate of other Hispanics. (White House Initiative on Educational Excellence, Risk to Opportunity, 2002, March, p. 3)

◆ Nearly 40 percent of Mexican immigrants 16 to 19 years old are dropouts.

◆ A lack of English-language ability is the prime characteristic of Latino dropouts. Almost 40 percent do not speak English well. The 14 percent of Hispanic 16- to 19-year-olds who have poor English language skills have a dropout rate of 59 percent.

◆ The unemployment rate for U.S.-born Latino dropouts is 26 percent, slightly better than for white dropouts.

Limited English Proficiency

Children from homes where the primary language is not English are placed at a disadvantage.

◆ In 1995, of those 16- to 24-year-olds who spoke a language other than English at home, the dropout rate of those who had difficulty speaking English (44 percent) was substantially higher than that of those who did not have difficulty speaking English (12 percent) (U.S. Department of Education, 1997).

◆ Young people from non–English-language backgrounds are one and one-half times more likely to leave school than those from English-language backgrounds. Thus, while high school dropout rates have been declining, the trend for Hispanic students is the opposite. In 1992, roughly 50 percent of Hispanics ages 16 to 24 dropped out of high school, up from 30 percent in 1990. The higher Hispanic dropout rate should be coupled with the fact that one-third of the Hispanic immigrant group who came to the United States by 1995 without a high school diploma had not entered an American school (Day, 1993).

◆ The dropout rate for Hispanics who do not speak English is three to four times as high as the rate for those who do (Day, 1993). The large increase in the number of foreign-born Hispanic immigrants with little or no English language skills may help explain the current high dropout rates among this group.

Urban Schools

Young people in the inner city often face additional challenges: violence, gangs, drugs, poverty, alcohol abuse, overcrowded classes, decaying schools, limited school supplies and books, and limited access to computers both at home and at school. Because classes are often overcrowded, teachers cannot supply the attention many of these students need. Because schools in poverty-stricken areas with minority populations tend to have difficulty obtaining certified teachers, classroom teachers may not know their subject material. As a result, students are bored. In Philadelphia, students considering dropping out of school listed boredom as the number one reason; stress and poor performance in school ranked second and third (Snyder, 2003).

Due to the concentration of minorities, low-income families, and first-generation immigrants, over 50 percent of urban young people do not graduate in four years. Many others receive an alternative certificate or a GED degree, which has little value in the labor market. (Civil Rights Project, 2003).

Rural Schools

Children who attend the nation's rural schools are often at a disadvantage because their schools lack the money, staffing, and programs to meet their needs. The Rural School and Community Trust (2003) reports these data:

- Almost one third (31 percent) of the public schools in America are in rural areas. Eight million children (21 percent) attend them. More than one in six American children attends a school in a community with fewer than 2,500 people.

- These schools are under increasing pressure to comply with the No Child Left Behind legislation. Because they generally offer lower salaries than competing urban and suburban areas, they have difficulty attracting the mandated "highly qualified" teachers—but communities with a low tax base cannot afford to raise teacher salaries. On average, rural teachers make 86 cents for every dollar earned by their urban counterparts. In 13 states, rural teacher salaries lag behind urban/suburban salaries by more than $5,000. In some states, the gap is even wider: $8,573 in Illinois, $7,896 in New York, $7,573 in Pennsylvania, $6,868 in Iowa (Tompkins, 2003).

- The Supreme Courts in Arkansas, Ohio, and Tennessee have ruled that the state funding systems were unconstitutionally depriving rural schools of equal funding.

- Many rural areas have poverty levels as high as those seen in urban centers in the same state. Overall, 13.8 percent of rural children live in poverty—but the rate in some states can range from 20 percent to over 25 percent.

- Minorities comprise 18.6 percent of all students enrolled in rural schools. These children are at greater risk merely because of where they attend school.

Teen Sexual Activity

In a 1999 study (Henry J. Kaiser Family Foundation, 2002), researchers found:

- Eight and three-tenths percent of students admitted having sex before age 13.

- Approximately one in four sexually active teens gets an STD every year, and approximately half of all new HIV infections occur in people under the age of 25.

- One quarter of sexually active students in grades 9 through 12 reported using alcohol or drugs during their most recent sexual encounter.

- Although the teen pregnancy and birth rates declined during the 1990s and teen pregnancy rates are at their lowest levels in 20 years, the United States still has the highest rates of teen pregnancy, birth, and abortion in the industrialized world.

- Four in ten girls become pregnant at least once before age 20—more than 900,000 teen pregnancies annually. There are nearly half a million teen births each year. That amounts to nearly 100 teen girls getting pregnant and 55 giving birth each hour.

- About 40 percent of pregnant teens are 17 or younger.

- Nearly eight in ten teen pregnancies are not planned.

- Seventy-nine percent of births to teen mothers are out of wedlock.

According to the National Campaign to Prevent Teen Pregnancy (2002), teen pregnancy and parenthood are linked to other critical social issues:

- Hispanics now have the highest teen birth rate nationally. Birth rates for Hispanic teens have increased in a number of states. If current Hispanic fertility rates remain the same, we will see a 26 percent increase in the number of pregnancies and births among teenagers.

- Teen childbearing costs taxpayers at least $7 billion each year in direct costs associated with health care, foster care, criminal justice, and public assistance, as well as lost tax revenues.

- Teen mothers are more likely to end up on welfare. Almost one-half of all teen mothers and over three-quarters of unmarried teen mothers began receiving welfare within five years of the birth of their first child.

- Some 52 percent of all mothers on welfare had their first child as a teenager.

- Teen mothers are less likely to complete the education necessary to qualify for a well-paying job; only 41 percent of mothers who have children before age 18 complete high school, compared with 61 percent of similarly situated young women who delay childbearing until age 21.

- Virtually all of the increase in child poverty between 1980 and 1996 was related to the increase in nonmarital childbearing.

- Nearly 80 percent of fathers of children born to teen mothers do not marry the mothers. These fathers pay less than $800 annually in child support, often because they are quite poor themselves.

- Children of teen mothers do worse in school than those born to older parents. They are 50 percent more likely to repeat a grade, are less likely to complete high school than the children or older mothers, and have lower performance on standardized tests.

- The sons of teen mothers are 13 percent more likely to end up in prison.
- The daughters of teen parents are 22 percent more likely to become teen mothers themselves.
- Although only three out of ten out-of-wedlock births in the United Sates are to teenagers, 48 percent of all nonmarital first births occur to teens—the largest single group.
- Nearly 80 percent of teen births are to unmarried teens, up from 15 percent in 1960.
- Boys and girls without involved fathers are twice as likely to drop out of school, twice as likely to abuse alcohol or drugs, twice as likely to end up in jail, and nearly four times as likely to need help for emotional and behavioral problems.
- Teen fathers have lower levels of education and earn 10 to 15 percent less annually than teens who do not father children.
- Teen parents and their children are less likely to graduate from high school. In fact, fewer than four in ten teen mothers who begin their families before age 18 ever complete high school.

Teenagers who get pregnant tend to drop out of school. It has been estimated that 30 to 40 percent of female teenage dropouts are mothers (Annie E. Casey Foundation, 1998). Women who drop out of high school are more likely to become pregnant and give birth at a young age and more likely to become single parents than women who graduate from high school. A child whose mother dropped out of school is twice as likely to drop out of school as the child of a mother who is a high school graduate (*Nevada KIDS COUNT Data Book*, 2000).

Tracking

The debate about the kinds of skill students need upon graduation continues. In the past, a small elite minority of students went on from high school to college. Other students, tracked into vocational programs, often ended up with low-paying, meaningless, dead-end jobs. Today, the expectation is that all students will be prepared to enter college. Yet according to the United States Department of Labor, only 20 percent of jobs in the future will require traditional baccalaureate degrees, while 70 percent will require some form of postsecondary school training (Coeyman, 2003).

Vocational education programs—now called *career technical education*—offer young people a valuable employment opportunity if they are linked to a strong academic component. Effective career technical training can make learning more interesting for those students who learn better from hands-on experience than from books. Nancy O'Brien, senior director of public policy for the Association for Career and Technical Education, believes that many businesses are crying out for American workers with technical skills (Coeyman, 2003).

Disruptive Students

Students who disrupt the classroom hinder their own learning and that of others. Some may find the environment too structured; others may have been promoted based on "seat time" rather than achievement. When these students demand more attention and need more services than their teachers can provide, they are frequently suspended or discharged. In school year 2000–2001, the state of Massachusetts excluded 1,621 students—a jump of almost 15 percent in one year and the highest number in six years (Vaishnav, 2003).

Under the provisions of No Child Left Behind, such student removals will have to be disaggregated by race, gender, and school system. Current research indicates that black and Latino male students are excluded more than whites, Asians, or females (Appalachia Educational Laboratory).

What accounts for the increase in exclusions? Possible factors include these (Appalachia Educational Laboratory):

- Schools may not be meeting the learning needs of these students.
- Students tend to show less respect in the classroom.
- Societal violence is on the rise.
- Alternative schools provide options for students excluded from traditional schools.
- In-school suspension programs remove students from their "normal" classroom.
- Schools may be getting tougher on disruptions.
- Students may be acting out more frequently.
- Budget cuts reduce supplemental school services like counselors, psychologists, and social workers.
- More students live in dysfunctional homes.
- Students lack role models for appropriate behavior.
- Latchkey children have less adult contact at home.

Children with Special Needs

Special education students drop out at a significantly greater rate than regular education students. According to the National Council on Disability Education, using data from the twenty-third annual report to Congress on the implementation of the Individuals with Disabilities Education Act, the

1998–1999 differential percentage comparing special education dropouts to regular education dropouts ranges from 2.4 times greater (Arizona: 8.4 percent regular dropouts; 20.3 percent special education dropouts) to 8.4 percent greater (Iowa: 2.5 percent regular education dropouts; 21.4 percent special education dropouts). According to the reporting states, the special education dropout rate was 3.762 times greater than the regular education dropout rate (National Council on Disability Education, 2002).

- ◆ "Special education" once indicated predominantly physical disability. Increasingly, the term identifies those unable to function in a traditional school or classroom. These students are often labeled "learning disabled."

- ◆ Minority students generally comprise the majority of learning-disabled special education students.

- ◆ Students with sensory, physical, cognitive, emotional, or behavioral disability can be considered for special education. The vast majority of children receiving special education today are described as learning disabled, emotionally disturbed, mildly mentally retarded, or having speech and language problems. During the past ten years, the number of children classified as having learning disabilities has increased by almost 38 percent, and over half of all children receiving special education in the United States are characterized as having a learning disability (InFocus, 2002).

- ◆ Graduation rates for students aged 14 and older with disabilities have grown steadily (in 1998–1999, the graduation rate was 57.4 percent). During the same time, the dropout rate has declined. In 1993–1994, the special-education dropout rate was 34.5 percent. By 1998–1999, the rate was 28.9 percent.

- ◆ Special-education dropout rates vary by racial/ethnic group: Asian/Pacific Islander special-education students had the lowest dropout rate (18.8 percent), followed by whites (26.9 percent), Hispanics (33 percent) and blacks (33.7 percent). The highest dropout rate occurred among American Indian/Alaska Native special-education students, at 44.0 percent.

- ◆ Graduation rates for students age 14 and older with disabilities varied by disability category; students with visual impairments had the highest graduation rate (75.1 percent), while students with emotional disturbance had the lowest graduation rate (41.9 percent).

- ◆ About 50 percent of students identified under the Individuals with Disabilities Education Act (IDEA) as having emotional and behavioral disorders drop out of school. Once they leave school, these lack the social skills necessary to be successfully employed; they suffer from low employment levels and poor work histories.

♦ Black students with disabilities exceeded their representation among the resident population.

♦ As of 1 October 1999, 12,241 funded positions were left vacant or filled by substitutes because qualified special-education teachers could not be found. Superintendents cited insufficient salary and benefits and the district's geographic location to explain this shortage (U.S. Department of Education, 2001).

♦ Research shows that mental retardation does not occur in any one race, ethnicity, or gender more than any other; thus, the demographics of a district's mentally retarded students should reflect that of the overall population. Yet in Connecticut, black girls are five times as likely to be identified as mentally retarded as white boys. In Stanford, blacks represent about half of the district's mentally retarded students but only a quarter of the student body (Overton, 2003).

Geographic Location

The dropout rate is higher in the inner cities than in suburbs and nonmetropolitan areas. In some districts, the rate is double the national average.

♦ The dropout rate is higher in the southern and western states than in the mid-Atlantic and New England states. "In 1998, status dropout rates in the Midwest (8.0 percent) and Northeast (9.4 percent) were significantly lower than dropout rates in the South (13.1 percent) and West (15.3 percent)" (U.S. Department of Education, 1998, p.14).

♦ Approximately 88 percent of the young adults in the Northeast and Midwest have completed high school, compared to 83.4 percent in the South and 80.4 percent in the West.

Predicting Dropouts Isn't That Simple

Although certain social, economic, ethnic, or racial characteristics increase the statistical likelihood that students will drop out, nobody can predict with any degree of certainty that particular students who have these characteristics will drop out, or that others who do not fit the profile won't.

A 1994–1995 Texas dropout report listed the top ten reasons students in Texas decided to leave school. As reported by school districts, the reasons were (in order of frequency):

♦ poor attendance,

- to enter a non–state-approved GED program,
- employment,
- low or failing grades,
- age,
- to get married,
- pregnancy,
- suspension/expulsion,
- failed exit examinations/did not meet graduation requirements,
- to enter a non–state-approved alternative program.

(U.S. Department of Education, online Publications and Resources)

The Oregon Department of Education tracked a cohort of students from 1991 to 1995. At the end of the four-year period, 24.5 percent of the students had dropped out before graduating. The most frequent reason given by students for deciding to leave was "irrelevant coursework." Other reasons were peer pressure, teaching that didn't match student learning styles, and teachers' lack of personal attention (U.S. Department of Education, online Publications and Resources).

Dropouts Are a Systemic Problem

Some view dropping out as an occurrence. Educators realize it is a process. Frequently the process begins in primary school. As students go through school, an accumulation of negative experiences increases the likelihood that they will drop out. Since students cannot physically leave school in the primary grades, the dropout problem first surfaces in middle or high school. However, there is a growing perception that the needs of at-risk students can and should be addressed as soon as they are identified.

The dropout problem begins long before the actual event of leaving school adds another number to the statistics. Furthermore, the dropouts reflected in the statistics do not represent the full extent and complexity of the problem. We can distinguish three types of dropouts:

- Dropouts—students who are leaving or have left school.
- Tune-outs—students who stay in school but disengage from learning.
- Pushouts—those who are suspended or expelled.

The first group is highly visible—easy to identify and measure. These students are the ones most frequently addressed in prevention, retention, and recovery programs.

The second category is less readily apparent. These students may attend school regularly, or not. Some pass their classes, earn credits, are promoted, and even get relatively good grades. School may be easy for them; it may be boring; it may not meet their needs at all. Unless they cause problems or disrupt classes, they are tolerated, even ignored. Some may eventually drop out. But even if these students complete high school, does the diploma stand for something of value?

The third group contains the troublesome students—those who refuse to follow school rules, or who are involved in crimes either inside or outside school. Rebellious, disruptive, alienated, these students don't fit the system, and they are encouraged—or told—to leave. The school's problem is solved; the student's problem, and our society's problem, is not.

It's time to recognize that the dropout problem is a systemic problem that can be addressed effectively only by a systemic approach. We must look at everything we do in schools with a fresh eye. Our primary goal is not simply to keep students in our classrooms until they graduate, but to provide them with an education that prepares them for a full and productive life beyond the classroom. Each one of our nation's children is a unique and valuable resource. What can we do in schools to make the most of this potential national treasure?

Conclusion

The foregoing chapter asked that, before addressing the problem of dropouts, we take a long, hard look at the characteristics of this segment of the population. As we do this, several aspects of the issue come to light that were not necessarily part of our initial belief system. Not only do we find that the identity of dropouts differs from the predictable, but also we encounter an array of varying criteria for measuring the problem. Indeed, the more we study dropouts, the more complicated the research becomes.

References

Appalacia Educational Laboratory Regional Educational Library (n.d.). *Schools for Disruptive Students: A Questionable Alternative?* Charleston, WV.

Annie E. Casey Foundation (1998). *Kids Count Data Book.* Baltimore, MD.

CNN Students' News. (2002, October 11). Census: Hispanic dropout numbers soar.

Coeyman, M. (2003, July 8). Practical skills vs. three R's: A debate revives. *Christian Science Monitor,* www.csmonitor.com/2003/0708/p13502-lepr.htm.

Day, J. (1993). *Population projections of the United States, by age, sex, race, and Hispanic origin: 1993 to 2050.* U.S. Bureau of the Census, Current Population Reports, Series P25–1104. Washington, DC: U.S. Government Printing Office.

Edley, C., & Wald, J. (2002, December 16). The grade retention fallacy. *Boston Globe,* p. A19.

El Nasser, H. (2003, June 19). 39 million make Hispanics largest minority group. *USA Today,* p. A1.

Fry, R. (2003). *Hispanic youth dropping out of U.S. schools: Measuring the challenge.* Washington, DC: Pew Hispanic Center.

Henry J. Kaiser Family Foundation. (2002). *Teen sexual activity.* Washington, DC: Author.

InFocus. (2002, April 12). *An in-depth analysis of emerging issues in health in schools.* Retrieved [June 1, 2003] from www.healthinschools.org.

Kiagas, C. (2003). *Status and trends in the education of Hispanics.* (NCES 2003-2008). Washington, DC: U.S. Department of Education, National Center for Educational Statistics.

Left unsupervised: A look at the most vulnerable children. (May 5, 2003). *Child Trends Research Brief* (n.d.) www.childtrends.org.

McBay, S. M. (2003, summer). Still underserved after all these years. *Issues in Science and Technology* online. Retrieved November 29, 2003, from http://www.nap.edu/issues/19.4/mcbay.html.

Murnane, R., & Tyler, J. (2000, May 3). The increasing role of the GED in American education. *Education Week on the Web.* Retrieved from www.edweek.org.

National Campaign to Prevent Teen Pregnancy. (2002, February). *Not just another single issue: Teen pregnancy prevention's link to other critical social issues.* Washington, DC: Author.

National Council on Disability Education: Revised Data Brief for August 27, 2002—Dropout Rates. www.ncd.gov.

National Educational Goals Panel Monthly. (2000, August). 2, No. 19, p. 2.

Nevada KIDS COUNT Internet Data Book. (2000). "High school dropouts and graduates." Center for Business and Economic Research, University of Nevada, Las Vegas. Available at http://kidscount.unlv.edu/kc_dbcontents_2000.html.

Offner, P., & Holzer, H. (April 2002). *Left behind in the labor market: Recent employment trends among young black men.* Washington, DC: Center on Urban and Metropolitan Policy, The Brookings Institute.

Overton, P. (2003, August 19). School districts receive warning: At issue is education of mentally retarded. *The Hartford Courant* Online, August 19, 2003, www.ctnow.com.

Poor children in working families continue to lag. (June 11, 2003). *Child Trends Research Brief* (n.d.) www.childtrends.org.

Rural School and Community Trust. (2003). *Why rural matters.* Retrieved from http://www.ruraledu.org.

Slavin, R. E., & Madden, N. A. (1989). Effective classroom programs for students at risk. In R. E. Slavin, N. L. Karweit, and N. A. Madden (Eds.), *Effective programs for students at risk.* Boston: Allyn and Bacon.

Snyder, S. (2003, August 6). Boredom cited as a reason for thoughts of dropping out. *Philadelphia Inquirer* Online, www.philly.com/mld/inquirer/.

The Civil Rights Project. (2003, June 2). *Missing children: Confronting the problem.* Cambridge, MA: Harvard University.

Tompkins, R. B. (2003, March 26). Leaving rural children behind. *Education Week,* p. 44.

U.S. Department of Education, National Center for Educational Statistics. (1997). *The condition of education 1997: The social context of education.* Washington, DC: U.S. Government Printing Office.

U.S. Department of Education, National Center for Educational Statistics. (1997). *The condition of education 1999*. (NCES 1999-022). Washington, DC: U.S. Government Printing Office.

U.S. Department of Education, National Center for Educational Statistics. (2003). *The condition of education 2003*, (NCES 2003-067). Washington, DC: U.S. Government Printing Office.

U.S. Department of Education, National Center for Educational Statistics. (2001, November). *Dropout rates in the United States: 2000*. Washington, DC: U.S. Government Printing Office.

U.S. Department of Education, National Center for Education Statistics. (1989). *High school and beyond survey, sophomore cohort*. Washington, DC: U.S. Government Printing Office.

U.S. Department of Education, Office of Educational Research and Improvement. (1999, November). *Dropout rates in the United States: 1998*. Washington, DC: Author.

U.S. Department of Education, Office of Educational Research and Improvement. (1997, March). *Key statistics on public elementary and secondary schools and agencies: School year 1995–1996*. Washington, DC: U.S. Government Printing Office.

U.S. Department of Education, Office of Educational Research and Improvement. (2001, November). [CB]need date*Reaching the goals: Goal 2, high school completion*. Washington, DC: Author.

U.S. Department of Education. (2001*). Twenty-third annual report to Congress on the implementation of the Individuals with Disabilities Education Act*. Washington, DC: U.S. Government Printing Office.

U.S. Department of Education. (2003, April, 28). *Publications and resources: Information and research on dropouts and dropout prevention strategies*. Retrieved November 29, 2003, from http://www.ed.gov/programs/dropout/dropoutprogram.html.

Vaishnav, A. (2003, March 12). Student suspensions leap in state. *Boston Globe* online www.boston.com/globe.

Viadero, D. (2001, February 7). The dropout dilemma. *Education Week*.

White House Initiative on Educational Excellence for Hispanic Americans, Risk to Opportunity: Fulfilling the Educational Needs of Hispanic Americans in The 21st Century, March 2003.

A School and Community Perspective

4

Systemic Renewal: What Works?

Patricia Cloud Duttweiler

Barriers to Change

If an unfriendly foreign power had attempted to impose on America the mediocre educational performance that exists today, we might well have viewed it as an act of war. As it stands, we have allowed this to happen to ourselves.... We have, in effect, been committing an act of unthinking, unilateral educational disarmament.

National Commission
on Excellence in Education (1983), p. 5

It would be comforting to think those words from *A Nation at Risk* do not apply to education in the United States in 2003. Over the years, however, educational systems in the United States have doggedly engaged in patchwork improvement, layering program after program onto existing structures. Twenty years after the release of *A Nation at Risk*, the most widely implemented recommendation from the Commission report is the one that stated "standards of achievement... should be administered at major transition points from one level of schooling to another." Yet, today's standards and accountability programs do not replace the ones that came before; they are simply added to them.

Many policy makers and educators seem to believe that accountability strategies (e.g., making promotion to the next grade or receiving a high school diploma contingent on passing the assessments) will motivate principals to lead their schools more effectively, teachers to teach better, and students to work harder at learning. However, the difficulties schools are faced with preclude simple, easy solutions. When combined with a student population increasingly composed of students whom schools have traditionally failed, the multifaceted educational changes required to meet current standards-based reform mandates have increased the already overwhelming complexity of schooling. While today's reform efforts dictate top-down standards for the content of schooling, they fundamentally leave the process of school change up to the discretion of local educators. In many ways, expecting local educators to reinvent the process of educational reform, school by school, is both unrealistic and unfair (Borman, Hewes, & Brown, 2002).

Students in at-risk situations must cope with personal, health, family, and/or community situations that contribute to their low academic performance. Circumstances in the schools too often compound these problems and hinder student learning. In spite of more stringent standards and tests of achievement, schools are still failing to provide students with the support, skills, and knowledge they need to succeed academically and graduate. Students do not suddenly decide in high school to drop out. For the most part, students have traveled a rough road of frustration and failure before they can legally leave. A report prepared by the General Accounting Office ("School Dropouts: Education Could Play ...", 2002) cites research studies that show dropping out is a long-term process of disengagement that begins in the earliest grades. The crucial point is that we cannot set higher standards and hold students accountable while we continue along the same, familiar educational path.

Organizational Barriers to School Improvement

Today's standards and accountability mandates rarely replace the programs that are already in place; they are simply added to them. A report by the Progressive Policy Institute (Hill, 2003) points out that few programs or initiatives ever go away entirely. The report mentions that in an Eastern city, principals saved all the directives they received from the central office during one 180-day school year. The stack contained 400 items, all signed by various senior district officials and issued under the authority of the school board. The report suggests that the result of such bureaucratic redundancy is to isolate problems and diffuse responsibility.

According to a study of twenty restructuring dropout prevention programs around the country conducted by Mathematica Policy Research, Inc. (Dynarski & Gleason, 1998), the organizational structure in which the programs operated affected their ability to function and adapt effectively. The programs brought something new into an existing local educational environment, yet were inserted into an organizational structure that provided few rewards or incentives for outstanding teaching while penalizing deviations from traditional forms of schooling. The report posed the question of whether dropout prevention programs—relatively small in comparison to their host schools or districts—could be implemented and accepted in a setting long noted for its resistance to change.

The Edna McConnell Clark Foundation began working with Jefferson County Public Schools (JCPS) in 1989, providing a series of grants over a six-year period to improve student achievement in three low-performing middle schools. The foundation provided larger grants to the whole district beginning in 1995 when the district adopted standards-based reform. After a decade and millions of dollars, the three middle schools remained at the bottom in achievement when the foundation's support ended in 1999. Reports from an independent research organization suggested that there was a lack of vision and that too many of the district's leaders believed that economically disadvantaged students could not excel. There were not enough accomplished teachers, not enough principals who were leaders, and not enough inspired support people and central office administrators who believed that greater gains were possible and knew how to achieve them. Although a core group of educators in the district knew what it would take to make all schools successful, they were too often stymied by powerful systemic forces resistant to the changes necessary to achieve the desire results ("Goodbye, Yellow Brick Road," 2000).

Professional Capacity

Many policy makers assume that teachers and administrators have a much greater capacity to implement reforms than is actually the case (Mizell, 2000). The study conducted by Mathematica Policy Research, Inc. (Dynarski & Gleason, 1998) of 20 dropout prevention programs found that even though many programs helped some students, "most programs made almost no difference in preventing dropping out in general." The study found that few principals and teachers were eager to change what they were doing even though students were dropping out in response to it. The report stated:

> Change would have been easier to promote if teachers or principals believed that how they did things contributed to the problem. The evaluation rarely found this to be the case. The evaluation commonly observed instruction in restructuring schools that was repetitive, boring, and even sometimes demeaning, but teachers and principals were either oblivious to this or ignored it. (p. 15)

Examples of Systemic Renewal

Systemic renewal is about continuous, critical inquiry into current practices, identifying innovations that might improve education, removing organizational barriers to that improvement, and providing a system structure that supports change. Systemic renewal necessitates creating a flexible, responsive organization that enables teachers, school administrators, students, parents, and community members to collaborate in providing within each school the experiences students need to achieve academic success. Schools and districts that engage in comprehensive school reform should be committed to developing a system-wide strategy that affects teaching, learning, accountability, governance, and professional development (Schwartzbeck, 2002).

Comprehensive, whole-school school reform is currently the closest approximation we have to systemic renewal. One of the first and most powerful of these efforts was the New American Schools (NAS) initiative launched in 1991. NAS, a nonprofit corporation supported by the private sector, funded design teams to create *break the mold* school designs and to provide implementation support to schools that adopted the designs (Berends, Bodilly, & Kirby, 2002). NAS selected seven designs for national scale-up (i.e., implementation and technical assistance). From 1995 through 1998, NAS led a scale-up phase in ten school districts that agreed to partner with NAS and to get approximately 30 percent of their schools to use the designs ("A Decade of Whole-School Reform," 2002). The RAND Corporation was chosen to monitor the initiative, assess the level of implementation, analyze changes to the designs, identify factors that impeded or encouraged implementation, and measure the outcomes (Berends, Bodilly, & Kirby, 2002).

The federal government's Comprehensive School Reform Program (CSRP), funded by Congress in 1998, has its roots in the NAS initiative. Schools receiving funding from CSRP are expected to implement effective, schoolwide reform efforts that are derived from scientifically based research and effective practices and that enable all children, particularly low-achieving children, to meet challenging academic standards. Over 1,800 schools in all 50 states, the District of Columbia, Puerto Rico, and schools funded by the Bureau of Indian Affairs (BIA) received grants as part of the original 1998 cohort. An additional 1,000 schools were funded through a funding increase in 2000. Additional schools were expected to receive funds from the 2001 and 2002 funding allocation ("About CSR," 2003).

What Have We Learned?

New American Schools Initiative

The final report on the New American Schools initiative (Berends, Bodilly, & Kirby, 2002) drew together the findings from RAND's various studies and discussed the lessons learned from this initiative and the implications for future school reform efforts. The findings were reported in three broad areas: the evolution of designs, the implementation observed in the NAS sites, and student outcomes.

Evolution of the Designs

The research literature on educational reform efforts has documented the complexity of planned educational change. Research on using external designs as blueprints for reform in K through 12 education has shown that as externally developed interventions are implemented, they tend to change significantly as they are adapted to local conditions and contexts. The result is that implementation and outcomes vary considerably across sites.

The RAND study found that the NAS designs were adapted to local conditions over time. Some of the design changes—for example, the increase in technical assistance packages and the further development of curricular units—helped schools improve. In addition, the development of a basic skills curriculum was positive when it was well integrated with the principles of the design and not simply added to meet district demands.

Other changes weakened the designs. When schools were required to adapt to district and school policies, the results in some schools were an unaligned and incoherent mix of standards, assessments, curriculum, instruction, and professional development. The consequences of such considerable local adaptation led observers to question the resulting unifying or coherent nature of the design ("A Decade of Whole-School Reform," 2002).

Design Scale-Up Implementation

There were large differences in implementation among school districts across all of the NAS sites. Two years into implementation, only about half of the sample sites were implementing designs at a level consistent with the expectations of NAS and the design teams. Achieving high levels of implementation proved to be difficult within schools facing a host of problems related to poverty, achievement, and school and district policies.

High levels of implementation were related to clear communication with and strong assistance from the design teams, school administrators and teachers who felt that their choices were well informed, and teacher support and buy-in. Furthermore, teachers viewed the principal's leadership as the most important predictor of the implementation level achieved. Implementation was higher in elementary schools than in secondary schools and was higher in smaller schools than in larger ones.

In general, implementation was higher in those districts that (a) had a stable district leadership that backed the reform and made it central to its improvement efforts; (b) were not burdened with crises such as budget shortfalls or redistricting; (c) had a coherent program of reform; (d) had resources dedicated to the implementation effort; (e) had significant school-level autonomy; and (f) had trusting relationships among school, district, and union staff ("A Decade of Whole-School Reform," 2002).

Student Outcomes

After three years into scale-up, the RAND study analyzed performance across the school sites. The analyses focused on whether NAS schools made any gains in test scores relative to their respective jurisdictions. The study found that, of the 163 schools for which there were data allowing comparisons in performance relative to the district or state, 81 schools (50 percent) made gains in mathematics relative to the district and 76 schools (47 percent) made gains in reading relative to the district ("A Decade of Whole-School Reform," 2002).

General Findings of the Study

The hypotheses posited by the study and the conclusions drawn by the researchers include the following:

- The initial hypothesis—*that a school could improve its performance by adopting a whole-school design*—was largely unsupported. Many schools had difficulty implementing the design; many showed no significant improvement.

- The hypothesis *that the designs alone were not helpful to schools and that schools needed assistance* in implementation was proven correct. Strong assistance from external design teams yielded higher levels of implementation. Conditions within the schools and districts and the manner of selection also made a difference.

- The scale-up hypothesis *that a district that converted 30 percent of its schools using whole-school approaches would become high performing and not revert to unproductive practices* was disproved. Districts such as Memphis quickly reverted to their former status after changes in their administrations.

- The scale-up hypothesis *that a district needs to provide a supportive environment* was dramatically proven. School staff also pointed to the difficulties inherent in simultaneously adopting multiple reforms, high-stakes testing regimes, and new school designs ("A Decade of Whole-School Reform," 2002).

The study found that implementation is likely to lag far behind in schools without strong principal leadership, without teachers who support the designs and have a strong sense of efficacy, without district leadership and support, and without clear communication and provision of materials and staff support on the part of external design teams. There is a basic inequality among schools in terms of capacity to undertake reform efforts. It is essential to develop leadership and staff capacity as a precursor to undertaking comprehensive school reform (Berends, Bodilly, & Kirby, 2002).

Comprehensive School Reform Program

The focus of the federally-funded Comprehensive School Reform Program (CSRP) is to raise student achievement using proven schoolwide methods and reform strategies that support ongoing state and local efforts to connect higher standards and school improvement (Borman, Hewes, and Brown, 2002). Externally developed CSRP models provide a direction for designing and supporting the process of school reform rooted in research, packaged, and delivered to each school. Schools that receive funding through CSRP are required to implement a comprehensive school reform program that ("About CSR," 2003):

- Employs proven methods and strategies based on scientifically based research,
- Integrates a comprehensive design with aligned components,
- Provides ongoing, high-quality professional development for teachers and staff,
- Includes measurable goals and benchmarks for student achievement,
- Is supported within the school by teachers, administrators and staff,
- Provides support for teachers, administrators and staff,
- Provides for meaningful parent and community involvement in planning, implementing and evaluating school improvement activities,
- Uses high-quality external technical support and assistance from an external partner with experience and expertise in schoolwide reform and improvement,
- Plans for the annual evaluation of strategies for the implementation of school reforms and for student results achieved,
- Identifies resources to support and sustain the school's comprehensive reform effort, and

- Has been found to significantly improve the academic achievement of students or demonstrates strong evidence that it will improve the academic achievement of students.

Although CSRP grants allow the use of locally-developed models as long as the model incorporates the eleven components listed above, many schools do not have the capacity to create their own comprehensive effort; they seek externally developed ones. A difficulty is that few of the well-known models have the requisite research base to show effectiveness in improving student achievement. The American Institutes for Research (AIR) developed a guide to provide accurate, objective information on whether the 24 most popular schoolwide approaches improve achievement in such measurable ways as higher test scores and attendance rates. Only three of the approaches—Direct Instruction, High Schools That Work, and Success for All—have sufficiently rigorous research to offer strong evidence of positive effects on student achievement. Four other approaches—Community for Learning, Core Knowledge, Different Ways of Knowing, and Expeditionary Learning/Outward Bound—provided promising evidence (Educational Research Service, 1999).

The Center for Research on the Education of Students Placed At Risk (CRESPAR) (Borman, Hewes, & Brown, 2002) conducted a thorough meta-analysis of 232 studies of comprehensive school reform models. The evidence included the following findings:

- Comprehensive school reform is still an evolving field. Taken as a whole, however, there were a sufficient number of reasonably high-quality studies to evaluate its overall effects on achievement and to inform policy.

- The overall effects of comprehensive school reform were statistically significant, meaningful, and appeared to be greater than the effects of other interventions that have been designed to serve similar purposes and student and school populations.

- The models meeting the highest standard of evidence—Direct Instruction, the School Development Program, and Success for All—were the only comprehensive school reform models to have clearly established, across varying contexts and varying study designs, that their effects are relatively robust and that the models, in general, can be expected to improve students' test scores.

- The number of years of model implementation has very important implications for understanding comprehensive school reform effects on student achievement. The strong effects of comprehensive school reform beginning after the fifth year of implementation may be explained in two ways: Perhaps schools experience stronger effects as they continue implementing the models, or perhaps the schools experiencing particular success continue implementing the reforms while the schools not experiencing as much success drop them after the first few years.

Effective Implementation and Best Practices

Based on their analyses of research studies and reviews of comprehensive school reforms and the processes of school change, Borman, Hewes, and Brown (2002) identified several common substantive factors that have a bearing on the success or failure of externally developed reforms.

♦ Most importantly, for external models of school change to make an important impact within schools, *teachers and administrators must support, buy into, or even help co-construct the reform design*. Steve Ross (Schwartzbeck, 2002) described his experiences in studying schools in Memphis, Tennessee: "For every model there was a successful school and an unsuccessful school, and some of those were a half-mile away, receiving the same professional development and the same resources. One took off and the other didn't, and the reason one took off is because they wanted to do it."

♦ *The quality of the CSRP model implementation matters*. Although some reform models have been criticized because their prescriptive designs may suppress teacher creativity and require an inordinate amount of preparation time, externally developed reforms that are more clearly defined tend to be implemented with greater fidelity and, in turn, tend to have stronger effects on teaching and learning than reforms that are less clearly defined.

♦ In addition, *the reforms must build capacity*. Well-implemented reforms tend to have strong professional development and training components and effective follow up to address teachers' specific problems in implementing change within their classrooms.

Conclusion

Context matters; reform cannot occur in an environment that is indifferent or hostile to it (Mizell, 2000). The recent research on attempts at school improvement reinforces the findings of early research on federally funded innovations in education: The critical variables related to improvement, change, and effectiveness are organizational rather than individual or programmatic in nature (Berman & McLaughlin, 1978). The failure of many comprehensive school reforms has been due to "powerful systemic forces resistant to the changes" that create barriers to effective implementation. Successful systemic renewal efforts should include the following elements:

- *Consensus*—Gain consensus that change is needed among those who must carry out the change within the district and the schools. Make sure there is a willingness and determination to improve throughout the district.

- *Assess needs and assets*—Use both data and professional experiences to assess needs and survey assets.

- *Build capacity*—Build professional capacity within the schools and across the district to plan and carry out the reform.

- *Involvement*—Have those who must implement the reforms select or create a model and develop a process for change.

- *District change*—Systemic renewal and comprehensive school reform are not add-ons; what happens at the district level must change as much as what happens at the school level.

- *Leadership*—Provide a broad base of leadership and leadership stability.

- *Resources*—Ensure that there are sufficient resources to implement and sustain the effort.

- *Monitor and assess*—Monitor both the process of implementation and the desired results; collect data and embark on the assessment at the beginning of the effort.

- *Technical assistance*—Call on expert technical assistance for planning, developing capacity, and assessing the effort.

- *Sufficient time*—Provide sufficient planning and start-up time. Do not expect to obtain significant improvement results in student achievement before three to five years into the implementation of the effort.

While it is true that powerful systemic forces and resistance to change can maintain the status quo no matter how damaging it is to our students, in systemic renewal, powerful forces can also be mustered to support comprehensive school reform and improvement. If change and improvement efforts are to be effective and successful, they must be initiated and implemented from within the system and they must be systemwide. The strategies described in this book can provide a guide to choosing a comprehensive school reform model or used to help create a model tailored specifically for the needs of the schools in a district.

The purpose of changing the system is to create an academic environment that builds the capacity of teachers to help students learn. From preschool to high school, students must find effective school leaders, knowledgeable teachers, caring and commitment, and instruction that is exciting, involving, and challenging. Students with difficulties must not be abandoned to travel that rough road to frustration and failure, but must be guided and nurtured to academic success and graduation. As educators, it is our job to create an enriching, culturally sensitive, relevant, and academically stimulating environment for all children. We must not just write vision statements that parrot the phrase "all children can learn"; we must shape our classrooms, our schools, our districts, and our communities so that it becomes a reality.

References

A decade of whole-school reform: The New American Schools experience. (2002). Available online at www.rand.org/publications.

About CSR. (2003). Available online at www.ed.gov/offices/OESE.

Berends, M., Bodilly, S. J., & Kirby, S. N. (2002). *Facing the challenges of whole-school reform: New American Schools after a decade.* Santa Monica: The RAND Corporation.

Berman, P., & McLaughlin, M. W. (1978). *Federal programs supporting educational change, Vol. III: Implementing and sustaining innovations.* (R-1589/8-HEW). Santa Monica: The RAND Corporation.

Borman, G. D., Hewes, G. M., & Brown, S. (2002). *Comprehensive school reform and student achievement.* (Report Number 59). Baltimore, MD: Center for Research on the Education of Students Placed At Risk.

Dynarski, M., & Gleason, P. (1998). *How can we help? What we have learned from evaluations of Federal dropout prevention programs.* Princeton, NJ: Mathematica Policy Research, Inc.

Educational Research Service. (1999). *An educator's guide to schoolwide reform.* Arlington, VA: Educational Research Service.

Goodbye, yellow brick road. (2000, Spring). Changing Schools in Louisville, 4(1), pp. 2:15. New York: Edna McConnell Clark Foundation.

Hill, P. T. (2003). *School boards: Focus on school performance, not money and patronage.* The Progressive Policy Institute 21st Century Schools Project. Available online at www.ppionline.org.

Mizell, H. (2000, April 5). Educators: Reform Thyselves. *Education Week.*

National Commission of Excellence in Education. (1983). A nation at risk: The imperative for educational reform. Washington, DC: U.S. Government Printing Office.

School dropouts: Education could play a stronger role in identifying and disseminating promising prevention strategies. (GAO Report # GAQ-02-240). Washington, DC: General Accounting Office.

Schargel, F. P., & Smink, J. (2001). *Strategies to help solve our school dropout problem.* Larchmont, NY: Eye on Education, Inc.

Schargel, F. P. (2003). *Dropout Prevention Tools,* Larchmont, NY: Eye On Education, Inc.

Schwartzbeck, T. D. (2002, February). Choosing a model and types of models: How to find what works for your school. *Research Brief,* National Clearinghouse for Comprehensive School Reform. Available online at www.goodschools.gwu.edu.

5

The Power of School–Community Collaboration in Dropout Prevention

Sam F. Drew Jr.

For any school program to assure the high academic achievement of all children, there must be an active partnership between the school and community to address the social and personal, as well as the academic, needs of children. As Jehl, Blank, and McCloud (2001) conclude in *Lessons in Collaboration*, a paper commissioned by the National Housing Institute, educators and community builders differ about the goals and scope of schools. Educators tend to see educational reform as focused on promoting the academic achievement of young people. Community builders (and some educators) focus on academic achievement in a broader context that includes social and personal development. One researcher (Sylvester, 1990), writing ten years after a national report calling for reform, suggested why school reform was not going well:

> School reform—simply improving the way teachers teach and
> the ways schools are structured—is not enough. Teachers must

now find ways to cope with children who live in dysfunctional families, who are victims of violence, who use drugs, who do not speak English, who are pregnant, who are homeless. Teachers, even the best ones, cannot help these children by themselves (p. 32).

His words ring true today. Most reform has focused on academics but has failed to make the community connections necessary to address the broader needs of students. Even in a time of economic prosperity, many young people may be left behind because they lack the support networks that youths in more advantaged communities take for granted. Disadvantaged youths may not experience the benefit of business people and community leaders as mentors, participate in community cultural or recreational activities, receive quality medical care, or have help addressing family or personal problems (U.S. General Accounting Office, 2000). To keep young people in school and help them achieve greater academic success, their family, social, work, and academic needs all must be addressed. Schools simply cannot do the job alone. Schools can no longer be islands in communities with no bridges to the mainland. Bridges must be built to connect schools, homes, and communities (Center for Mental Health in Schools, 2001). Districts must plan strategically to keep students in school by focusing on strategies that go beyond the classroom. The very foundation for these strategies must be school–community collaboration.

Strategies for dropout prevention work best when built on a foundation of school–community collaboration and implemented in the context of a strategic plan. A systems approach is needed to give attention to the infrastructure that supports program delivery. Without that emphasis, schools and communities generally end up with a smorgasbord of prevention efforts that lack unanimity of focus, direction, and effectiveness (Hays, 2002). A single strategy—tutoring a child having difficulty in a subject area or counseling a child with a problem—may help in the short run. But for the duration, multiple strategies must be applied strategically and over time to keep students in school and achieving at high levels. A community-wide dropout prevention system provides an interconnected web of supports for youth and families. A school that develops a plan on its own—without establishing a strong working relationship with parents, community agencies, faith-based organizations, businesses and civic organizations—diminishes its chances of success. The diagram below establishes a framework within which to view the relationship of school–community collaboration to the other strategies discussed in this book.

Figure 5.1: A Framework for School–Community Collaboration in Dropout Prevention

In our framework, community collaboration forms the foundation for involving the appropriate partners in comprehensive implementation of the strategies for dropout prevention. Systemic renewal through strategic planning activities wraps around and integrates the other strategies.

This chapter focuses on the importance of community collaboration, not only as a solitary strategy, but also as an effective way to unite and mobilize the school and the surrounding community in implementing all the strategies outlined in a strategic plan for youths at risk of school failure. Community collaboration, as addressed in this book, is not an option. It is the driving force for developing the supports that enable children and youth to learn and succeed and help families and communities thrive. School–community collaboration can transform a community into what Denton (1989) termed the *educative community*. The educative community is an ecosystem of educating institutions—school, home, places of worship, television, press, museums, libraries, businesses, factories, and more. In the educative community, parents, human service agencies, businesses, and other community agencies and organizations share in the responsibility of providing and being held accountable for quality education for all citizens.

What Is Collaboration?

Collaboration—a widely used term—means different things to different people. Collaboration can mean coordination, integrated services, school-linked and school-based services, any focus on non-educational or supportive services, public-private partnerships with businesses and community groups, parental or family involvement. Collaboration also can be defined through existing educational programs that emphasize and utilize partnerships, such as school-to-work, service learning, extended learning, and before- and after-school programs (Boyd, Brown, & Hara, 1999, pp. 8–9).

London (1995) offers the simplest definition of collaboration as derived from its Latin roots *com* and *laborare:* to work together. In *Collaborative Leadership*, Chrislip and Larson (1994) suggest a more comprehensive definition: "It is a mutually beneficial relationship between two or more parties who work toward common goals by sharing responsibility, authority, and accountability for achieving results" (p 2).

Still other definitions (Drew, 1991; Hogue, 1993) place collaboration on a continuum of relationships. While the elements of the various continuums vary, one continuum (Drew, 1991) is illustrated in the following diagram:

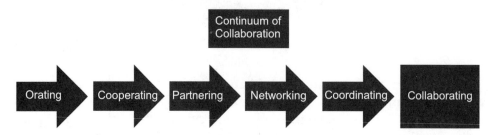

The continuum progresses from an emphasis on individual or personal needs (orating) through various forms of uniting of people and agencies toward a common purpose. It ends with true collaboration: building interdependent systems to achieve a common goal that cannot be achieved by each agency working alone. Thus, we view collaboration as a means of bringing the school and community into an interdependent working relationship to address and solve problems that no single agency can solve. One such problem is that of young people dropping out of school.

The scope of this chapter does not permit an in-depth discussion of the specific research findings. It is clear, however, that a strong research base exists for inclusion of school-community collaboration as a foundation strategy for keeping young people in school and achieving at higher levels. One research synthesis (Henderson and Mapp, 2004) reveals much evidence of the impact of school-family-community connections on student achievement. The synthesis included findings on the impact of connections:

◆ "Taken as a whole, these studies found a positive and convincing relationship between family involvement and benefits for students, including improved academic achievement.… Although there is less research on the effects of community involvement, it also suggests benefits for schools, families and students, including improvement in achievement and behavior" (Henderson and Mapp, 2004, p. 24).

and findings about the nature of the connections themselves:

◆ "When schools build partnerships with families that respond to their concerns and honor their contributions, they are successful in sustaining connections..." (Henderson and Mapp, 2004, p. 7).

A recent U.S. General Accounting Office (GAO) (2000) study of federal programs targeted toward school–community initiatives revealed a general lack of rigorous evaluation to determine the effectiveness of these programs on student achievement or success in later life (the dual goals that generally mark these programs). Programs that have been studied show positive results on higher academic achievement, behaviors and attitudes of students, reduced incidence of vandalism, and other destructive behaviors, higher aspirations and credits earned, and more positive mental health. One such program showed that among students at high risk of school failure, attendance rates rose and dropout rates declined significantly (GAO, 2000, p. 15).

The GAO study found that many programs produced anecdotal data that demonstrate strong community support for the programs. In cases where funding is threatened, communities have fought to keep these programs. Evaluation presents challenges for evaluators because school–community initiatives are complex. In addition, students participate in them to varying degrees. The community support generated by the programs creates commitment, dialogue, and new decision-making structures within the community for retaining students who are at risk of failure in school. Ultimately, community support helps these students achieve academically and prepares students for life as productive citizens.

The report *Building New Futures for At-Risk Youth* (Center for the Study of Social Policy, 1995) supports these findings. Operating in five cities across the United States, the project attempted to reduce the school dropout rate, improve students' academic performance, prevent teen pregnancies and births, and increase the number of youth who go on to a job or college. Significant interim steps were taken in the project communities that may lead to improved outcomes for students. Specifically, the communities

◆ raised awareness about the problems of at-risk youth,

◆ started a new dialogue among leaders and community representatives who had not previously sat down together,

◆ developed rich school-based information systems,

◆ created a new body of knowledge around collaboration and local government,

◆ demonstrated how to build substantive relationships between public and private sectors by combining leadership and money, and

◆ launched a new ongoing community-based decision-making structure.

(Center for the Study of Social Policy, 1995, as reported in Schargel & Smink, 2001)

These studies suggest that simply forming school–community collaborations does not automatically and immediately effect changes in student success in school. Collaborative relationships themselves must be nurtured, and this takes time. Once in place, these school–community collaboratives provide a strong and unifying foundation for incorporating all of the strategies we know to be effective in keeping young people in school and helping them to achieve and become healthy, active citizens.

Features of Successful School–Community Collaboration

The Sense of the Geese illustrates the key elements of collaboration.

When geese head south for the winter they fly along in small groups or flocks in a "V" formation. As each bird flaps its wings, it creates uplift for the bird immediately following. By flying in a "V" formation, the whole flock achieves a greater flying range than if each bird flew on its own.

1. Collaborative groups share a common vision, purpose and direction.
2. Collaborative groups are composed of interdependent stakeholders.
3. Successful collaboration is done in smaller groups rather than large groups.
4. Successful collaboration requires consensus on all agreements for action.

If a goose falls out of formation, it suddenly feels the drag and resistance of trying to go it alone; quickly, it gets back into formation to take advantage of the power of the flock.

5. Collaborative groups are inclusive, drawing power from individual strengths.
6. Collaboration is characterized by achieving more through the group venture than each partner could have achieved alone.
7. Shared information gives power to the collaborative.

When the goose that is leading the flock tires, he rotates back in the wing and another goose assumes the lead position.

8. Successful collaborative groups are self-governed with facilitative, shared leadership.

The geese honk from behind as they fly to encourage those up front to keep their speed.

When a goose gets sick or is wounded by a gunshot from a hunter and falls out, two geese fall out of the formation and follow the injured goose down to help and protect him. They stay with him either until he is able to fly or until he is dead; then they link up with another formation to catch up with their group.

9. Collaborative members encourage and support one another to energize the collaborative and keep it moving forward.

10. Collaborative groups have the power to implement final actions.

11. Collaborative members are committed to the individual, the group, and the process.

12. Collaborative members are committed to work over the long term.

Limitations of and Barriers to Collaboration

Collaborations are not easy to build or maintain. Barriers or obstacles can be expected; knowing some of those obstacles at the outset can help a collaborative succeed. Of course, just knowing the obstacles will not guarantee success. The partners must actively work to address and overcome the barriers. In a study of after-school collaborative programs, the National Assembly (2000), with funding from the Charles Stewart Mott Foundation, administered a survey to a group of school and community partner grantees to identify common barriers. Key findings:

- ◆ Levels of satisfaction with the collaborative experience varied; school partners were more satisfied than community partners.
- ◆ Three obstacles to collaboration were identified by both school and community partners: different attitudes and philosophies about how children learn and develop, different perceptions of accountability, and disagreements over turf.
- ◆ Community partners attached more importance to certain obstacles than school partners did. These included different attitudes and philosophies about how children learn and develop, unclear delineation of roles and responsibilities, differences in contracts and work rules, use of facilities and space, and negative experiences with prior collaborations.

- Community partners were particularly concerned about differences in goals and expectations, desired outcomes and the lack of training in the process of collaboration.

- School partners were particularly concerned about the addition of activities to their busy schedules, different traditions about how things are done, and the lack of availability of their community partners.

- Collectively, the barriers identified by both school and community partners suggested differences in philosophies, organizational cultures, and operating practices.

While formidable, all of the barriers identified can be overcome. The purpose of a collaborative is to create new structures to address a common vision for solving specific problems. As the saying goes, doing what we have always done will get what we have always gotten. No one suggests that collaboration is an easy process.

A Successful
School–Community Collaboration

Assessing Collaboration

It is important to distinguish between a collaborative and some other form of partnering that may be referred to as a collaborative. True collaborative ventures attempt to unite the school and community agencies to do what none could do alone. The collaborative must follow the central principle for organizational design: Form follows function. While designs may differ, the successful collaboration most often is created around a problem area.

School–community collaborations typically strive to improve and strengthen schools, families, and student learning. For such collaborations, the following indicators (adapted from the National Standards for Parent/Family Involvement Programs and the National Parent-Teacher Association, 1997) represent hallmarks of success:

- Information is regularly distributed regarding cultural, recreational, academic, health, social, and other resources that serve community members.

- Partnerships are developed with local businesses and student groups to advance student learning and assist schools and families.

- Employers are encouraged to adopt policies and practices that promote and support adult participation in prevention and education.

- Student participation in community service is fostered.

- Community members are involved in school volunteer programs.
- Information about school programs and events is disseminated to the community.
- Collaboration with community agencies helps to provide family support services and adult learning opportunities that enable parents/caregivers to more fully participate in prevention and education.
- Staff members are informed about the resources that are available in the community and strategies for utilizing those resources.

Three checklists developed by Blank & Langford (2000) for the Coalition of Essential Schools are helpful in assessing the development of an individual school–community partnership. While school–community partnerships may not meet the more comprehensive definition of collaboration as discussed in this chapter, they are vital in the continuum toward true collaboratives. The checklists are intended as planning tools to help strengthen local partnerships and existing coordination of services as well as to expand levels of support.

For example, the first checklist focuses on partnership assessment and asks participants to rate eight items on a scale of 1 (disagree) to 5 (agree). The items focus on

- the development of a clear vision;
- the joint identification of the results to achieve for children, youth, families, and the community;
- the successful engagement of a broad base of partners representative of the community;
- the development of strategies for coordinating and linking the array of supports and opportunities for children, youth, families, and community members that are available at or connected to the school;
- the development among all partners of an understanding of who the partners are, what organizations they come from and what those organizations do;
- the establishment of regular communications among all partners to keep them informed about the work of the partnership;
- the engagement of the partnership in activities to create awareness about the work of the partnership and increase support for its work; and
- the identification and mobilization of financial and other resources from the partner organizations and other entities in the community.

Starting a School–Community Collaboration?

Several formal models integrate the steps for starting a school–community collaboration into a series of specific training activities. This is not a one-size-fits-all endeavor, but the steps, although they differ among the various models, are very similar. This chapter focuses on the major steps and activities. Once understood, these steps allow a community to tailor its own approach to addressing the needs of at-risk students in its schools.

Winer and Ray (1994) outline four steps and 15 activities for developing and sustaining collaborations:

1. Envisioning results
   - Criteria for membership are decided and people are brought together to get to know one another.
   - Trust among the participants is enhanced by sharing knowledge, disclosing self-interests, ensuring that all stakeholders' needs are met and letting people feel their participation is justified by producing visible results.
   - A shared vision statement is developed that indicates where the group wants to go.
   - Desired results are specified in the form of goals and objectives that are jointly developed.

2. Empowering the effort
   - Authority for the group to act is obtained, roles are clarified, and commitments are secured, and each agency knows what contribution it is expected to make.
   - Conflict is expected and addressed by having a conflict resolution process in place to clarify issues, focus on goals, and explore alternatives.
   - The effort is organized by forming a structure that determines roles and staffing and secures resources.
   - Members are supported by establishing a decision-making protocol and communications plan, and recognizing and rewarding participants.

3. Ensuring success
   - Work is managed by establishing an action plan based on vision and goals, developing collaborative work habits, and determining accountability for all activities.
   - Where necessary, collaborating agencies make necessary policy and procedural changes to ensure responsiveness to the other agencies and support the collaborative.

- Multiple methods of assessment are used to evaluate and continuously improve the effort.
- The collaborative remains flexible and adaptable to changing conditions.

4. Endowing continuity
   - The collaborative is made visible by publicizing and promoting results, and involving the media.
   - Participation is sought from the wider community, including youth groups, businesses, and grassroots community organizations.
   - The effort is sustained by periodically reassessing the mission and vision, involving new leadership, and securing diverse funding.

PERC (*Planning Effectively for Resource Collaboration*) is one formal process developed and used successfully to help schools and communities develop collaborative work. PERC outlines a three-phase process to developing a school–community collaborative: matrix planning, fission (analysis), and fusion (synthesis). The PERC planning framework can be modified to meet the needs of different types of communities, agencies, and school districts. The intent is to engage people and agencies in planning that stimulates thinking about ways individual people and programs can connect to strengthen service delivery. When this process is focused on dropout prevention, existing services can be enhanced and additional resources can be created for at-risk students. Future needs are identified and become a part of the budget planning process. A built-in support group is formed to encourage and promote school boards and other funding agents to allocate sufficient resources to meet the needs identified for addressing the dropout problem (Drew, 1991).

The PERC mapping process endeavors to link—across programs (within an agency) and across agency lines—services that are similar or that closely complement each other. The process is based on the development and analysis of a "target population–agency matrix" and a series of mapping exercises to explore the nature of the interagency relationships. PERC ends in an interagency action planning session.

PERC relies on several assumptions:

- that each agency or organization is unique and effective in carrying out its own specific mission;
- that many of these missions connect directly with the missions and activities of other agencies; and
- that by working together, agencies and organizations can maintain their own autonomy, individuality, and focus, and can accomplish

more than would be possible if each agency continues to work alone.

Ultimately a successful collaborative focuses on changing the system, with a focus on integrated services (Anderson, 1996). The new system of integrated services allows the school and community to address problems related to dropout prevention that each working alone could not adequately address.

Conclusion

School-community collaboration is a foundation strategy for helping young people stay in school and succeed academically. Collaboration is the most integrated strategy along a continuum of community partnering activities that include agency cooperation, networking, and service coordination. In a true collaboration, agencies partner in ways that allow them to accomplish goals that no agency could accomplish alone.

School–community collaboration should be deployed within the context of a strategic plan, with specific goals of the collaborations focused on the research-based early intervention, core basic and classroom strategies discussed in this book.

Collaboration is a difficult task, with many barriers to overcome. However, the resulting communication among community agencies and schools, unity of vision within the community, integration and enhancement of agency services, and community support of common goals are well worth the effort. School–community collaboration is essential to providing the comprehensive academic and social services needed for youth at risk of dropping out of school to succeed academically and in later life.

References

Anderson, R. T. (1996). *Beyond "one-stop shopping": An integrated service delivery system for job seekers and employers.* Pewawkee, WI: Waukesha County Workforce Development Center.

Blank, M. J., & Langford, B. H. (2000). *Strengthening partnerships: Community school assessment checklist.* Washington, DC: Coalition of Community Schools.

Boyd, W. L., Brown, C., & Hara, S. (1999). *State education agency support for school–community collaboration in the mid-Atlantic states.* Publication Series No. 3 report by the Laboratory for Student Success at Temple University Center for Human Development and Education.

Center for Mental Health in Schools. (2001). *School–community partnerships: A guide.* Los Angeles: Author.

Center for the Study of Social Policy (1995). Building new futures for at-risk youth, as reported by Schargel, F., and Smink, J. *Strategies to help solve our school dropout problem*, 2001.

Chrislip, D. D., & Larson, C. E. (1994). *Collaborative leadership: How citizens and civic leaders can make a difference.* San Francisco: Jossey-Bass.

Denton, W. (1990). Restructuring school and community relationships. Unpublished monograph. Clark Atlanta University.

Drew, S. (1991). *PERC: Planning effectively for resource collaboration.* Unpublished training manual.

Hays, C. (2002). The systems approach to community prevention. *Prevention Forum (22)*3.

Henderson, A., & Mapp, K. (2002). *A new wave of evidence: The impact of school, family, and community connections on student achievement.* Austin, TX: Southwest Educational Development Laboratory.

Hogue, T. (1993). *Community based collaboration: Community wellness multiplied.* Retrieved December 10, 2003, from http://crs.uvm.edu/nnco/collab/wellness.html.

Jehl, J., Blank, M., & McCloud, B. (2001, July/August). Lessons in collaboration: Bringing together educators and community builders. *National Housing Institute, ShelterForce Online.* Retrieved from http://www.nhi.org/online/issues/ 118/Jehl blankmccloud.html.

London, S. (1995). *Collaboration and community.* Retrieved December 10, 2003, from http://www.scottlondon.com/reports/ppcc.html.

National Assembly. (2000). *21st Century Community Learning Centers collaborative survey.* Washington, DC: National Assembly National Collaboration for Youth.

National Parent Teacher Association. (1997). *National standards for parent/family involvement programs.* [Booklet.] Chicago, IL: Author.

Sylvester, K. (1990). New strategies to save children in trouble. *Governing (3)*8.

U.S. General Accounting Office. (2000, October). *At-risk youth: School–community collaborations focus on improving student outcomes.* GAO Report to the Honorable Charles B. Rangel, House of Representatives.

Winer, M., & Ray, K. (1994). *Collaboration handbook: Creating, sustaining, and enjoying the journey.* St. Paul, MN: Amherst H. Wilder Foundation.

6

Creating Safe
Learning Environments

Ronald D. Stephens

No task is more important than creating safe learning environments for our nation's children. Without safe schools, it is difficult, if not impossible, for learning to take place. In a safe school, students can learn and teachers can teach in a warm and welcoming environment free of intimidation, violence, and fear. Behavior expectations are clearly communicated, consistently enforced and fairly applied. Such an educational climate fosters a spirit of acceptance and care for every child.

Students, staff, and parents deserve schools that are safe, secure, and peaceful. Children are compelled by state law to attend school. Keeping young people in school requires a clear, consistent, and systematic plan to create an educational climate conducive to learning. This is especially true for students at risk of academic failure. Some states, such as California, have passed legislation that endows students with the "inalienable right to attend schools that are safe, secure, and peaceful...." Nearly 30 states have passed legislation that either mandates or recommends that every school develop a safe school plan. Schools that fail to create such plans open themselves for a variety of lawsuits and potential litigation.

Parents, citizens, and lawmakers are now demanding to know what schools are doing to create a positive school climate that will provide for the safety of their children. Schools that fail to provide that setting risk being labeled as "persistently dangerous" under the No Child Left Behind Act. Under this legislation, students who attend persistently dangerous schools or are victims of a violent crime while in their school can choose to transfer to a safe school within their district. Schools that want to avoid losing students must do a better job of protecting their students.

A welcoming climate is important for all students, particularly struggling learners who may need additional support and care to support their academic success, or students in at-risk situations outside of the school setting. School officials are charged with two tasks: keeping trouble away from kids and keeping kids away from trouble. It has been said that 90 percent of success comes from simply "showing up." For schools to be effective, students must attend school.

The No Child Left Behind Act allows students to leave schools that are identified as persistently dangerous. Unfortunately, some students in that situation decide to leave school altogether. School attendance remains a major challenge, particularly for high-risk students. It is difficult to graduate if you don't come to school.

Old and New Concerns

Keeping schools safe has been one of the top education goals of the past decade. While the data indicate that schools are safer than ever before, the public's perception is different. A series of serious school shootings in the late 1990s, followed by the terror attacks against the United States on 11 September 2001 and the ongoing homeland security threat, have generated a new wave of concerns among school officials, students, and parents.

Average students and their caretakers worry about bullying, violence in the community, and the possibility that a troubled classmate could attack the school. The threat of international terrorism only increases the need for schools to have appropriate partnerships, crisis response plans, and emergency resources in place.

According to the series of Youth Risk Behavior Surveys sponsored by the Centers for Disease Control (2003, Physical Fighting: Youth Risk Behavior Survey: http://www.cdc/ncipe/pub_res/pdf/sec3/pdf), nearly one out of twelve young people who have been the targets of bullying and intimidation stay away from school because of fear. Truancy of this nature frequently occurs in the wake of a fight or some other type of physical or emotional confrontation. When negative behaviors are allowed to persist, kids who are otherwise successful and well behaved stay away from school.

Bullies can terrorize individual students, teachers, classrooms of students, a whole school, and an entire community. Violence in schools is a threat or criminal act against school personnel, students, or property that

- creates immediate or prolonged fear/anxiety,
- manipulates the actions/reactions of others,
- causes primary and/or secondary victimization, and
- may result or does result in death, bodily injury, or significant property damage.

Consider the similarities between the definition of terrorism in school and the following definition of terrorism. Terrorism is

- the systematic use of fear,
- using the threat of violence,
- committed for political, ideological, or religious purposes, and
- with a desire to alter the behaviors of others.

Experts tell us that teens see bullying as the threat that most frightens them and interferes with their education.

With all of these threats, concerns, and issues facing today's schools, keeping kids in school has become a major challenge. It is extremely important to create a school climate where terrorism, bullying, and intimidation are not allowed, where safety and security are promoted, and where a positive learning climate can be maintained.

School officials and communities have not been able to guarantee the safety and well-being of all students, but excellent progress is being made in this area. Placing school safety on the educational agenda is a necessary first step. Implementing safe school plans and developing close working partnerships with students, law enforcement, the community, and the courts are also important components.

The focus of this chapter is to address those strategies that foster a safe and welcoming school climate and promote student attendance. The discussion that follows will give school officials the tools and strategies they need to create a safe learning environment that will support the success and development of all of America's children.

Safe School Planning

It's not easy to find the right balance between creating a safe and secure school and maintaining a welcoming and nurturing environment. Successful administrators choose creative ways to address this challenge. They face three demanding responsibilities. The first task is assessment: accurately identifying where the school is in terms of school violence and school crime prevention issues. This includes assessing the threats and the assets of the school within the context of the greater community. The second step is to identify where the school wants to be—in other words, set goals. The third phase, implementation and strategy, describes how the school will move from where it is to where it wants to be. A safe school plan can guide the school and community in creating a vision that is consistent with the community's will and a process that allows the school to achieve the type of school climate it desires.

To shape a successful safe school plan, administrators must be able to interpret the effects of myriad factors and to articulate local issues. This chapter provides a compendium of assessment strategies designed to assist school officials in their quest for definition, direction, development, and execution of a safe and welcoming school climate. Assessment tools have been gathered from a variety of sources across the country. They are offered here as a resource to complement the efforts of school officials in developing and implementing their own unique assessment, planning, and evaluation instruments.

Safe school planning is not a one-time event. It is an ongoing, broad-based, systematic, and comprehensive process. A safe school plan includes both behavioral aspects and property aspects of crime prevention. The best safe school plans integrally involve the entire community. Students, parents, law enforcement, mental health professionals, business and community leaders, and a wide array of community members should be included in the planning forum. Safe school planning is an inclusive and cooperative activity.

Safe school planning is all about the "art of the possible." The safe school planning process is not confined to this set of guidelines or any other special constraints. Each community has the opportunity to shape the type of school climate it wishes to create. More than anything else, a safe school plan is a function of the community's will, its priorities, and interests. Only the imagination, creativity, energy, and commitment of the community limit the components and confine the process.

Essential Components of the Plan

The specific planning components mandated in a safe school plan may vary from state to state and school to school. Schools should check local and state laws for direction and guidance. Local and state law enforcement officials may provide guidance. Planners should consider defensible needs, good practice, and reasonable judgment as they decide whether and how to include the following basic elements:

- behavior/conduct/discipline policies and codes;
- supervision, security, and surveillance plans;

- the use of crime prevention through environmental design (CPTED) principles;
- systems for school crime reporting, tracking, and analysis;
- partnerships and agreements among the school, law enforcement and other community agencies;
- the use of Homeland Security issues and resources;
- crisis response and emergency evacuation plans;
- participation in community disaster preparedness plans;
- student transportation management;
- special event management;
- screening and selection of staff;
- staff training;
- parent participation;
- student leadership and involvement;
- student attendance (truancy and dropout prevention);
- curricula/strategies that address bullying, crime, and violence, drug use, social skills development, cultural awareness;
- extracurricular activities and recreation;
- health and social services;
- programs for community service/outreach;
- media and public relations;
- corporate/business partnerships;
- nuisance abatement;
- legislative outreach and contact;
- restitution programs for student offenders;
- evaluation and monitoring.

As school safety plans and issues are considered, several additional components may also emerge. Safe school planning affords each community a unique opportunity for introspection, followed by the opportunity to customize strategies and priorities for each program component chosen for examination. Limitless opportunities and strategies exist.

California Education Code Section 35294 describes safe school planning as a seven-step process:

1. Identify your safe school planning committee members.
2. Assess data on school crime.
3. Identify school safety strategies and programs.

4. Ensure that school procedures comply with existing laws related to schools.

5. Hold a public meeting before your school adopts the plan.

6. Make the plan available for public review.

7. Amend the plan once a year, as needed.

Legal Aspects of Safe School Planning

An essential preliminary step is to conduct a legal review of federal, state, and local statutes pertaining to student management and school order. This review should also include relevant court cases, district policies, and operations manuals along with labor contracts. Nearly every major school safety issue is embedded in existing law.

Planners should start by examining federal laws, such as:

- the No Child Left Behind (NCLB) Act of 2001 (the most recent reauthorization of the Elementary and Secondary Education Act)
- the Federal Gun-Free School Zone Act of 1994
- the Family Educational Rights to Privacy Act (FERPA) and its recent amendments
- the Drug-Free Schools and Communities Act of 1986
- the Individuals with Disabilities Education Act (IDEA).

They should also review relevant U.S. Supreme Court cases. The next step is to consider state and local laws pertaining to safe school planning, crisis prevention and management, and school disorder. As a minimum, planners should check the following codes:

- the state constitution,
- education code,
- health and safety code,
- penal code,
- vehicle code,
- child welfare and institutions code,
- fire code,
- municipal code,
- school district code, and
- recent local court decisions.

Some states, such as North Carolina, have instructive legislation regarding the content, process and leadership responsibilities for the planning process; for example, North Carolina mandates that the superintendent take the lead on safe school planning. The State of New York outlines specific plan components that are required by law; for instance, every school system in New York must have a district-wide plan for bully prevention. Consequently, reviewing these kinds of laws is a necessary beginning step.

During the review of the laws and court decisions, it is important to recognize that some laws, and/or policies developed in response to these laws, may be inconsistent with one another. For instance, while it may be tempting to control campus access by chaining closed certain doors, such action may create a fire code violation, setting the stage for a serious liability problem. It is essential not to create new conflicts or legal problems by establishing incompatible policies or issuing contradictory legal and procedural directives.

District policy and procedure manuals will also provide further insight as to what each local school board may require. Planners should make certain to review all federal, state, county, local, and other municipal ordinances before they develop a safe school plan. Once the plan is developed, the school attorney should then provide a complete legal review to ensure that the components of the plan are fair, reasonable, consistent with other policies, and that they do not promise more than they can deliver.

The National School Boards Association recommends that school districts consider the following questions as they develop violence prevention policies:

- Is the content of the policy within the scope of the board's authority?
- Is it consistent with local, state, and federal laws?
- Have legal references been included?
- Does it reflect good educational practice?
- Is it reasonable?
- Does it adequately cover the issue?
- Is it limited to one policy topic?
- Is it cross-referenced to other relevant policy topics?
- Is it consistent with the board's existing policies?
- Can it be administered?
- Is it practical in terms of administrative enforcement and budget?

Asking these questions will save school administrators and their school boards a great deal of anguish as well as protect them from liability.

A Framework for Planning

Safe school planning initiatives are best established by community coalitions of school, law enforcement, and community leaders. The safe school team is the driving force behind the planning process. This group should involve a wide variety of key individuals within the community who touch the lives of children. Examples of essential team members include the superintendent of schools, chief of police, presiding juvenile judge, chief probation officer, prosecutor, health and welfare providers, parents, business leaders, mayor, city manager, church and community leaders, representatives from neighborhood service organizations and from mental health, corrections, parks and recreation, and emergency response teams. Planning teams that place students at the heart of the process find that they provide tremendous insight and direction.

The development of a school safety plan is a complex issue. To ensure a broad constituency, planners may involve the following individuals:

- local and state law enforcement people,
- the state superintendent/commissioner or their representative,
- the district superintendent,
- the district's lawyer,
- parent representatives,
- community representatives, and
- business people.

States that require safe school planning often have provisions that guide the planning process. Reviewing state laws streamlines the safe school planning process and gives it focus. We have mentioned California's constitutional amendment stating the "inalienable right" to schools that are safe, secure, and peaceful. Such proclamations can help set the stage for effective safe school planning.

Georgia law requires that school safety plans shall be prepared with input from enrolled students, parents or legal guardians, teachers, community leaders, other school employees, school district employees and local law enforcement, fire service, public safety, and emergency management agencies.

Oklahoma state law not only identifies who must be on the team but also mandates various substantive components. Oklahoma requires each public school site to establish a Safe School Committee composed of at least six members. The Safe School Committee shall be composed of an equal number of teachers, parents of the children affected, and students. The Safe School Committee is directed to study and make recommendations to the principal regarding unsafe conditions, possible strategies for students to avoid harm at school, student victimization, crime prevention, school violence, and other issues that prohibit the maintenance of a safe school.

Ohio code requires each school board to adopt a comprehensive safe school plan for each school building under its control. The board must examine the environmental conditions and operations of each building to determine potential hazards to safety and propose operating changes to promote the prevention of potentially dangerous problems and circumstances. Community law enforcement and safety officials, parents, teachers, and other employees assigned to the building must be involved in designing the plan for each building. The board must consider incorporating remediation strategies into the plan for any building where documented safety problems have occurred.

Leadership of the Planning Team

Anyone in the community may lead the safe school team. Most generally, the superintendent of schools leads the team. The safe school team provides an excellent opportunity for the chief school officer to take an active leadership role in the community. At the site level, the school principal is the recommended professional for this leading role. In some communities, the presiding juvenile judge may be the key leader. In other areas, it may be the chief of police or a school board member.

Each community should capitalize on the people, the resources, and the levels of commitment that they are able to engage at the planning table. Larger school systems may prefer a tiered approach. A multilevel/multifaceted network can significantly enhance the safe school planning process. On the first tier, agency heads—such as the police chief, the superintendent of schools, or the presiding juvenile judge—lead, empower, and support the team as needed. A second tier may include agency and organization representatives who meet regularly to discuss issues, define problems, and develop solutions. A third tier might be a broader advisory committee composed of community and school representatives who would meet perhaps monthly or quarterly. They would provide input and direction to the various agencies and organizations that serve young people. Such options increase participation and can improve the quality and quantity of good ideas. Most importantly, such diverse efforts send a message to the community that school safety is not merely a school problem, but a community issue—that the school expects and needs the community's full support, but also that the problem requires a broad-based community response.

For any plan to succeed, the safe school team must draw upon the cultural diversity of the community it represents. Overlooking opportunities to include diversity can severely limit the team's ability to develop wide-ranging solutions.

Once the team is formed, members need to educate themselves and the community about school crime and violence prevention. It's a good idea to choose two or three talented people from the team to undergo specialized training in violence prevention. Groups like the National School Safety Center provide certified training in school safety leadership. Individuals who have been through such training can then coach other team members and community members.

The Work of the Safe School Team

Articulating the Mission Statement

A beginning point for safe school planning is the development of the educational mission. The educational mission establishes the tone and climate for the development of policies and procedures that create and promote safe and welcoming schools. School safety should be incorporated into educational goals. This can be accomplished by adding a phrase to the mission statement: "It is the goal of the school to provide a quality education in a safe and secure environment free of intimidation and fear." This language establishes the legal basis and rationale for the development and application of strategies, policies, and programs to support the educational mission.

Section 22-32-1091 of the Colorado law states, "Each school district board of education shall adopt a mission statement for the school district"; this statement includes making safety a priority in each public school of the school district. The legislation also requires principals to submit annual written reports to local school boards concerning the learning environment in that school. The report includes information about violations involving dangerous weapons, tobacco, alcohol and other drugs, criminal acts, and other conduct and discipline violations.

Conducting a Site Assessment

Every school should conduct an annual school safety assessment. States such as Virginia and Ohio already require such reviews by law. A school safety assessment is a strategic evaluation and planning tool used to determine the extent of a school safety problem. A school safety assessment, in broadest terms, is a comprehensive review and evaluation of the educational program of a school or school district. Various issues are examined to ascertain how they affect school climate, school attendance, personal safety, and overall school security. Such an assessment evaluates

- the current school safety plan and planning process,
- the crisis response plan,
- the existing educational plan and its support for a positive school climate,
- the school/law enforcement partnership,
- community support,
- the presence of gangs or weapons in school,
- student drug or alcohol abuse,
- the existence of schoolyard bullying,

- the condition and safety of the facilities,
- the use of environmental design to prevent crime,
- student discipline problems, policies, procedures and practices at both the school site and district level,
- compliance with local and state laws,
- employee recruiting, selection, supervision and training criteria as they pertain to school safety,
- parent attitudes,
- student attitudes and motivation,
- student activities and extracurricular programs,
- student health services,
- other emerging school climate trends and concerns, and
- other areas that may be deemed necessary in the evaluation of the district or site.

The assessment can be as broad or as narrow as may be required by state law or as may be dictated by the interests and needs of the local board and/or community. Safe school planning is about creating customized strategies and plans that respond to the specific needs of the local community.

The assessment process entails reviewing and analyzing the following kinds of information:

- all security and safety-related policies of the district,
- the student handbook,
- the teacher handbook,
- labor contracts/agreements that address the safety of classified and certified staff,
- a site plan showing the campus boundaries and access points,
- a floor plan of school buildings,
- campus crime reports for the previous year,
- student discipline records/reports for the previous year, including suspension and expulsion data,
- student progress reports,
- identified safety and security concerns of the staff, students, parents, and community members,
- the school's media file of previous news coverage,
- log of police "calls for service" generated from the school or dispatched to the school
- property loss, vandalism and insurance reports,

- maintenance/work orders related to vandalism or graffiti, and
- list of students who have been sent to school as a condition of probation and the terms of the probation.

Collecting Data

The data collection process includes five essential components. The first component involves a general review of school and community facts and trends. Sample questions that might be used in this assessment process include the 20 questions listed below. As indicators of critical campus management issues, these questions get the evaluation process started. They are by no means comprehensive. They reflect key issues or concerns that should be considered in evaluating school safety. The questions aim to heighten awareness about how the campus is managed and to help identify community factors that influence the daily management of the school. Local school administrators will likely wish to develop an evaluation tool customized to their specific needs.

- Do you have an open campus?
- Is your community transient rate increasing?
- Do you have an increasing presence of graffiti in your community?
- Is your truancy rate increasing?
- Are your suspension and expulsion rates increasing?
- Have you had increased conflicts relative to dress styles, food services, or types of music played at special events?
- Do you have an increasing number of students on probation at your school?
- Have you had isolated racial fights or gang-related incidents?
- Have you reduced the number of extracurricular programs and sports at your school?
- Are parents withdrawing students from your school because of fear?
- Has your professional development budget for staff been reduced or eliminated?
- Are you discovering more weapons on your campus?
- Do you lack written screening and selection guidelines for new staff at your school?
- Are drugs easily available in or around your school?
- Has your community crime rate increased over the past 12 months?
- Does your annual staff turnover rate exceed 25 percent?

- Have you had a student demonstration or other signs of unrest within the past 12 months?

- Are more than 15 percent of your work orders vandalism-related?

- Has there been an emergence of an underground student newspaper?

- Do you have terrorist or "hate groups" operating in your community?

The second assessment component involves reviewing school crime and discipline reports. Every school should have a comprehensive and systematic process for maintaining and analyzing written records about school crime and disciplinary incidents. The data should provide for some means of analysis to determine what incidents may be linked to other incidents on the campus. Maintaining such records can serve as a valuable student management tool. These reports should be complemented by community crime data obtained from local law enforcement officials.

A third component in data collection involves conducting a campus safety audit of the physical plant. The goal of this step is to identify unsafe places on campus, particularly those places that are often overlooked because people assume that they are safe or consider them routinely trouble-free. Components of this assessment include the examination of environs, site design, building design, interior spaces, procedures, and systems/equipment. Planners might search the Internet for sample checklists; for example, the National School Safety Center lists resources at www.nssc1.org.

A fourth component in data collection involves surveying teachers, students, parents, staff and community members regarding their perceptions of behavior and safety issues. The survey document should not only ask specific questions, but also provide for some open-ended input. Sample questionnaires are available from various state departments of education, such as Texas, California, Kentucky, South Carolina, and Florida. A sample student survey follows.

The fifth and perhaps most important data collection component is to talk with students individually and in focus groups. Typically students will not report their victimization or feelings about school safety on their own to teachers, school administrators, law enforcers, or parents. If adults want to find out what is going on, they must ask. The following questions are excellent icebreakers:

- Are there areas of the campus you avoid?

- What types of initiation rites exist for incoming students?

- Are drugs easily available on your campus?

- Have you ever seen a weapon at school?

It is important to dialog with students and establish a climate of trust. Students will offer some incredible insights—not only to the problems but also to their recommended solutions. Good information and insight improve the quality of our decisions about student management.

Make an inventory of the school safety strategies and programs already in place. It is good practice and good public relations to share these programs and their successes with your constituency. In case of litigation that the district may face, it is prudent to keep written records of the proactive and preventive steps the community has taken to promote safe schools. This may include documenting your conflict resolution program, gang prevention curriculums, bullying prevention, student courts, community service, and other extracurricular activities.

When developing your plan, summarize the threats within the district. Threats may include the presence of known gangs or "hate groups" in the local community. By the same token, identify the assets. Develop partnerships and memoranda of understanding with emergency responders, law enforcement agencies, and hospitals, among others. Set reasonable goals, and flank those goals with clear objectives that are specific, measurable, achievable, realistic, and time-oriented. For instance, if the goal is to reduce the number of assaults or threats on campus, indicate the yardstick of measure, the person(s) responsible, and a specific target date for reaching the goal.

Once your safe school plan is developed, have the county or district counsel review it to make certain that the policies and programs are in compliance with local, state, and federal laws. After legal review, hold a public meeting to announce the plan and provide the local community with at least 30 days to review the program. Safe school planning is very much about "community will." Community buy-in is essential for success. Finally, review the plan at least once a year. Make modifications or changes as necessary. Safe school planning is a changing process that requires new ideas, new insights, and new plans.

The materials that follow provide educational leaders with a variety of resources and tools for assessing school safety and keeping schools safe. School districts can adapt these strategies or adopt their own.

School Safety—Sample Student Questionnaire

1. Do you feel a major violent incident, such as a shooting, could occur at your school?
   - ☐ Yes
   - ☐ No

2. Have you ever seen a weapon at your school?
   - ☐ Never
   - ☐ 1–5 times
   - ☐ 6–10 times
   - ☐ Over 10 times

3. If you saw a weapon while on campus today, would you:
   - ☐ Say nothing?
   - ☐ Tell a friend?
   - ☐ Report it to school officials?
   - ☐ Call the police or police hotline?

4. Are there any cliques or groups that bully students or groups in your school?
   - ☐ Yes
   - ☐ No

5. During the past year have you been threatened, or intentionally hit, in a way that harmed you or made you feel afraid?
   - ☐ Yes
   - ☐ No

6. Do you know anyone on your faculty to whom you could turn if you knew of potential violence in your school?
   - ☐ Yes
   - ☐ No

7. How long would it take to get a gun in your community?
   - ☐ A few hours
   - ☐ A day
   - ☐ A few days
   - ☐ Weapons aren't available

8. Have you every heard a student make a death threat on your campus?
   - ☐ Never
   - ☐ 1–5 times
   - ☐ 6–10 times
   - ☐ Over 10 times

9. Have you ever had someone bully or threaten you at school?
   - ☐ Never
   - ☐ 1–5 times
   - ☐ 6–10 times
   - ☐ Over 10 times

10. Have you ever bullied or threatened someone else at school?
    - ☐ Never
    - ☐ 1–5 times
    - ☐ 6–10 times
    - ☐ Over 10 times

11. Have you stayed away from school because you were afraid?
    - ☐ Yes
    - ☐ No

12. Whom do you trust the most at school?
    - ☐ A specific teacher
    - ☐ A specific administrator
    - ☐ A classmate
    - ☐ Someone you are dating

13. What is the best way to reduce or eliminate school violence?
    - ☐ Use metal detectors
    - ☐ Hire security personnel
    - ☐ Use surveillance cameras
    - ☐ Increase communication among students and school staff

14. What percent of violent acts at your school do you think were communicated to others by the perpetrator before they occurred?
    - ☐ Up to 15 percent
    - ☐ Up to 30 percent
    - ☐ Up to 50 percent
    - ☐ More than 50 percent

15. Do you feel safe at your school?

☐ Yes

☐ Sometimes

☐ Seldom

☐ Never

16. Who is most responsible for creating safe schools?

☐ Students

☐ Teachers

☐ Parents

☐ Police

17. Whom do you perceive to be your greatest potential threat at school?

☐ Someone coming from off campus

☐ A fellow student

☐ A school employee

Prepared by National School Safety Center
141 Duesenberg Drive, Suite 11
Westlake Village, CA 91362
805-373-9977
web site: www.nssc1.org

Early
Interventions

7

Family Engagement

Karen L. Mapp

For the past four decades, researchers, educators, policy makers, and community members have investigated the connections between parent[1] engagement and successful academic outcomes for students. In the spring of 2001, Anne Henderson and I, with the support of the Southwest Educational Development Laboratory's (SEDL) Center for Family and Community Connections with Schools, set out to analyze recent research on the relationship between parent and community connections with schools and student academic achievement. Our findings were published in 2002 (Henderson & Mapp) as *A New Wave of Evidence: The Impact of School, Family, and Community Connections on Student Achievement*, a synthesis of 51 research studies conducted since 1994. The studies covered a wide range of areas:

- early childhood through high school,
- all regions of the country,
- diverse populations (income, race/ethnicity, educational level, and occupation),
- community as well as parent and family involvement,
- a variety of methods, both quantitative and qualitative

1 The terms "parent" and "parents" and "family" and "families" are used interchangeably throughout this document. The terms refer to any adult caretaker, including biological parents, siblings, grandparents, aunts, uncles, and "fictive kin" who may be friends or neighbors.

- different sources of data (survey research, evaluations, case studies, experimental and quasi experimental studies, and research reviews).

The 51 studies fell into three categories:

- studies on the impact of family and community involvement on student achievement,
- studies on effective strategies to connect families, schools, and communities,
- studies on parent and community organizing efforts to improve schools.

This chapter offers a subset of the findings and recommendations from the *Evidence* synthesis. The research presented here reveals what we know about the relationship between family involvement and student outcomes such as graduation from high school and enrollment in postsecondary opportunities and about effective strategies to connect families and schools. In particular, this chapter highlights findings about the impact of family engagement on the achievement of students placed at risk due to circumstances such as poverty and lack of access to community resources. The chapter concludes with recommendations for putting the findings into action.

The Impact of Family Involvement on Student Achievement

One overarching conclusion emerged from the first group of studies:

> Taken as a whole, there is a positive and convincing relationship between family involvement and benefits for students, including improved academic achievement. This relationship holds across families of all economic, racial/ethnic, and educational backgrounds and for students at all ages.

The findings from the *Evidence* publication support and add to the sizeable research base suggesting a strong link between parent engagement in the educational development of children and improvements across various measures of student achievement[2] (Henderson & Mapp, 2002).

When families are engaged in children's learning, students are more likely to

---

2 The research does not suggest that parent engagement is all that is necessary to produce high student achievement. Studies of high-performing schools identify several characteristics such as high standards, effective leadership, *and* parent and community engagement as characteristics associated with improved achievement.

- earn higher grade point averages and scores on standardized tests or rating scales,
- enroll in more challenging academic programs,
- pass more classes and earn credits,
- attend school regularly,
- display more positive attitudes about school,
- graduate from high school and enroll in postsecondary programs,
- refrain from destructive activities such as alcohol use and violence.

The new studies also shed light on the kinds of involvement that have the greatest influence on positive student outcomes. They reveal how family involvement is important at all stages of a child's life—from preschool to high school—and how involvement activities shift as children progress through school.

> Parent and community involvement that is linked to student learning has a greater effect on achievement than more general forms of involvement. To be effective, the form of involvement should be focused on improving achievement and be designed to engage families and students in developing specific knowledge and skills.

Engagement programs that are *logically linked* to student learning have the best outcomes. "Logically linked" means that however families and community are involved, improving achievement is always a main focus of the programs (Henderson & Mapp, 2002). For example, Early Head Start, a program designed to prepare low-income preschoolers for school, supported new mothers with information on early education and parenting skills and with comprehensive health services. The researchers found that the parents in the Early Head Start program were more likely to support cognitive, language, and literacy development. Early Head Start children also showed modest but greater gains than children in the control group in areas such as vocabulary development and sentence completion (Mathematica Policy Research, Inc., & Center for Children and Families at Teachers College, Columbia University, 2001).

Workshops and other outreach strategies that provide parents with information about what their children are learning in school and with techniques and activities about how to help their children at home are also examples of programs that are linked to learning. Epstein, Simon, and Salinas (1997) examined the impact of the Teachers Involve Parents in Schoolwork (TIPS) interactive homework process on student achievement in the middle grades. The students were sixth and eighth graders in two schools in Baltimore, Maryland, that served a majority African-American population. Both schools were among the lowest achieving in the city. The TIPS process enabled teachers to design homework that requires students to talk to someone at home about their assignment. School staff engaged with families to build parents' skills to monitor, interact, and support their children with homework activities. The researchers found that students' test scores and grades in writing and language improved when their families participated in TIPS learning activities at home. Parent participation in TIPS added significantly to students' writing scores over the course of the year, and completing more TIPS homework positively affected language-arts report card grades at the end of the school year.

At the high school level, family involvement that is linked to learning continues to have a positive relationship to student achievement. Simon (2000) studied predictors of high school and family partnerships and the influence of these partnerships on student success. Simon used the long-term national database, the National Educational Longitudinal Study (NELS:88), to explore family and community connections with high schools, the effects on student achievement, and the influence of high school staff outreach on family involvement.

Simon concluded that parent engagement at the high school level does have an impact on student academic success. The types of activities parents engaged in at the high school level vary from those in middle and high school, and involvement increased with support from the school. When school staff contacted parents about these opportunities, parents were more likely to

- attend planning workshops and talk to their teenagers about college and employment,
- volunteer as audience members at school activities,
- work more often with their teenagers on homework,
- talk to teenagers more often about school.

Parent engagement activities were related to higher grades in English and math, more completed course credits in English and math, better attendance and behavior, and increased preparedness for class. Simon (2000) found stronger relationships between parent involvement activities that were logically linked to learning, such as talking to students about college, and student outcomes.

> The continuity of family involvement at home appears to have a protective effect on children as they move through school. The more families support their children's learning and educational progress, the more their children tend to do well in school and continue their education.

Students are more likely to continue their education when their parents stay engaged. Miedel and Reynolds (1999) analyzed interviews from 704 low-income parents of eighth graders in Chicago. In addition to their background and expectations for their children, parents reported on their involvement when their children were in preschool and kindergarten. Seventy percent had been engaged in Chicago Parent Centers. The Centers offered workshops and information to parents about children's learning as well as activities to help parents be involved at school.

Miedel and Reynolds compared results for students based on how much their parents had been involved. Between first and eighth grades, students whose parents took part in a greater number of activities did consistently better in school. They tended to earn higher scores on reading tests, spend less time in special education, and pass from one grade to the next. These findings held across all family backgrounds.

In his analysis of NELS:88 data, Trusty (1999) found a similar protective influence. Parent involvement in eighth grade, as reported by students, influenced students' expectations to finish college six years later. Students who felt that their parents communicated with them and supported their learning were more likely to continue studies past high school. In other words, the more students felt their parents' involvement and support, the longer they planned to stay in school.

> Families of all cultural backgrounds, education and income levels encourage their children, talk with them about school, help them plan for higher education, and keep them focused on learning and homework. In other words, all families can, and often do, have a positive influence on their children's learning.

The message emanating from these findings is that all families, regardless of their background or economic circumstances, engage in some form of involvement with their children's education. Families from economically distressed circumstances or families from ethnic or racial groups different from school staff are often labeled "hard to reach," but it is more often the case that schools and programs are inaccessible to these families. Regardless of their socioeconomic status or family composition, families do engage in their children's learning.

Clark (1993) surveyed families of 1,171 third-graders of all backgrounds in Los Angeles. After dividing the students into high and low achievers based on standardized test scores, he correlated the ways they spent their out-of-school time with grades, family background, and other factors. Clark discovered that the way children spent their time at home, not the family's income or education level, predicted their success in school. Most parents reported that they talked to their children about homework, read to their children, and made sure they did their homework assignments. However, Clark found differences in the *type* of activities parents engaged in. Families with high achievers reported more time engaged in home learning activities than families with low achievers. For example, high-achieving children spent more time on homework, reading, and using materials like the dictionary.

Clark identified four variables that comprise what he calls "parents' press for academic success." Together, these factors explained 47 percent of the variation between low- and high-achieving students in the study:

- ◆ parent knowledge about homework assignments,
- ◆ parent perception of child's engagement in homework,
- ◆ child knowledge of how to use a dictionary, and
- ◆ parent expectations for child's education.

Low-achieving students tended to come from households where the parents were younger, did not work outside the home, had not attended college, and were low-income. Even though higher-achieving students often had parents who were not home to monitor their late afternoon activities, having parents in the work force was related to higher test scores.

Despite the relationship between achievement and family resources, Clark found that high-achieving students came from a wide variety of family backgrounds. More than half (51.3 percent) of the mothers of high achievers in Clark's study possessed no more than a high school education. Almost 40 percent lived in single parent households. Almost 43 percent of the high achievers were Hispanic and 21.8 percent were black.

In their study of NELS:88 data, Ho Sui-Chu and Willms (1996) found that although children from higher income families tend to do better in school, students of all backgrounds gain when their parents are involved. Ho Sui-Chu and Willms found that higher-income families were slightly more involved in some ways, but the effect was small. On the whole, the researchers concluded, higher-income and two-parent families were *not* more involved with their children's education than lower-income and single-parent families.

Effective Strategies
to Connect Families and Schools

The previous section addressed the important relationship between family involvement and outcomes for students. This section will summarize the research on strategies that lead to successful school/family engagement initiatives.

From these studies, one overarching conclusion emerged:

> When programs and initiatives focus on building respectful
> and trusting relationships among school staff, families, and

community members, they are effective in creating and sustaining family and community connections with schools.

These studies revealed that *relationships matter* (Henderson & Mapp, 2002). How parents are viewed and treated by school staff—as assets to the process of raising student achievement rather than liabilities—surfaced as a theme throughout the studies. Parents must trust school staff before positive relationships and effective communication can be established. Often, schools focus on the programmatic elements of a family involvement initiative without focusing on the relationship-building aspects of a program. Parents will not participate in engagement initiatives designed to support students if they distrust or feel disrespected by staff. The findings that follow define the components of successful school/family programs.

Programs that successfully connect with families invite involvement, are welcoming, and address specific parent needs.

Parents need to feel that school staff value their involvement, welcome them into the school community, and address their needs. Educators sometimes make the mistake of creating programming for parents without first asking parents for their feedback or about their needs. Peña (2000) explored how parents in one urban elementary school in Texas were or were not involved in their children's education and the factors that influenced their involvement. The school population was 95.5 percent Mexican. Peña interviewed 28 parents of children in pre-kindergarten/kindergarten and third/fourth grade classes. She also conducted observations of a range of meetings and activities and examined school documents regarding parent involvement.

Peña found that parent involvement was influenced by several factors: language, parent cliques, parents' educational level, attitudes of school staff, cultural influences, and family issues such as childcare. She emphasized the importance of school staff taking the time to gain the trust of parents and informing them of how they could be involved. In the study, parents not only identified factors that they felt influenced their involvement, but also offered suggestions for improving parent involvement:

- Make the parents feel more welcomed.
- Change the attitudes of school staff so that they recognize the advantages of teachers and parents working together.
- Consider the educational level, language, culture, and home situation of parents.
- Give teachers time to plan and organize parent activities.
- Take parents' interests and needs into consideration when planning activities.

- Recognize that even if parents cannot be present at school, helping their children at home is also a valuable contribution.
- Provide parents with knowledge about how to be involved in a range of involvement opportunities.

Starkey and Klein (2000) also found that parent programs and interventions work best when the strategies respect the needs of families. They studied the impact of a math intervention with Head Start parents on pre-kindergarten children's math development. The intervention respected the needs of parents by addressing common barriers to parent involvement such as childcare, transportation, and scheduling conflicts. These barriers were overcome by

- providing childcare at the program during the class,
- arranging carpools,
- encouraging family members to send a substitute family member to a class when necessary, and
- providing math kits for use at home.

When programs honor the needs of parents, parents respond by engaging in the activities.

> Parent involvement programs that are effective in engaging diverse families recognize, respect, and address cultural and class differences.

With many public schools in the United States facing rapid changes in the socioeconomic, ethnic, and cultural mix of their students, educators must connect with families from diverse cultural and class backgrounds. A study by Scribner, Young, and Pedroza (1999) looked at the relationships between parents and school staff at eight high-performing Hispanic elementary and secondary schools located in the Texan borderlands. Of the students in these schools, 95 percent were Hispanic, 70 percent were from low economic backgrounds, 10 percent were recent immigrants, and 20 percent were migrants. The researchers identified five "best practice" strategies used by school staff and parents to build collaborative relationships:

1. Learn about and build on cultural values of Hispanic parents.
2. Stress personal contact with parents.
3. Foster communication with parents.
4. Create a warm environment for parents.
5. Facilitate structural accommodations for parent involvement.

These schools recognized and implemented dynamic strategies to address language and cultural differences.

Chrispeels and Rivero (2000) studied the impact of a program intervention called the Parent Institute for Quality Education (PIQE) on a group of Latino immigrant parents. The overarching research question was, "How do Latino parents define their role and perceive their place in their children's education and their relationship with the school?" The authors examined the impact of PIQE by assessing parents' perceptions of their role and place in their children's education before and after their participation in the program.

The program consisted of eight 90-minute sessions using a curriculum translated into the parents' language. An important component of the training was the use of PIQE instructors who acted as "cultural brokers." The researchers adopted this term from Delgado-Gaitan (1996), who used it to refer to a white educator who, because of his affiliation with the Latino community, was able to translate between his ethnic and cultural group and the Latinos. The instructors selected for the program were from backgrounds and life experiences similar to those of the participants, had succeeded in the U.S. system, and could interpret this system to the Latino parents.

Parents developed higher levels of engagement with their children and with the school, especially with teachers, as a result of participation in the PIQE program. Chrispeels and Rivero (2000) emphasized the role of the instructors as cultural brokers between parents and the schools. The instructors built relationships with the parents and acted as the connecting force between parents and the schools.

> Effective programs to engage families and community embrace a philosophy of partnership. The responsibility for children's educational development is a collaborative enterprise among parents, school staff, and community members.

Some of the study findings suggest that the best way to engage families and communities with school is through a philosophy of *partnership*. Schools where staff and families act as partners—where the responsibility for educating children is a shared enterprise—see positive effects on students and on school quality and successful implementation of initiatives.

Wang, Oates, and Weishew (1997) reported on three "case scenarios" to illustrate the potential of the Community for Learning program (CFL) to improve student learning in urban schools. Described as a "broad-based, school-family-community-linked coordinated approach," the CFL design was based on two programs, the Adapted Learning Environments Model and James Comer's School Development Program (p.176). The CFL program seeks to improve student achievement particularly for students at the margins of the achievement distribution, for example, bilingual, Chapter I, and special needs students. In the area of parent involvement, CFL supports a shared partnership approach. The program encourages schools to actively involve families through "communication and cooperation between home and school" (p.17).

The achievement data over two years showed that in schools and classrooms that implemented the CFL program, fewer students than expected were in the bottom 20 percent of reading and math. More students than expected scored in the top 20 percent (with one exception). Attendance increased in the middle school. Student perceptions about the learning environment in their classroom and school were generally higher than those of students in comparison schools and classrooms.

The authors stressed that no one practice of the CFL approach accounted for student improvement. Rather, the key was an integrated system of delivery that combined several practices, including family involvement.

Putting the Findings into Action

The following is a summary from the *Evidence* publication of how the findings can be converted into action steps to create programs that support student outcomes and that effectively connect with families:

1. Recognize that all parents, regardless of income, education level, or cultural background, are involved in their children's education and want their children to do well in school.

Assume that all families can help improve their children's performance in school and influence other key outcomes that impact student achievement. Families respond to helpful information and support about how to help with their children's learning. Refrain from blaming families for low achievement and have high expectations for families as well as students.

2. Link family and community engagement efforts to student learning.

Programs and practices that engage families should be focused in some way on improving achievement. Some activities can be designed to assist students to develop their knowledge and skills. Other activities can have different goals, such as building working relationships between families and teachers.

Examples of programs that are linked to learning include family literacy programs, interactive homework, and programs that engage families in math and science activities. Initiatives should incorporate aspects of programs that research has linked to gains, for example:

◆ Demonstrate an activity for parents, engaging parents in role-playing the parts.

◆ Give materials to each family, offering advice as they use them.

- Help parents assess children's progress and steer children to next steps.
- Lend materials to use at home.

Redesign school's traditional family engagement programs to include activities that link to learning:

- Incorporate information on standards and exhibits of student work at open houses and back-to-school nights.
- Engage parents and students in math and reading games at Family Nights. Engage in a dialog with families, with user-friendly language, about where students' skills need to be stronger. Use scoring guides with projects and let parents know what a scoring guide is and how to use it.
- Use the school newsletter to offer helpful hints to parents about supporting learning at home, explanations of test results, and what students are doing to meet higher standards.

3. Create initiatives that will support families to guide their children's learning, from preschool through high school.

The following are examples of preschool, elementary, middle, and high school strategies to support families' efforts to guide their children's learning.

Examples of preschool strategies:

- Home visits from trained parent educators with cultural backgrounds similar to their own, or with knowledge of their culture.
- Lending libraries that offer games and learning materials to build skills at home.
- Discussion and/or support groups with other families about children's learning.
- Classes on how to stimulate their children's mental, physical and emotional development.

Examples of elementary and middle school strategies:

- Interactive homework assignments that involve parents with their children's learning.
- Workshops on topics that families suggest.
- Regular calls from teachers, not just when there are problems, about how their children are doing in class. Lead with positive information.
- Learning packets in reading, science, and math, as well as training in how to use them.

- Meetings where parents and teachers *share* information about children's progress and what they're learning.

Examples of high school strategies:

- Regular meetings with parents, teachers, and counselors work together to plan their children's academic program.

- Information to parents about program options, graduation requirements, test schedules, and postsecondary education options and how to plan for them.

- Explanations of courses students should take to be prepared for college or other postsecondary education.

- Information about financing postsecondary education and applying for financial aid.

4. Develop the capacity of school staff to work with families.

Increase the opportunities for professional development on how to connect with families. Several studies highlighted the importance of the relationship between school staff and families as key to developing effective connections.

In several studies, an intervention was introduced to teachers or other school staff that shifted the level and nature of the contact between themselves and families. Staff were encouraged to see families as their children's first teachers and to elicit and value parents' feedback about their children's skills and challenges (Mapp, 2002). These shifts in practices changed the way families felt about the school, affected their relationship with teachers, and influenced how they were involved in the educational life of their children. School staff need more support in developing ways to reach out to families and use resources available to them in the local community.

Few teacher preparation programs include instruction on how to partner with parents and community. Such programs must include a focus on the importance of partnership with parents and community to improve student achievement. All school staff, from the principal to the custodian, need opportunities to learn more about this area.

Design pre- and in-service educational opportunities for all school staff that

- help all staff recognize the advantages of school, family, and community connections,

- explore how trusting and respectful relationships with families and community members are achieved,

- enhance school staff's ability to work with diverse families,

- enable staff to make connections with community resources, and

◆ explore the benefits of sharing power with families and community members.

5. Focus efforts to engage families on developing trusting and respectful relationships.

A consistent theme in the studies is that relationships are key. Any attempt to form genuine collaborations among school staff and families must start with building relationships of respect. The building of relationships must be intentional and consistent. When outreach efforts reflect a sincere desire to engage parents as partners in children's education, the studies show that students, parents, and the schools all benefit from the partnership.

Respecting cultural and class differences is an important step towards building trusting relationships with families. The studies suggest that educators must make every attempt to learn about the concerns of families and how they define and perceive their role in the school. Chrispeels and Rivero (2000) point out the value of teachers' learning how to become cultural brokers and cross-cultural boundaries.

6. Embrace a philosophy of partnership and be willing to share power with families. Make sure that parents and school staff understand that the responsibility for children's educational development is a collaborative enterprise.

Adopt a philosophy of partnership where the contributions of all constituents are valued and where power is shared. Several studies found that when school/family initiatives were a part of a comprehensive plan to improve student achievement, the programs engaged and sustained the involvement of families. Engage families in the process of planning, establishing policy, and making decisions. Families lose interest in working with schools when they realize that their participation is token.

Conclusion

The research from the *Evidence* synthesis indicates that when students feel support from both home and school, they tend to do better in school (Henderson & Mapp, 2002). Students state that they have more self-confidence and feel school is more important. The research suggests that they also are less disruptive, earn higher grades, and are more likely to go to college (Gutman and Midgley, 2000; Sanders and Herting, 2000; Shumow and Lomax, 2002; Trusty, 1999). Engaging families in student learning through partnerships with schools must be recognized as a critical component to improve educational outcomes for all children. Susan Swap (1993) summarizes the importance of partnerships and family engagement:

Home–school partnership is no longer a luxury. There is an urgent need for schools to find ways to support the success of all of our children. One element that we know contributes to more successful children and more successful schools across all populations is parent involvement in children's education. When our focus is on improving the achievement of all children at academic risk, partnership with families is not just useful—it is crucial.

References

Chrispeels, J. H., & Rivero, E. (2000). *Engaging Latino families for student success: Understanding the process and impact of providing training to parents.* Paper presented at the Annual Meeting of the American Educational Research Association, New Orleans, LA.

Clark, R. M. (1993). Homework-focused parenting practices that positively affect student achievement. In N. F. Chavkin (Ed.), *Families and schools in a pluralistic society* (pp. 85–105). Albany, NY: State University of New York.

Delgado-Gaitan, C. (1996). *Protean literacy: Extending the discourse on empowerment.* London: Falmer Press.

Epstein, J. L., Simon, B. S., & Salinas, K. C. (1997). Involving parents in homework in the middle grades. *Research Bulletin No.18,* 4 pages, http://www.pdkintl.org/edres/resbul18.htm.

Gutman, L. M., & Midgley, C. (2000). The role of protective factors in supporting the academic achievement of poor African American students during the middle school transition. *Journal of Youth and Adolescence, 29*(2), 223–248.

Henderson, A., & Mapp, K. (2002). *A new wave of evidence: The impact of school, family, and community connections on student achievement.* Austin, TX: Southwest Educational Development Laboratory.

Ho Sui-Chu, E., & Willms, J. D. (1996). Effects of parental involvement on eighth-grade achievement. *Sociology of Education, 69* (2), 126–141, (ERIC Document Reproduction Service No. EJ533315).

Mapp, K. (2002). *Having their say: Parents describe how and why they are involved in their children's education.* Paper presented at the Annual Meeting of the American Educational Research Association, New Orleans, LA.

Mathematica Policy Research, Inc., & Center for Children and Families at Teachers College, Columbia University (2001). *Building their futures: How early Head Start programs are enhancing the lives of infants and toddlers in low-income families.* Washington, DC: Administration on Children, Youth, and Families, Department of Health and Human Services http://www.acf.dhhs.gov/programs/core/ongoing_research/ehs/ehs_reports.html.

Miedel, W. T., & Reynolds, A. J. (1999). Parent involvement in early intervention for disadvantaged children: Does it matter? *Journal of School Psychology, 37*(4), 379–402, (ERIC Document Reproduction Service No. EJ607658).

Peña, D. C. (2000). Parent involvement: Influencing factors and implications. *Journal of Educational Research, 94*(1), 42–54, (ERIC Document Reproduction Service No. EJ615791).

Sanders, M. G., & Herting, J. R. (2000). Gender and the effects of school, family, and church support on the academic achievement of African-American urban adolescents. In M. G. Sanders (Ed.), *Schooling students placed at risk: Research, policy, and practice in the education of poor and minority adolescents* (pp. 141–161). Mahwah, NJ: Lawrence Erlbaum Associates.

Scribner, J. D., Young, M. D., & Pedroza, A. (1999). Building collaborative relationships with parents. In P. Reyes, J. D. Scribner, & A. Paredes-Scribner (Eds.), *Lessons from high-performing Hispanic schools: Creating learning communities* (pp. 36–60). New York: Teachers College Press.

Shumow, L., & Lomax, R. (2001). *Parental efficacy: Predictor of parenting behavior and adolescent outcomes.* Paper presented at the Annual Meeting of the American Educational Research Association, Seattle, WA.

Simon, B. S. (2000). *Predictors of high school and family partnerships and the influence of partnerships on student success.* Unpublished doctoral dissertation, Johns Hopkins University.

Starkey, P., & Klein, A. (2000). Fostering parental support for children's mathematical development: An intervention with Head Start families. *Early Education and Development, 11*(5), 659–680, (ERIC Document Reproduction Service No. EJ618579).

Swap, S. M. (1993). *Developing home-school partnerships: From concepts to practice.* New York: Teachers College Press.

Trusty, J. S. (1999). Effects of eighth-grade parental involvement on late adolescents' educational experiences. *Journal of Research and Development in Education, 32*(4), 224–233, (ERIC Document Reproduction Service No. EJ598231).

Wang, M. C., Oates, J., & Weishew, N. L. (1997). Effective school responses to student diversity in inner-city schools: A coordinated approach. In G. D. Haertl & M. C. Wang (Eds.), *Coordination, cooperation, collaboration* (pp. 175–197). Philadelphia, PA: The Mid-Atlantic Regional Educational Laboratory at Temple University.

8

Early Childhood Education

Dolores Stegelin

The value of early childhood education as an effective dropout prevention strategy is compelling. The concept of *prevention* applies to the critical role of good early learning experiences: young children who engage in hands-on, exploratory experiences that validate their sensory, cognitive, emotional, social, and verbal development are much more likely to stay in school and make consistent contributions to the larger society (Jones, 1998; Barnett, 1995; Campbell & Ramey, 1994; Christie, 1990; Lazar, Darlington, Murray, Royce, & Snipper, 1982). The positive impact of high-quality early childhood education is most notable for young children from lower socioeconomic status families, children with disabilities and special needs, and other young children whose life circumstances place them at risk for academic success and positive life outcomes.

The value of high-quality learning experiences to enhanced cognitive and social development is confirmed in recent brain research. Brain scans of toddlers raised in stimulating, engaging environments versus brain scans of toddlers deprived of cognitive, nutritional, social, and language stimulation are quite convincing evidence (Begley, 2000; O'Donnell, 1999). Early stimulation is absolutely essential if young children are to develop optimally and take their places in society as constructive, contributing, and creative citizens (Shore, 1997).

Defining high-quality early childhood education is documented through the research over the past twenty years. Derived from the theoretical frameworks of Froebel, Dewey, Piaget, Vygotsky, and more contemporary theorists such as Howard Gardner and Marian Diamond, the parameters for quality early childhood education are distinct and measurable (Morrison, 2001; Gardner, 1983; Vygotsky, 1978; Piaget, 1952). High-quality early childhood education is reflected in both research and practice as nurturing, consistent, stimulating, hands-on, exploratory, and holistic learning experiences and interactions with caring adults and peers (Bredekamp, 1987). High-quality early childhood education cuts across all domains of child development—physical, cognitive, social, emotional, and creative—and integrates interactive learning experiences across curriculum areas, such as language arts, science, math, social studies, and the creative arts (Jones, 1998; Perry & Rivkin, 1992; Bredekamp, 1987).

Documenting the Effectiveness of Early Childhood Education

One of the greatest challenges for early childhood professionals is documenting the long-term impact of early learning experiences. Studying infants, toddlers, and preschool children presents both ethical and practical challenges. However, policy makers have justifiably demanded "proof" of the value of high-quality early childhood education (Stegelin, 1992). This proof has evolved over the past 30 years and in many different forms. Head Start, birthed in 1964 as America's first national venture into early childhood education, provided a critical window of opportunity for both short-term and longitudinal research on the outcomes of early childhood education for at-risk young children. Conceptualized as a means to raise the intelligence quotients (IQs) of at-risk preschoolers, Head Start was established within the context of Lyndon B. Johnson's Great Society. From the beginning, government agencies demanded evidence that this massive early intervention program was worthy of funding. This research evidence came in several venues, but among the most famous were the Perry Preschool Study (Barnett, 1995) and the Consortium of Longitudinal Studies (Lazar et al., 1982).

The Consortium of Longitudinal Studies compared intervention approaches across Head Start programs, and it served a valuable role in defining the specific outcomes of behavioral versus maturationist versus constructivist approaches (Lazar et al., 1982). The famous longitudinal Perry Preschool Study, conducted by Drs. David Weikart and Lawrence Schweinhart and spanning nearly 40 years, continues to document the positive outcomes of former Head Start children who participated in a constructivist, hands-on, exploratory early childhood education program associated with the High/Scope Foundation of Ypsilanti, Michigan. Among the findings of this noted longitudinal study is a range of benefits to the larger society. While long-term gains in IQ were not documented through this longitudinal research, the significance of this research lies in the qualitative, social, and preventative outcomes for these young children as they progressed through adulthood.

The Perry Preschool Study confirms that at-risk four-year-old children who participated in a high-quality, developmentally appropriate Head Start program gained such significant social benefits as decreased levels of school dropout, lower levels of truancy and delinquency, reduced rates of teen pregnancy, and lower levels of welfare dependency and incarceration. *Taken together, these factors enabled the Perry Preschool Longitudinal Study researchers to document that one dollar invested into high-quality early childhood education programs by policy makers results in a return of seven dollars in preventative costs associated with incarceration, truancy, school dropout, and teen pregnancy.* This significant longitudinal study represents a critical reason for the passage of state-funded preschool programs during the 1980s and 1990s. After all, a return rate of $7 to $1 is significant, and policy makers have utilized these research outcomes to justify the millions of dollars currently being committed to high-quality, state-funded early childhood programs.

A more recent form of evidence of the effectiveness of early childhood education as a dropout prevention strategy lies in the brain research (Diamond & Hopson, 1998). The recent explosion of neuroscientific research is increasing our understanding of the effects of early stimulation (Wolfe & Brandt, 1998), although there is still much interpretation to do. In 1989, President Bush proclaimed the 1990s as the Decade of the Brain. During this decade, hundreds of research studies were conducted and interpreted, shedding much insight into the explosive and critical brain growth period of the first 36 months of life. The field of brain science is a growing field, and we have learned more about the brain in the past five years than in the previous hundred years (Wolfe & Brandt, 1998).

In simple yet explicit terms, the brain research documents that a young child's brain at birth has all the cells or neurons it will ever have (Morrison, 2001). How these billions of neurons develop will be determined by the interactions of this young child with his/her immediate environment. We are still sorting out all of the factors that influence this rapid brain growth, but at the top of the list are such critical variables as quantity and quality of daily nutrition, motor development and movement, exposure to visual and auditory stimuli, meaningful verbal exchanges with nurturing adults and peers, consistent and safe daily routines, and emotionally supportive and caring exchanges (Diamond & Hopson, 1998). According to Diamond, an enriched environment:

- includes a steady source of positive emotional support,
- provides a nutritious diet with enough protein, vitamins, minerals, and calories,
- stimulates all the senses (but not necessarily all at once!),
- has an atmosphere free of undue pressure and stress but with a degree of pleasurable intensity,
- allows social interaction for a significant percentage of activities,
- promotes the development of a broad range of skills and interests that are mental, physical, aesthetic, social, and emotional,
- gives the child an opportunity to choose many of his or her efforts and to modify them,
- provides an enjoyable atmosphere that promotes exploration and the fun of learning,
- allows the child to be an active participant rather than a passive observer (Diamond & Hopson, 1998).

Best Practices in Early Childhood Education in Diverse Settings

What constitutes "best practices" in early childhood education can be described through the lens of developmentally appropriate practice (Bredekamp, 1987). Developmentally Appropriate Practice, DAP, represents a consensus in the field of early childhood education about what constitutes well-rounded, holistic, and high-quality early childhood education. DAP is designed to provide a paradigm for decision making for teachers, administrators, and parents, and it applies to home-, school-, and community-based settings for young children (Goffin & Stegelin, 1992). Developmentally Appropriate Practice is currently being applied to childcare settings of all types (family, group, and center; for-profit and non-profit; public and private); before- and after-school programs; pre-K and kindergarten settings in public and private sectors; and primary learning settings in both private and public venues. In addition, DAP takes into consideration the increasingly developmentally diverse and multicultural settings for young children. DAP applies to rural, suburban, and urban neighborhoods, and it can be used by parents as a guide for establishing more stimulating home environments also. DAP is the basis for National Association for the Education of Young Children (NAEYC) accreditation processes and for school-based early childhood education programs.

The three dimensions of DAP are (1) age-appropriate, (2) individually appropriate, and (3) culturally appropriate. Always under review and scrutiny, DAP continues to be examined and refined in order to reflect the existing needs of contemporary families, children, communities, and schools.

From our vast knowledge of early brain development, combined with the research over the past three decades on social, emotional, cognitive, and language development, we now know which practices are associated with optimal child development. Following are descriptions of best practices for infants, toddlers, preschoolers, and kindergarten/primary children.

Figure 8.1. Best Practices for Infants and Toddlers (Birth to 3 years)

Infants and toddlers in both home and childcare settings have complex and comprehensive developmental needs that can best be met through the following:

- ☐ Safe, healthy environments that are secure and allow for exploration as well as rest
- ☐ Up-to-date immunizations and well-baby checkups, with attention to nutrition
- ☐ Conversations with adults that are interactive, stimulating, and nurturing
- ☐ Soothing, comforting, and nurturing interactions with caring adults
- ☐ Consistency in routines with opportunities to develop language, cognitive, social, and physical development
- ☐ Exposure to books, stories, poems, music, singing songs, listening to CDs, and other animated interactions with both adults and peers of same and multi-age
- ☐ Integration of children with special needs into typical settings
- ☐ Exposure to social settings that expand the child's understanding of their own and other cultures
- ☐ Consistent routines that create a sense of predictability and psychological safety
- ☐ Interactions that provide for both individual and small group experiences
- ☐ Programs that establish reciprocal interactions with parents and families
- ☐ Routines that encourage self-help skills, problem-solving, autonomy, and independence
- ☐ Toddler routines that encourage much physical activity and exploration, such as climbing, crawling, walking, rolling, running, kicking, and manipulation
- ☐ Daily routines that include both active and quiet activities throughout the day

Figure 8.2. Best Practices for Preschool Children (3 to 5 years)

Young children from three to five years of age spend many hours in the home as well as in childcare settings. Faith-based and state-funded preschool programs have grown rapidly over the past 20 years, and childcare options abound also. Whether a preschooler is in a home or care setting, the developmental needs remain the same. Following are practices for optimal preschool development:

☐ Provide concrete materials to help children see and experience concepts and processes.

☐ Incorporate sensory experience that involve listening, tasting, feeling, pouring, counting, smelling, auditory, visual, and oral experiences.

☐ Use hands-on activities that give children opportunities for active involvement in their learning (i.e., measure a live cat rather than just read about one).

☐ Plan many and varied experiences throughout the day that range from physically active to quiet and reflective play and activity.

☐ Model appropriate tasks and behaviors, as young children learn a great deal through observation and imitation of language, social, problem-solving, and daily routines.

☐ Create a print-rich environment that encourage the preschool child to learn about the alphabet and number systems.

☐ Give young children choices of activities that encourage in-depth project work and exploration.

☐ Provide quiet spaces for children to engage in books, quiet conversations with peers, rest, and reflection.

☐ Provide opportunities for children to draw, write, paint, trace, color, and experience early literacy experiences.

☐ Encourage dialogue between children so that they learn empathy for one another and can develop conflict resolution skills.

☐ Create holistic learning environments that value emotional intelligence as well as cognitive and language skills.

☐ Use play as the major means for learning and exploring, and establish learning centers that engage the child in active play.

Figure 8.3. Best Practices for Kindergarten and Primary Children (5 to 8 years)

Froebel brought the concept of kindergarten to the United States from Germany in the 1850s. Along with Dewey, Froebel helped to share the philosophy of play-based and active learning environments for five-year-olds. Today's kindergarten and primary settings have become more academic, but they should include the following dimensions in order to be developmentally appropriate:

- ☐ Provide materials for a wide range of children's abilities, keeping in mind developmental and cultural differences.
- ☐ Children should be focused and engaged in active learning centers either in individual work or in small, cooperative learning groups.
- ☐ Curriculum should be integrated and should be sensitive to linguistic and cultural differences.
- ☐ A balance of active and quiet learning should take place, and the teacher should take cues from each of the children in shaping the content and format of the curriculum and lessons.
- ☐ Assessment should involve multiple strategies and should be balanced between required standardized testing and a variety of authentic assessment strategies.
- ☐ Children should be encouraged to make choices in their learning activities and they should learn to work in-depth as an individual and in small groups.
- ☐ Hands-on, exploratory, and concrete learning activities should be planned and implemented.
- ☐ Children should learn alphabet, number concepts, social and science concepts within real-life contexts.
- ☐ Encourage children to have conversations with one another and with adults; adults should model conflict resolution techniques.
- ☐ Teachers should spend time with individual children and with small groups of children rather than primarily with the entire group of children.
- ☐ Create project work so that children can become immersed in a theme or topic that they love and have chosen to explore in-depth.
- ☐ Balance active and quiet time, provide outdoor play, and encourage maximum physical activity.
- ☐ Model and encourage a love of books and a positive disposition for reading.

Early Childhood Intervention and Dropout Prevention

The statistics presented in Chapter 3 paint a vivid picture of who drops out and why. Researchers have identified the factors that place children at risk of dropping out. Educators have learned to recognize the signs that a child faces a rocky road in school. Early intervention can make a difference.

One of the most effective ways to improve the likelihood of students staying in school is to provide competence, skills, and confidence through early childhood programs (Wishon, Huang, & Needham, 1987). Early intervention effects—documented in research projects completed since the 1960s—reflect positive outcomes for young children that include stronger commitment to staying in school, higher levels of academic achievement, fewer special education services, and lower rates of grade retention. Most notably, early intervention for young children who are at risk for school failure also alleviates dropout problems and diminishes the inclination toward juvenile delinquency (Schweinhart & Weikart, 1985).

Components of effective early intervention programs include motivated teachers and students, learning within a regular (versus special needs) classroom context, high-quality program design and implementation, parental involvement, staff supervision, in-service training, teacher planning and collaboration, positive staff relationships, ongoing evaluation, and administrative leadership. Perhaps the most important component is that of a caring classroom. Research establishes that many teachers behave less favorably toward students who come from lower socioeconomic status homes, are lower academic achievers, speak other than Standard English, and come from ethnic minority backgrounds (Martinez, 1986).

Conclusion

The role of early childhood education as an effective strategy to dropout prevention is critical. Based on the concept of prevention, high-quality early childhood education programs are most valuable and effective for those young children from disadvantaged and marginalized families. Over a period of four decades, the research clearly documents the positive outcomes of early childhood education, and these outcomes represent both cognitive and social dimensions. Further research is needed in the areas of disabilities and special needs. Historically, research in these areas has focused on cognitive outcomes. However, what is still needed is research that can document the broad developmental trajectories for young children with disabilities. In addition, further research is needed in the area of curriculum development, implementation, and consequent child developmental outcomes. In other words, which curricula work best for which child populations? Finally, qualitative research is needed that further explains the relationship between high-quality early childhood education programs, the families that are a part of these child populations, and outcome measures not just for the child but for the family as a system. Does early childhood education also enhance family communication, literacy routines, attitudes toward reading and learning, adult attitudes toward completion of education, and other variables that directly connect the child, the family, and positive outcomes of high-quality early childhood education?

The 1960s marked a significant demarcation for the field of early childhood education. Federal initiatives in Head Start and new legislation to serve young children with disabilities combined to set a precedence and emphasis on the value of early intervention. The new millennium marks another turning point for young children as states begin to strengthen their role in providing high-quality early childhood education. With dwindling federal and state funds, the commitment to educating young children must remain steadfast. The outcomes for young children who experience systemic, high-quality early childhood education are clearly documented. Early childhood education remains one of the most essential and valuable effective strategies for dropout prevention.

References

Barnett, W. S. (1995). Long-term effects of early childhood programs on cognitive and school outcomes. *The future of children: Long-term outcomes of early childhood programs, 5*(3), 25–50.

Begley, S. (2000, Fall/Winter). Wired for thought. *Newsweek*, pp. 25–30.

Bredekamp, S. (1987). *Developmentally appropriate practice in early childhood programs serving children from birth through age 8*. Washington, DC: National Association for the Education of Young Children.

Campbell, F. A., & Ramey, C. T. (1994). Effects of early childhood intervention on intellectual and academic achievement: A follow-up study of children from low-income families. *Child Development, 65*, 684–698.

Christie, J. F. (1990). Dramatic play: A context for meaningful engagements. *The Reading Teacher, 43*, 542–545.

Diamond, M., & Hopson, J. (1998). *Magic trees of the mind: How to nurture your child's intelligence, creativity, and healthy emotions from birth through adolescence*. New York: Penguin Putnam.

Gardner, H. (1983). *Frames of mind: The theory of multiple intelligences*. New York: Basic.

Goffin, J., & Stegelin, D. (1992). Changing kindergardens: Four success stories. Washington, DC: National Association for the Education of Young Children.

Jones, R. (1998). Starting early: The why and how of preschool education. *The American School Board Journal, 17*, 20–25.

Lazar, I., Darlington, R., Murray, H., Royce, J., & Snipper, A. (1982). Lasting effects of early education: A report from the consortium for longitudinal studies. *Monographs of the Society for Research in Child Development, 47* (Serial No. 195).

Martinez, R. (1986). *Minority youth dropouts: Personal, social and institutional reasons for leaving school.* Colorado Springs, CO: Center for Community Development and Design.

Morrison, G. (2001). *Early childhood education today, 8th ed.* Columbus, OH: Merrill/Prentice-Hall.

O'Donnell, N. S. (1999). Using childhood brain development research. *Child Care Information Exchange, 75,* 58–62.

Perry, G., & Rivkin, M. (1992). Teachers and science. *Young Children, 47*(4), 9–16.

Piaget, J. (1952). *The origins of intelligence in children.* New York: International Universities Press.

Schweinhart, L. J. & Weikart, D. P. (1985). Evidence that good early childhood programs work. *Phi Delta Kappan, 66,* 8.

Shore, R. (1997). *Rethinking the brain: New insights into early development.* New York: Families and Work Institute.

Stegelin, D. A. (1992). Early childhood education: Policy issues for the 1990s. Greenwich, CT: Ablex.

Vygotsky, L. (1978). *Mind in society: The development of higher psychological processes.* Cambridge, MA: Harvard University Press.

Wishon, P., Huang, A., & Needham, R. (1987). School discontinuance prevention through early intervention, *Dimensions, 15*(2), 22–23.

Wolfe, P., & Brandt, R. (1998). What do we know from brain research? *Educational Leadership, 16,* 8–13.

9

Early Literacy Development

Linda B. Gambrell

The failure of many children to develop early literacy skills that lead to both academic and social success continues to be a national concern. Students who experience early reading failure typically experience difficulty in the later grades and in life. According to Stanovich (1986), students who acquire early literacy skills have the tools to exponentially develop in their knowledge and skills, while those who fail to develop early literacy skills fall further and further behind. With respect to literacy development, Stanovich (1986) used the term "Matthew Effect" to describe this phenomenon of "the rich get richer and the poor get poorer." By the later elementary years, students who experience severe reading failure are often given the label of "learning disabled" (Haager & Windmueller, 2001) and by the middle school years are in jeopardy of dropping out of school because of academic failure.

Most young children enter first grade with well-developed knowledge about language and print (Snow, Burns, & Griffin, 1998). They speak in complex sentences and have an oral vocabulary of approximately 5,000 words (Roberts, 1998). Both the quality and the quantity of preschool literacy experiences influences a child's knowledge of language and print, as well as "preparedness" for academic success (AACTE, 2002).

Literacy:
Common Elements of Reading and Writing

While definitions of literacy vary, most of them acknowledge the common elements of print, language, and comprehension. There is general agreement that literacy is a constructive and interactive process. That is, literacy is viewed as a meaning-making process that involves not only the student and the text, but the contextual setting as well (Gambrell, 1996; Guthrie, 1996, Vygotsky, 1978). In this constructive-interactive view of literacy, both reading and writing are recognized as cognitive processes that are nurtured and developed using a multitude of instructional practices and assessment techniques.

Literacy is a continuum that begins at birth and continues throughout life. This perspective acknowledges that reading and writing develop concurrently and interrelatedly in young children (Teale & Sulzby, 1987). For example, Harste (1989) showed that writing improved young children's reading skills and decoding skills. According to Teale and Sulzby (1988), children do not first learn to read and then learn to write; rather, reading and writing develop in concert. Therefore, it seems appropriate that we build on the close and complementary relationship between reading and writing in the literacy experiences we provide for young children.

Factors Associated with Early Literacy Development

A range of factors have been found to be related to learning to read and write successfully, including storybook reading, exposure to environmental print, and home-school connections.

Storybook Reading

Students with a high risk of reading failure are often those children who have had limited access to books and book sharing experiences. The single most important literacy activity for building a strong foundation for literacy development is having an adult who reads aloud to the child on a continuing basis (Anderson, Hiebert, Scott, & Wilkinson, 1985). Children make the most literacy growth when the materials that are being read aloud are slightly above the child's vocabulary and syntax level (Chomsky, 1972). It is the interactive nature or the engagement between the adult and the child that makes the most substantial contribution to literacy development (Adams, 1990). Parents or other adults support and nurture children's literacy development during read-aloud experiences when they build on the child's comments about the text; pose challenging questions; suggest alternative interpretations of the text; encourage personal reactions; draw attention to letters, words, and illustrations; and engage in extended discussions about the text (Adams, 1990; Teale, 1984).

According to Clay (1979) and Smith (1988) the read-aloud experience helps children learn about the features of written language. They learn that print is different from oral language, that print generates meaning, and that printed words on a page have sounds. In addition, the behaviors of the adult during read-aloud experiences have been found to be associated with literacy development. Flood (1977) found that the following parent behaviors were among the best predictors of children's reading achievement: number of questions asked by the parent before and during the story reading, number of evaluative questions asked by the parent following the story reading, and positive verbal comments offered by the parent.

Research has documented the positive effect of read-aloud experiences on a number of literacy skills: children's interest in reading (Cullinan, 1992: Huck, 1992), familiarity with book language (Anderson et al., 1985), awareness of story structure (Morrow & Weinstein, 1982), verbal expression and vocabulary (Purcell-Gates, 1988; Whitehurst & Lonigan, 1998), and story comprehension (Morrow & Weinstein, 1982; Wells, 1986). Consequently, many current intervention programs for young children who are at risk of reading failure incorporate an emphasis on interactive storybook reading, as well as increased access to books, both of which have resulted in positive gains in children's literacy growth (Morrow & O'Connor, 1995; Gambrell, Almasi, Xie, & Heland, 1995).

Environmental Print

A variety of literacy events that occur in homes afford children with opportunities to learn about print. Reading and writing experiences include demonstrations of reading text on cartons, containers, flyers, coupons, advertisements, and television notices; writing grocery lists; signing names; and written communications with family and others (Purcell-Gates, 1996). Research suggests that the frequency of literacy events in the home and the degree of children's participation can be associated with young children's literacy motivation and knowledge about the functions of print (Baker, Serpell, & Sonnenschein, 1995). However, if parents and their children do not view print as useful within their own culture, environmental print may contribute little to emergent literacy development (Purcell-Gates, 1994).

Home-School Connections

Recent research has begun to focus on home-school connections, or the lack of home-school connections, and their effects on children's literacy learning. Heath (1983) conducted an influential study that shed light on the influence of home-school connections. She found that cultural mismatches between parent-child and teacher-child linguistic interactions affected children's performance in school. The home and community, as well as preschool literacy experiences, can shape children's literacy knowledge and may impede or facilitate learning in school (Neuman & Roskos, 1997).

Swap (1993) has argued that some parent involvement programs assume a "deficit" model, that is, non-mainstream-culture families are "deficient" and are in need of remediation regarding how they can "fit" the practices in schools. An "anti-deficit" model, on the other hand, is grounded in the view that children will benefit from experiences and instruction that draw upon their home and community life. If we believe in the associative capacity of human cognition, then a range of home and community experiences can be viewed as relevant and meaningful for classroom literacy instruction.

Best Practices in Early Literacy Instruction

Becoming a successful reader is a complex task. The young child must orchestrate many areas of awareness, master specific skills, and acquire both decoding and comprehension strategies. Reading is first and foremost a meaning-getting process, therefore children must have adequate and accurate concepts about what print is and what words are. Children also need to learn to decode well and be able to move from letters to sounds to real words and, ultimately, to comprehend the meaning of the text they read. The following section provides an overview of several factors associated with becoming a successful reader.

Early Readers and Writers can Distinguish the Sounds They Hear in Spoken Words

Phonemic awareness means that the child is aware of the sounds that make up spoken words. Phonemic awareness—conscious attention to the sound elements of language—has been identified as a critical predictor of later literacy. A number of phonemic awareness training activities enhance reading achievement for children who are at risk of reading failure. Evidence suggests that the ability to isolate and manipulate the sound elements of language is developed through word play training that includes activities such as comparing and contrasting rhyming words (for example, "Do book and cook rhyme?"), generating rhyming words (for example, "Can you tell me a word that rhymes with bake?), blending (cat = k-a-t), syllable-splitting (run-ning; bea-u-ti-ful), phonemic segmentation (gr-een; cl-ip) and deleting or adding phonemes to create new words (see Adams [1990] for descriptions of these tasks). It is not difficult to understand how phonemic awareness is related to literacy development. A child who either does not consciously realize that words are made of sounds or is unable to hear or manipulate sounds in words will most likely have difficulty linking letters to sounds (as in reading) or sounds to letters (as in writing).

In a study by Ayres (1995), direct instruction in phonemic awareness was more effective than indirect instruction, and direct instruction was most effective when provided during the second half of the kindergarten year. It should be noted that even the most enthusiastic supporters of direct instruction in phonemic awareness, such as the National Reading Panel (2000) report, suggest that training is more effective when instruction

- is offered in small group settings,
- is tied to letter sound instruction, and
- does not exceed 18 hours of training.

Early Readers and Writers Know the Alphabet and the Sounds the Letters Represent

Alphabetic understanding refers to the knowledge that letters represent sounds and that whole words have a structure consisting of individual sounds and patterns of groups of sounds. It appears that children's ability to simply recognize and name the letters in the alphabet is not as important as their ease and fluency in doing so (Adams, 1990). A number of reasons have been put forth as to why letter-naming speed and accuracy is advantageous in learning to read. One reason may be that children who are able to rapidly and accurately name letters have a deeper and more thorough knowledge of letters and are therefore better able to focus on patterns within words. Conversely, children who cannot rapidly and accurately name letters appear to spend greater cognitive energy on letter discrimination. Because letter names are closely related to sounds, children who are able to name letters quickly will be better able to associate letters with sounds.

Through independent print-related explorations as well as direct instruction, children begin to explore the alphabet as they learn the letter names and sounds, as well as high-frequency spelling patterns (Richgels, Poremba, & McGee, 1998). Knowledge about the alphabet is developed as teachers demonstrate the relationship between speech sounds and letters during shared reading lessons, and help children spell words by stretching the sounds they hear during shared writing lessons.

Early Readers and Writers Know the Sounds that are Represented by Letters and Combinations of Letters

The term *letter-sound correspondence* refers to the child's ability to link discrete sounds with individual letters or patterns of letters. Phonics is the formal process of teaching letter-sound relationships. In the early stages of reading and writing development, children develop an awareness of letter-sound correspondence in a variety of naturally occurring literacy events. For many children the interest and desire to write precedes interest in reading. Children will often ask, "How do I write *mommy*? or "How do I spell *helicopter*?"

In their early attempts to write, children use the letter names they hear in words, such as "kr" for car, or "apl" for apple (Harste, Burke, & Woodward, 1982). The invented spellings of young children appear to be attempts at mapping the sound system rather than a means for identifying words. Young children often "sound out" the initial letter or letters in a word they are attempting to read, for example, they will voice the sound of "d" in the word dog or the "t" in top. There is converging evidence that a combination of training in phonemic awareness and letter-sound correspondence facilitates reading as well as spelling development (Adams, 1990; Mann, 1993; Snowling, 1991).

Research on what young children need to know about sounds in spoken words in order to be successful readers highlights the importance of learning letters and their sounds together. Ohnmacht's (1969) research revealed that teaching children to recognize letters of the alphabet produced little benefit unless the children were also taught the sounds the letters represent. Likewise, it appears that teaching children to recognize sounds in spoken words has little effect on reading unless children are also taught the printed letters that represent their spoken counterparts (Bradley & Bryant, 1983).

Early Readers and Writers Know that Print Carries Meaning

Research clearly indicates that the most significant factor underlying fluent word reading is the ability to recognize letters, spelling patterns, and whole words easily and automatically. It is equally important to keep in mind that the ultimate goal of both reading and writing is comprehension. As children engage in reading text, they interpret the meaning by gathering new information as they proceed through the text. New information is interpreted in light of what they already know and have experienced (prior knowledge). Comprehension is interactive in nature and depends as much on the readers' knowledge as it does on the information revealed in the text (Mason, 1984). In other words reading is a meaning-getting process. When young children engage in writing, it involves the process of meaning-giving, as they write about their thoughts and ideas.

Teachers and parents support the development of comprehension skills when they interact with children about the ideas in text. This occurs during teacher or parent read-aloud sessions when the talk centers on important ideas in the text (for example, mother asks "Why do you think Juan did that?"). In writing, focusing on the message helps children understand that they are communicating with others (for example, an adult is helping young child write a Father's Day card and asks, "What are some special things you would like to thank your father for? You can tell him in this note you are writing (drawing)").

Early literacy development depends upon a wide range of variables including the acquisition of the skills involved in phonemic awareness, alphabetic understanding, phonics, and comprehension. While there is no one-size-fits-all approach to literacy instruction, a robust research base suggests that these are the skills that children must learn in order to be successful readers and writers.

Instructional Implications for Early Literacy Development

Effective instruction in the early years is critical to the development of reading and writing, particularly for those children who at risk of failure. Below are some commonly agreed upon characteristics of effective literacy instruction (Flippo, 2001):

- **A book-rich literate environment.** The environment includes books and a variety of other reading materials, as well as displays of written work including charts, stories, words, and lists.

- **Teacher read-alouds.** The reading of outstanding children's literature is an important component of the curriculum, including the reading of big books, chart poems, picture books, pattern books, and predictable storybooks.

- **Students reading aloud to others.** Students need opportunities to read to the teacher and to peers, including the reading of stories they have written themselves.

- **Shared reading.** There should be many opportunities for students to participate in experiences such as reading along with the teacher, echo and choral reading, shared reading, daily silent reading, and rereading of familiar books.

- **Phonological awareness instruction,** including phonemic awareness and knowledge of the alphabet. This instruction includes knowing that words are made up of individual sounds and patterns and knowing how to work with or manipulate the sounds in words.

- **Phonics instruction.** Phonics instruction includes the teaching children letter-sound relationships and how to apply these skills when reading and writing.

- **Reading comprehension strategy instruction.** The teaching of strategies for constructing meaning and analyzing text supports the independent development of reading comprehension skills. These strategies include using background knowledge, understanding main ideas and supporting details, text structure awareness, drawing inferences, predicting outcomes, vocabulary development, questioning the author's purpose, clarifying information, and summarization (AACTE, 2002).

- **Writing strategy instruction.** Teacher or parent modeling of making lists, writing notes, cards, directions, and letters are examples of the kinds of early experiences that provide the foundation for success in writing.

- **Variety of reading and writing activities.** Effective teachers resist limiting their instruction to one particular strategy or narrowly defined paradigm and provide a variety of reading and writing experiences for their students (Duffy & Hoffman, 1999).

- **Time for reading and writing.** Providing time for reading and writing at home and at school facilitates the development of literacy skills. Having play corners where writing materials are available (for example, in the grocery store corner, have paper available for making grocery lists; in the doctor's office corner, have pads available for writing prescriptions) will support children in developing writing skills. Providing a special time for reading at home and in school will give children time to explore books with an adult and independently and will help them develop the reading habit.

In summary, research provides some insights about what promotes the development of early stages of literacy. *Research-Based Literacy Instruction*, a paper published by the American Association of Colleges for Teacher Education (AACTE, 2002), presents the following observations:

- Children learn the value and functions of print by observing its use by more sophisticated readers and writers.

- Children must have opportunities to engage actively in a variety of purposeful literacy activities, including occasions to read, write, and talk about text with a more knowledgeable mentor.

- It is generally accepted that by participating in experiences involved in acquiring literacy, children will also acquire a rich infrastructure of knowledge and skill that will enable increasingly more complex and sophisticated literacy performances.

- Teacher expectations are important because we know that children are more likely to achieve literate competence when their teacher expects that they will succeed (p. 6).

Finally, and perhaps most importantly, schools need to provide early intervention for children who experience problems learning to read and write. This additional instructional support is necessary and essential in helping struggling readers and writers "catch up with their peers early, before their difficulties become more intractable" (AACTE, 2002, p. 14). A number of programs such as reading recovery and book buddies have proven effective in accelerating the progress of struggling literacy learners (Invernizzi, Rosemary, Juel, & Richards, 1997; Pinnell, 1989). According to Pikulski (1994), the success of intervention programs for struggling readers and writers depends upon careful coordination so that the intervention program and the regular classroom literacy program complement each other.

References

AACTE (American Association of Colleges for Teacher Education). (2002). *Research-based literacy instruction.* Washington, DC: Author.

Adams, M. J. (1990). *Beginning to read: Thinking and learning about print.* London: MIT Press.

Anderson, R. C., Hiebert, E. H., Scott, J. A., & Wilkinson, I. A. G. (1985). *Becoming a nation of readers.* Champaign, IL: University of Illinois, Center for the Study of Reading.

Ayres, L. R. (1995). The efficacy of three training conditions of phonological awareness of kindergarten children and the longitudinal effect of each on later reading acquisition. *Reading Research Quarterly, 30*(4), 604–606.

Baker, L., Serpell, R., & Sonnenschein, S. (1995). Opportunities for literacy learning in the homes of urban preschoolers. In L. M. Morrow (Ed.), *Literacy connections in families, schools, and communities* (pp. 236–252). Newark, DE: International Reading Association.

Bradley, L., & Bryant, P. E. (1983). Categorizing sounds and learning to read–A causal connection. *Nature, 301,* 419–421.

Chomsky, C. (1972). Stages in language development and reading exposure. *Harvard Educational Review, 42,* 1–33.

Clay, M. M. (1979). *Reading: The patterning of complex behavior,* (2nd ed.). Exeter, NH: Heinemann.

Cullinan, B. E. (1992). *Invitations to read: More children's literature in the reading program.* Newark, DE: International Reading Association.

Duffy, G. G., & Hoffman, J. V. (1999). In pursuit of an illusion: The flawed search for a perfect method. *The Reading Teacher, 53* (1), 10–16.

Flippo, R. (2001). About the expert study: Report and findings. In R. Flippo (Ed.), *Reading researchers in search of common ground* (pp. 5–21). Newark, DE: International Reading Association.

Flood, J. (1977). Parental styles in reading episodes with young children. *The Reading Teacher, 30,* 864–867.

Gambrell, L. B. (1996). Creating classroom cultures that foster reading motivation. Distinguished Educator Series. *The Reading Teacher, 50,* 14–25.

Gambrell, L. B., Almasi, J. F., Xie, Q., & Heland, V. (1995). Helping first-graders get a running start in reading. In L. Morrow (Ed.)., *Family literacy: Connections in schools and communities* (pp. 143–154). Newark, DE: International Reading Association.

Guthrie, J. T. (1996). Educational contexts for engagement in literacy. *The Reading Teacher, 49* (6), 432–443.

Haager, D., & Windmueller, M.P. (2001). Early reading intervention for English language learners at-risk for learning disabilitites: Student and teacher outcomes in an urban school. *Learning Disability Quarterly, 24,* 235–251.

Harste, J. C. (1989). The basalization of American reading instruction: One researcher responds. *Theory into Practice, 28,* 265–273.

Harste, J. C., Burke, C. L., & Woodward, V. A. (1982). Children's language and world: Initial encounters with print. In J. A. Langer & M. T. Smith-Burke (Eds.), *Reader meets author/bridging the gap* (pp. 105–131). Newark, DE: International Reading Association.

Heath, S. B. (1983). *Ways with words: Language, life, and work in communities and class-rooms.* Cambridge, UK: Cambridge University Press.

Huck, C. S. (1992). Books for emergent readers. In C. E. Cullinan (Ed.), *Invitations to read: More children's literature in the reading program* (pp. 2–13). Newark, DE: International Reading Association.

Invernizzi, M., Rosemary, C., Juel, C., & Richards, H. (1997). At-risk readers and community volunteers: A 3-year perspective. *Scientific Studies of Reading, 1,* 277–300.

Mann, V. A. (1993). Phoneme awareness and future reading ability. *Journal of Learning Disabilities, 26*(4), 259–269.

Mason, J. (1984). A schema-theoretic view of the reading process as a basis for comprehension instruction. In G. G. Duffy, L. R. Roehler, & J. Mason (Eds.), *Comprehension instruction: Perspectives and suggestions* (pp. 26–38). New York: Longman.

Morrow, L. M., & O'Connor, E. (1995). Literacy partnerships for change with "at-risk" kindergartners. In R. Allington & B. Walmsley (Eds.), *No quick fix: Rethinking literacy programs in America's elementary schools* (pp. 97–115). New York: Guilford.

Morrow, L. M., & Weinstein, C. S. (1982). Increasing children's use of literature through programs and physical design changes. *Elementary School Journal, 83,* 131–137.

National Reading Panel. (2000). *Report of the National Reading Panel: Teaching children to read.* Rockville, MD: NICHD Clearinghouse. `

Neuman, S. B., & Roskos, K. (1997). Literacy knowledge in practice: Contexts of participation for young writers and readers. *Reading Research Quarterly, 32*(1), 10–32.

Ohnmacht, D. C. (1969, April). *The effects of letter knowledge on achievement in reading in the first grade.* Paper presented at the annual meeting of the American Educational Research Association, Los Angeles. Reviewed in Ehri, L. (1983). Summary of Dorothy C. Ohnmacht's study: The effects of letter knowledge on achievement in reading in the first grade. In L. M. Gentile, M. L. Kamil, & J. S. Blanchard (Eds.), *Reading research revisited* (pp. 141–142). Columbus, OH: Merrill.

Pikulski, J. (1994). Preventing reading failure: A review of five effective programs. *The Reading Teacher, 48,* 30–39.

Pinnell, G. (1989). Reading Recovery: Helping at-risk children learn to read. *Elementary School Journal, 90,* 161–183.

Purcell-Gates, V. (1988). Lexical and syntactic knowledge of written narrative held by well-read-to kindergartners and second graders. *Research in the Teaching of English, 22,* 128–160.

Purcell-Gates, V. (1994). Nonliterate homes and emergent literacy. In D. F. Lancy (Ed.), *Children's emergent literacy: From research to practice* (pp. 41–51). Westport, CT: Praeger.

Purcell-Gates, V. (1996). Stories, coupons, and the TV Guide: Relationships between home literacy experiences and emergent literacy knowledge. *Reading Research Quarterly, 31*(4), 406–428.

Richgels, D. J., Poremba, K. J., & McGee, L. M. (1998). Kindergarteners talk about print: Phonemic awareness in meaningful contexts. In C. Weaver (Ed.), *Practicing what we know: Informed reading instruction* (pp. 50–68). Urbana, IL: National Council of Teachers in English.

Roberts, B. (1998). "I No EvrethENGe": What skills are essential in early literacy. In S. B. Neuman & K. A. Roskos (Eds.), *Children achieving: Best practices in early literacy* (pp. 38–55). Newark, DE: International Reading Association.

Smith, F. (1988). *Joining the literacy club: Further essays into education.* Portsmouth, NH: Heinemann.

Snow, C. E., Burns, S., & Griffin, P. (Eds.). (1998). Preventing reading difficulties in young children. Washington, DC: National Academy Press.

Snowling, M. (1991). Words, nonwords, phonological processes: Some comments on Gathercole, Willis, Emslie, and Baddeley. *Applied Linguistics, 12*(3), 369–373.

Stanovich, K. E. (1986). Matthew effects in reading: Some consequences of individual differences in the acquisition of literacy. *Reading Research Quarterly, 21,* 360–406.

Swap, S. (1993). *Developing home-school partnerships.* New York: Teachers College Press.

Teale, W. (1984). Reading to young children: Its significance for literacy development. In H. Goelman, A. Osberg, & F. Smith (Eds.), *Awakening to literacy* (pp. 110–121). Exeter, NH: Heinemann Educational Books.

Teale, W., & Sulzby, E. (1987). Literacy acquisition in early childhood. In D. Wagner (Ed.), The *future of literacy in a changing world* (Vol. I, pp. 120–129). New York: Pergamon.

Teale, W., & Sulzby, E. (1988). *Emergent literacy: Writing and reading.* Norwood, NJ: Ablex.

Vygotsky, L. S. (1978). *Mind in society. The development of higher psychological processes.* Cambridge, MA: Harvard University Press.

Wells, G. (1986). *The meaning makers: Children learning language and using language to learn.* Portsmouth, NH: Heinemann.

Whitehurst, G. J., & Lonigan, C. J. (1998). Child development and emergent literacy. *Child Development, 69,* 848–873.

Basic
Core Strategies

10

Mentoring:
An Effective Strategy for
Youth Development

Jay Smink

Ask a student, "Why did you drop out of school?" The typical reply is, "No one cared if I stayed or left!" Students who lack strong personal support from a parent, a friend, a teacher—anyone who cares—are at risk of dropping out of school and possibly the community as well. In years past, two-parent families, nearby grandparents and other relatives, and close-knit neighborhoods offered more of the support and guidance that young people need. Mentoring is not a substitute for parental guidance; however, mentoring has resurfaced as an effective strategy for working with youth who need role models and a positive support system in today's world as well.

Mentoring has a long and proven history. The early Greeks practiced mentoring; today, it is as common in business and politics as it is in schools. A mentor is simply a wise and trusted friend with a commitment to provide guidance and support. Though many mentoring relationships involve tutoring in academic subjects, this is certainly not always the case. Traditionally, mentoring has taken the form of a one-to-one relationship, but a mentor may also work with a group. The Internet has even opened opportunities for telementoring.

Many groups promote mentoring as an effective strategy for youth development, and many different political and social constellations support the practice. For example, state legislators and governors in California, Connecticut, Texas, Massachusetts, and elsewhere have initiated statewide mentoring programs; Tom Osborne, who founded the TeamMates Mentoring program as a coach, still endorses and promotes the value of mentoring youth in his role as Nebraska's senator. Major organizations such as Big Brothers Big Sisters, 100 Black Men, and Communities In Schools, as well as national initiatives such as America's Promise, have spurred the widespread development of mentoring programs in our schools and communities.

Mentoring Is Effective with Troubled Youth

A host of research studies credit mentoring with changing the lives of children in general and troubled youth in particular. According to a recent *Child Trends Research Brief* (Jekielek, Moore, Hair, & Scarupa, 2002), mentoring is so popular and so effective that it should be considered a major strategy for youth development. Mentored youth are likely to have fewer absences from school, better attitudes towards school, fewer incidents of hitting others, less drug and alcohol use, better attitudes towards elders, and improved relationships with their parents. Furthermore, mentoring has proved its worth in a variety of countries, societies, cultures, age brackets, diversity groups, and program formats. This successful youth development strategy, applied with well-designed program structures and careful management, will work extremely well for high-risk youth.

Why Adolescents Need Mentors

Young people growing up today, especially adolescents, have to cope with many more personal and social pressures than any previous generation. The issues they face can cause lifelong problems or trigger immediate life-threatening situations. According to *The Commonwealth Fund 1998 Survey of Adults Mentoring Young People*, eight of ten young people in mentoring relationships have one or more problems that put their health, development, or success in school at risk. The five most prevalent problems reported in the survey were the young people's negative feelings about themselves, poor relationships with family members, poor grades, associating with the wrong crowd, and getting into trouble at school (McLearn, Colasanto, & Schoen, 1998).

Early intervention through a structured mentor program may be able to give young people the personal skills, practical tools, and support they need to be successful. A report from the State of California Resource Center, *Results From Mentoring Effectiveness Research* (1999), finds that mentoring has been effective in addressing the complex problems that face our youth today in such areas as drug use, academic failure, teenage pregnancy, and gang violence.

According to many parents and school counselors, today's youth face so many new and different social, psychological, and physical demands that what was once known as "normal adolescent development" may no longer exist. Any individual about to undertake the task of being a mentor must understand these problems and issues. The following brief discussion is adapted from the One to One Partnership Guidebook (1996).

Peer Pressure

One of the greatest forces acting on adolescents is the power and influence of their peers. This outside influence on personal attitudes and behaviors can be either positive or negative. Mentors should recognize the power of peer pressure. Although they cannot force their own beliefs on their young mentees, they should be able to help them learn decision-making skills and practice making good choices based on their own convictions.

Substance Abuse

The temptation to experiment with alcohol, tobacco, and drugs is a constant threat to each adolescent in today's world. Mentors should set an excellent example by avoiding the use of alcohol and tobacco in the presence of mentees, encourage discussions about the issues of substance abuse, and be very observant of mentee behaviors. If there is evidence that the mentee may have a problem in this regard, the mentor should seek professional intervention by a psychiatrist, social worker, or school counselor.

Sexuality and Teenage Parenting

Young people may turn to sexual relationships for a variety of reasons. This is a sensitive issue, and mentors must take great care in any discussions related to sexuality. Professional assistance is often helpful to the mentor.

Child Abuse and Family Violence

Physical or mental abuse, within the family or in any environment, will have an immediate effect on the mentee and also create long-lasting, negative attitudes and behaviors. Most states require that a school official report suspected abuse to the proper authorities. A mentor will need to seek professional help if observations indicate that this type of abuse may be occurring.

School Safety and Violence

Many young people are exposed to bullies or to other violent behavior in the school setting. This may lead to attendance problems or diminished academic achievement. An observant mentor should discuss this with the mentee and inform the school officials about the situation, being careful not to involve the mentee in the reporting process.

Depression and Suicide

When young people are overwhelmed by issues and situations they cannot resolve, serious depression may develop. Mentors should be sensitive to this possibility. Any indications of extreme depression or suicide must be referred to the professionals involved in the program.

Nutrition and Health Care

Many young people feel they are immortal and tend to ignore good health practices. In addition to modeling a healthy lifestyle, mentors can discuss these issues, initiate visits to health-related institutions, or engage in special activities that promote good health.

Faith and Religion

This issue is usually within the domain of the family, and mentors should be sensitive to family values and practices. However, this may be an area of great concern for the mentee, or the pair may share an interest that could foster positive discussions.

Social Activities and Time Management

Young people today often need to juggle schoolwork, extracurricular activities, family chores, leisure activities, and other social demands. Mentors should be able to assist them with helpful discussions about time-management techniques and related decision-making skills.

Career Exploration and Part-Time Work

Because most mentors are in the workforce, career exploration is usually a natural and easy issue to address. Discussions about employment opportunities and specific job skill requirements, as well as visits to work sites, are quite common in mentoring relationships. Talking about these school-to-work issues may be a good starting point that leads naturally into related mentor-mentee activities.

Goals and Expected Outcomes of Mentoring

Mentoring programs across the country have many different goals and objectives; however, most programs seek changes and benefits in the general areas of academic achievement, employment or career preparation, social or behavior modification, family and parenting skills, and social responsibilities. The specific benefits often expected include

- improved academic achievement scores,
- increase in extracurricular activities,
- increase in graduation rates,
- increase in school attendance,
- decrease in grade retention rates,
- decrease in discipline referrals,
- decrease in early pregnancy rates,
- increased self-esteem,
- increase in securing entry-level jobs, and
- increase in community service activities.

Mentoring can be very beneficial to low-performing students and students in at-risk situations. The *Mentoring Program Manual*, published by United Way of America, as part of the One to One Partnership guide (1996) lists four major tasks for which mentors are particularly valuable:

1. establishing a positive personal relationship
2. developing life skills
3. assisting in case management of families
4. increasing abilities of youth to interact with other social and cultural groups

School districts, organizations, businesses, or communities sponsoring mentor programs will vary greatly in their stated objectives and expected benefits. To cite a typical example, one successful 14-year program, the Kalamazoo Area Academic Achievement Program, aims to

- provide the youth with a positive role model,
- enhance the youth's self-esteem,
- instill a sense of responsibility by allowing youth to make decisions,
- develop a sense of accepting the need to improve academic performance,
- participate in recreational activities and other social settings,
- reinforce the efforts of the school and teachers,
- create an understanding for improved social and school behaviors
  (Kalamazoo Area Academic Achievement Program, no date)

The Impact of Mentoring

Regardless of the format, structure, or institutional host of the program, mentoring is both a youth development strategy and a community development program. Mentoring can change the direction of troubled youth, providing positive alternatives and opening doors to success in life. In addition, mentoring alters community structures, shifts institutional boundaries, and widens the mentee's horizon. Whether in a single school or across a state, this powerful human force can change the vision, the health, or the economic base of the community.

Mentors have the power and influence to change the negative cycles of their mentees and their families. A well-structured mentor program serves as a powerful low-cost, low-tech strategy to help rebuild the dreams of youth in at-risk situations. Mentoring is clearly an effective strategy for keeping students in school. Programs across the nation have an abundance of solid evidence supporting this fact. The most comprehensive national research evidence, from a thorough review of Big Brother Big Sister programs (Tierney & Grossman, 1995), shows these results:

- ◆ 46 percent decrease in initiating drug use,
- ◆ 27 percent decrease in initiating alcohol use,
- ◆ 38 percent decrease in number of times hitting someone,
- ◆ 37 percent decrease in skipped classes, and
- ◆ 37 percent decrease in lying to parents.

Another nationwide study, the Commonwealth Fund's survey of mentoring programs (McLearn, Colasanto, & Schoen, 1998) reported similar positive results:

- ◆ 62 percent of students improved their self-esteem,
- ◆ 52 percent of students skipped less school,
- ◆ 48 percent of students improved their grades,
- ◆ 49 percent of students got into less trouble in school,
- ◆ 47 percent of students got into less trouble out of school,
- ◆ 45 percent of students reduced their substance abuse, and
- ◆ 35 percent of students improved family relationships.

Nearly all mentoring programs collect data representing the number of relationships in place and contact hours completed by the mentor and mentee. One example of a local program reporting major accomplishments comes from California's San Luis Obispo County. During the 1998–99 school year, AmeriCorps members there provided over 52,000 hours of mentoring activities to 307 local teenagers (AmeriCorps, 2000). From these interventions, they reported the following results:

- 80 percent did not re-offend, as compared to 35–65 percent for similar offenders without mentors,
- 89 percent improved or maintained a good attitude toward life with the help of their mentor,
- 73 percent of juvenile offenders using alcohol or other drugs quit or decreased their use,
- 71 percent of substance-abusing youth stopped or decreased their use,
- 69 percent have shown improvements in school,
- 96 percent began participating in positive alternatives to drug use,
- 41 percent of teens who used tobacco decreased or stopped their use,
- 64 percent of mentored teens made improvements in school, including a 44 percent decrease in number of times tardy and a 56 percent increase in the amount of time spent doing homework,
- 38 percent of youth decreased sexual activity and 58 percent increased their use of birth control,
- 85 percent of youth sought employment; of those, 56 percent obtained employment,
- 58 percent of youth volunteered beyond mandated service requirements,
- 71 percent of youth state that their AmeriCorps mentor helped change the direction of their life, and
- 62 percent of youth claim they would be in a worse place today without their mentor.

The U.S. Department of Justice Office of Juvenile Justice and Delinquency Prevention, through its Juvenile Mentoring Program (JUMP), supports one-to-one mentoring projects that target youth at risk of becoming delinquent, being involved in gangs, failing in school, and dropping out of school. In one of these, Project SOAR, university and community college students work with students at risk of academic failure and with their families to promote personal and academic success. Project SOAR targets ethnically diverse families, with a primary focus on Hispanic, African-American, and Native American students. The impact is dramatic; 66 percent of the students improved their reading and math grades; 80 percent improved their study skills; discipline referrals decreased by 77 percent; and parents reported positive behavior changes with school work, less violence, and less gang participation (Waits, 2003). And in a meta-analysis of 55 evaluations of the effects of mentoring programs, DuBois, Holloway, Valentine, and Cooper (2002) found that youth from backgrounds of environmental risk and disadvantage appear most likely to benefit from participation in mentoring programs.

A vast majority of the respondents to an evaluation of YouthFriends, a school-based mentoring program in Kansas City, Missouri, believed YouthFriends is of great value not only to the students, but also to the volunteers, schools, and community. The parents gave a favorable 93 percent overall rating to the program; 81 percent indicated YouthFriends had a positive effect on their child's attitude, and 80 percent saw a positive effect on their behavior (YouthFriends 2000 Evaluation, 2001).

Key Components of a Mentoring Program

Many schools and communities across the country are initiating mentoring programs as school dropout prevention measures. The approaches vary greatly. Successful programs are based in schools, community organizations, businesses, and other institutions such as colleges and universities. Regardless of the setting, the sponsors, or the targeted youth groups, planners seeking the greatest impact on the mentees in their programs should be aware that some basic program components are critical.

In 1991, the National Mentoring Partnership developed a checklist, *Elements of Effective Practice*, to guide program planners. The first of its kind, this nuts-and-bolts checklist identified ten major components of successful mentor programs and served as the "gold standard" for more than a decade. A revised checklist, *Elements of Effective Practice*, published by the MENTOR/National Mentoring Partnership (2003), includes 35 items in four major program categories: design and planning, management, operations, and evaluation. (The detailed checklist is available at www.mentoring.org.) Reflecting the latest in mentoring policies, practices, experiences, and research, the revised *Elements* aims to serve program planners and managers in program types or formats that include traditional mentoring (one adult to one young person), group mentoring (one adult to up to four youth), team mentoring (several adults working with small groups of youth), peer mentoring (caring youth mentoring other youth), and e-mentoring (mentoring via e-mails and the Internet).

Research conducted by Public/Private Ventures (Herrera, Sipe, & McClanahan, 2000) confirmed several of these elements and provides additional guidance for program design. This research, which surveyed 722 mentoring programs nationwide, found a rapidly growing and changing field, both in traditional community-based programs and in the newer school-based programs. Despite the programs' operational and programmatic differences, the researchers identified eight factors as extremely important in the design, operations, and final impact of the program:

- engaging in social activities,
- engaging in academic activities,
- number of hours per month youth and mentors meet,
- decision making about the use of time,
- pre-match orientation and training,
- post-match training and support,
- mentor youth similarity of interests, and
- age of the mentee.

In addition, a recent meta-analysis of 55 evaluations of one-to-one youth mentoring programs (Dubois, Holloway, Valentine, & Cooper, 2002) delineated empirically based "best practices" in mentoring programs:

- monitoring of program implementation,
- access to community setting for mentoring activities,
- mentors whose background includes a helping role or profession,
- expectations for frequency of contact,
- ongoing training,
- structured activities for the mentors and youth, and
- parental support and involvement.

Need for Structured Forms of Mentoring

Mentoring occurs in many different settings and formats. However, most mentoring relationships can benefit from a structured program of support. Structured programs enable mentors to offer mentees a variety of helpful experiences designed to improve their attitudes, behaviors, and competencies.

A structured mentoring program is generally recognized as having

- a formal relationship between the mentor and mentee,
- an established pattern for contacts,
- recommended parameters for the meetings or activities,
- a commitment to a time frame (usually twelve months, or not less than a school year),
- an ongoing structured training program,
- monitoring and support by experienced professionals, and

◆ a consistent assessment and evaluation effort.

Although structured mentoring programs come in all shapes and sizes, including the groundbreaking Hewlett-Packard telementoring program (Field, 1999), some are generally regarded as more practical and more effective than others. The most common mentoring models or formats are characterized as follows:

Traditional mentoring generally matches one adult with one youth. They meet regularly, usually about once a week or twice a month, typically for one year (or at least the school year). Programs may be school-based, community-based, or site-based, depending on the sponsor. For example, YouthFriends is school-based, Big Brothers Big Sisters of America programs are mostly community-based, and Boys and Girls Clubs are usually site-based.

Group mentoring consists of one or several adults working with a group of youth, usually not larger than four. Contacts are usually weekly or twice a month, with a minimum commitment of one year. Campus Pals and AmeriCorps Chapters are examples of group mentoring.

Peer mentoring typically matches one older youth with a younger youth, monitored under adult leadership. Regular contacts include activities focused in special areas such as tutoring. The Coca Cola Valued Youth Program offers peer mentoring.

Team mentoring usually involves one or more adults working with several young people of mixed age. Contacts are on a regular basis for a fixed time period, usually not less than a year. Foster parents programs are examples of this format.

Intergenerational mentoring places senior volunteers in regular contact with youth, usually in focused areas such as tutoring, homework centers, or community-based projects. Retired Senior Volunteer Program/RSVP or Foster Grandparents programs are excellent models of this form.

Telementoring links one or several adults with one or more youth using the Internet as the basic communication tool. Some local programs are standard in their approach; however, several national programs focus on special areas such as math, science, or computer-related interests. Relationships may be for a special project assignment but typically last for a year or more. The Hewlett-Packard Telementor Program and the National Mentoring Partnership "Digital Heroes" are among the best programs using this model.

Other formats include variations of these models or reflect the specific goals or objectives of the project or the sponsors. These include faith-based programs, work-based programs, or "commitment-based" organizations such as the "I Have a Dream" Foundation.

Key Elements
of a Structured Mentor Program

The National Mentoring Center (NMC), created in 1998 with support from the Office of Juvenile Justice and Delinquency Prevention (OJJDP), U.S. Department of Justice, provides support to OJJDP-funded JUMP mentoring projects nationwide. The NMC recent report, *Foundations of Successful Youth Mentoring: A Guidebook for Program Development* (Garringer, Fulop, & Rennick, 2003), identifies 31 essential program elements across five broad categories of program design:

- ◆ strong agency capacity for service delivery,
- ◆ effective program practices,
- ◆ strong formal partnerships and informal collaborations,
- ◆ sustainable resource development and funding,
- ◆ useful program evaluation.

Among the many components of a structured mentoring program, the elements most critical to success are a clear statement of program purpose and goals, a recruitment and selection plan for mentors, a support and training program for mentors, and a monitoring and evaluation process for the program (Crockett & Smink, 1991). Of these tasks, most program planners find designing an effective training program and developing a comprehensive evaluation process to be the most daunting. Recognizing this, the National Dropout Prevention Center/Network at Clemson University developed and published *A Training Guide for Mentors* (Smink, 1999) to assist program planners.

Recruiting mentors is an ongoing challenge, especially for new programs and those without a national organization to lend assistance and credibility. One of the best resources to guide program managers with practical suggestions, worksheets, and forms is available from The National Mentoring Center (Jucovy, 2001). It includes ideas for developing a recruitment plan and special considerations for recruiting college students and older adults.

The Mass Mentoring Partnership offers additional hints on recruiting male mentors (Connelly, 2000):

- ◆ Recruit through companies that encourage volunteerism, especially in professions employing a high percentage of men.
- ◆ Consider programmatic changes that appeal to men.
- ◆ Emphasize that family and friends can be involved.
- ◆ Remember that word-of-mouth recruiting often works better than advertisements.

- Encourage female volunteers to recruit their male friends.
- Recruit through local colleges, especially their fraternities.

Regardless of the specific program objectives, the source of mentors, or the unique target groups being served, the key to effective mentoring relationships lies in the development of trust. Recent research confirms that building that trusting relationship requires time and a significant amount of effort on the part of both mentor and mentee. In addition, Sipe (1996) reports that effective mentors are more likely to engage in certain practices:

- Involve youth in deciding how the pair will spend their time together.
- Commit to being consistent and dependable and serve as a steady presence to the mentee.
- Take responsibility for keeping the relationship alive.
- Pay attention to the mentee's need for fun as a valuable part of the relationship.
- Respect the mentee's viewpoint.
- Seek assistance and advice from program staff when needed.

Limits of and Concerns about Mentoring Programs

For all the positive aspects of mentoring programs, they have some limitations. Program coordinators who recognize these can be watchful in their program planning and their mentor training programs.

Time

Goodlad (1995) notes several reasons for program failures, but by far the overwhelming deterrent is the very basic issue of time. Individuals who volunteer to be mentors naturally have other personal, family, and job-related commitments. As a result, their time is short, and often the quality of the available time is less than what it should be for each mentor-mentee activity.

Social Distance

A social distance between the mentor and mentee—differences in their socioeconomic status, culture, generation, language, or ethnic background—can present a challenge. If the mentor lacks the interest or persistence needed to bridge the gap, the relationship may falter. A more socially comfortable mentor-mentee relationship takes less effort and may get more frequent attention than the difficult relationship.

Isolation

Another problem often mentioned in mentor interviews is a feeling of isolation. Unless mentors are involved in a structured program with a strong initial and ongoing training and support program, they tend to feel alone and lack the encouragement they need. Although time remains an issue, mentors do value training and support and are willing to participate in these efforts to the extent that time is available.

Termination

When program coordinators are aware of any of the above challenges or other problems with the relationship, they must take immediate action either to provide the needed support or to end the mentoring relationship. Not all mentor-mentee relationships are successful. Procedures must be in place to halt a relationship that is not effective or creates a disruptive atmosphere in the overall program. Most program plans do have provisions for these situations. These plans should be written and be part of the local training program and guidebook for mentors.

Lack of Mentors

Recruitment of qualified mentors is a constant concern; a related issue is the everlasting problem of keeping mentors fully involved. The national experience of volunteerism suggests that most volunteers terminate their engagements on an average of every three years. Therefore, mentoring programs often have long waiting lists. For example, Big Brothers Big Sisters estimated that 45,000 youth nationwide were in a wait status in 1998; the average wait time was 18 months (Herrera, 1999).

Youth with Disabilities

According to Sword and Hill (2002), "Despite the increasing prevalence and importance of mentoring for youth in general, few of these programs, to date, intentionally include youth with disabilities." Though mentoring programs for youth with disabilities are few, those that prevail are generally successful. Program managers who address youth with disabilities must make some accommodations; most of these are outlined in the students' IEPs. Because disabilities vary widely, program managers should seek professional assistance when designing these programs.

Telementoring

The rapid growth and flexibility of the Internet has made telementoring an important vehicle for exposing youth to a wider range of mentors and experiences. However, telecommunication is not necessarily the best way to provide more mentors or wider experiences. Telementoring programs are certainly growing, aided by national organizations and by innovative programs created in local school districts. Although some telementoring takes place strictly via the Internet, many programs use the Internet to supplement traditional one-on-one mentoring.

Telementoring is no longer new, but it is still undergoing development. Questions still arise about equipment costs and availability, and the issue of protecting personal and private communications is still widely discussed. Viable programs require thorough planning.

The E-Mentoring Clearinghouse (at www.mentoring.org) is the best source for planning e-mentoring programs. The E-Mentoring Tool Kit, developed by MENTOR/National Mentoring Partnership in collaboration with AOL Time Warner Foundation, provides all the program features and procedures for developing a new program.

Program Evaluation: A Real Concern

The program component that usually receives the least attention from program planners is the evaluation process. Measuring the progress of the program and its impact on students is critical for many different reasons, including the need to demonstrate evidence of results for the program's sponsors. If local expertise is not available to design an evaluation model, program leaders should solicit technical assistance from local universities or from an organization such as the National Dropout Prevention Center/Network or the National Mentoring Center. One prudent planning tip is to promote opportunities for providing success stories to the local media, policy makers, or sponsors who provide resources or make decisions about whether to continue the program.

Perhaps the most crucial aspects of the evaluation process are planning its design and selecting the indicators of success. The evaluation design should include mentor observations and opinions. In particular, an excellent program evaluation would seek evidence about the mentors and mentees in many different categories, such as

Change Categories		*Indicators of Change*
A	Attitudes	More interest in school, involvement in after-school activities, feels better about home life, etc.
B	Behaviors	Fewer discipline referrals, less absenteeism, etc.
C	Competencies	Improved test scores, new job-related skills, etc.
D	Developmental	Improvement in areas of mental and physical health, economics, drug use, etc.
E	Everything Else	Family participation, civic responsibility, parent involvement, recidivism rates, social interactions, team participation, etc.

Model Programs and Unique Ideas for Mentoring Programs

Alhough mentoring has many advantages, it should not be regarded as an independent intervention or offered as the only effective strategy for working with students in at-risk situations. Mentors are not miracle workers, and mentoring cannot provide an immediate cure for the problems young people face. Mentoring programs should work in conjunction with other programs, ideas, and strategies for helping youth at any stage of their development, and especially those youth at risk of academic failure.

Despite these limitations, the number of successful mentoring programs in the United States is vast. Local program planners can learn much from the programs already in place. The National Dropout Prevention Center/Network "model program" database (at www.dropoutprevention.org) presents many successful programs and several unique ideas that offer excellent models for consideration by local program planners. The database (brief program descriptions and contact information) is searchable using keywords.

References

AmeriCorps 1998–99 Annual Report. (2000). San Luis Obispo County, CA.

Connelly, C. (2000, Fall). Recruiting men as mentors. *The Connector.* Boston, MA: The Mass Mentoring Partnership.

Crockett, L., & Smink, J. (1991). *The mentoring guidebook: A practical manual for designing and managing a mentoring program.* Clemson, SC: National Dropout Prevention Center.

Dubois, D. L., Holloway, B. E., Valentine, J. C., & Cooper, H. (2002, April). Effectiveness of mentoring programs for youth: A meta-analytic review. *American Journal of Community Psychology, 39*(2), 157–161.

Field, A. (1999, January). Tech-mentor. In *How to be a great mentor,* (a guide produced by Kaplan/Newsweek/The National Mentoring Partnership). Washington, DC: Kaplan/Newsweek.

Garringer, M., Fulop, M., & Rennick, V. (2003). *Foundations of successful youth mentoring: A guidebook for program development.* Portland, OR: National Mentoring Center.

Goodlad, S. (Ed.). (1995). *Students as tutors and mentors.* London: Kogan Page.

Herrera, C. (1999). *A first look into its potential.* Philadelphia, PA: Public/Private Ventures.

Herrera, C., Sipe, C. L., & McClanahan, W. S. (2000, April). *Mentoring school-age children: Relationship development in community-based and school-based programs.* Philadelphia, PA: Public/Private Ventures.

Jekielek, S. M., Moore, K. A., Hair, E. D., & Scarupa, H. J. (2002, February). Mentoring: A promising strategy for youth development. *Child Trends Research Brief.* Washington, DC: Child Trends.

Jucovy, L. (2001). *Recruiting mentors: A guide to finding volunteers to work with youth.* Portland, OR: National Mentoring Center.

Kalamazoo Area Academic Achievement Program (KAAAP). (n.d.). *Mentoring handbook.* Kalamazoo, MI: Author.

McLearn, K., Colasanto, D., & Schoen, C. (1998, June). *Mentoring makes a difference.* Findings from The Commonwealth Fund 1998 Survey of Adults Mentoring Young People.

MENTOR/National Mentoring Partnership. (2003). *Elements of effective practice* (2nd ed.) Alexandria, VA: Author.

Mentoring: Elements of effective practice. (1991). One to One/The National Mentoring Partnership. Washington, DC.

One to One Partnership, Inc. (1996). *One to one start-up: A guide.* Washington, DC: Author.

Sipe, C. L. (1996). *Mentoring: A synthesis of Public/Private Venture's research: 1988–1995.* Philadelphia, PA: Public/Private Ventures.

Smink, J. (1999). *A training guide for mentors.* Clemson, SC: National Dropout Prevention Center.

State of California Resource Center. (1999). *Results from mentoring effectiveness research* (Publication No. (ADP) 99-1563). Sacramento, CA: Author.

Sword, C., & Hill, K. (2002, December). Creating mentoring opportunities for youth with disabilities: Issues and suggested strategies. *NCSET Issue Brief (1)4.*

Tierney, J. P. & Grossman, J. B. (with Resch, N. L.). (1995). *Making a difference: An impact study of Big Brothers/Big Sisters* (Executive Summary). Philadelphia, PA: Public/Private Ventures.

Waits, J. (2003, March). *Project SOAR: Mentoring at-risk youth and families.* Retrieved from The University of Arizona, College of Agriculture and Life Sciences web site: http://ag.Arizona.edu/impacts/.

YouthFriends 2000 evaluation shows positive results. (2001, Winter). *YouthFriends Compass, 5*(1).

11

Service-Learning: Engaging Students in Community-Based Learning

Robert Shumer and Marty Duckenfield

Dropping out of high school has been a perennial phenomenon in America for the past century. For many years, dropping out meant dropping into a decent job, but for the past several decades, dropping out has meant reduced lifetime wages (Doland, 2001), increased involvement in crime (Harlow, 2003), and generally lives of greater uncertainty (National Center for Educational Statistics, 2002).

Students drop out for many reasons; perhaps the most common are loss of connection to the school and loss of meaning in the educational process (U.S. Department of Education, 1990). According to a National Study of School Evaluation (1997), nearly two-thirds of students surveyed were "either neutral to the idea or did not look forward to school each day." Another 50 percent were either neutral to or disagreed with the statement "Students feel they fit in at our school." If our schools aren't places where students want to be and feel they belong, how can we expect them to stay there?

To put it bluntly, schooling in America—especially secondary education—tends to be passive, boring, and isolated. Any strategy that aims to engage students and keep them in school must address these three conditions. One effective strategy—service-learning—addresses all three at once.

Service-learning has been defined in many ways, but in essence, good service-learning programs involve students doing meaningful service—usually a project they select based on real community needs—that is linked to academic and personal learning.

- Service-learning is reciprocal; those who serve and those served learn from each other.
- Service-learning is active; students learn by doing and by reflecting on what they do.
- Reflection is a key component; students think about, write about, and discuss applications of theories in real-world contexts.
- Service-learning is interesting and exciting; students select their own initiatives and help design, implement, and evaluate their projects.
- Service-learning is connected to community; students engage in activities with community members or support community efforts through community-based learning projects.

Effectiveness of Service-Learning

Does service-learning work? The evidence to date is more than promising. When done well, implementing principles of good practice (National Service-Learning Cooperative, 1998; Shumer, 2000), service-learning enables students to engage positively in their surroundings, to effect change, and to improve conditions of social justice and fairness. Studies of the effects of service-learning on grades, attendance, and dropout reduction indicate the value of this strategy for students who have significant risk factors (Shumer, 1994; Follman, 1998; O'Bannon, 1999). Service-learning has the potential to reduce alienation (Yates & Youniss, 1996; Celebrese & Schumer, 1986), reduce risky behavior (Follman, 1998; Scales, Blyth, Berkas, & Kielsmeier, 2000), and provide students with positive attitudes toward school, community, and self.

Furthermore, service-learning is one of the most effective strategies for reducing teen pregnancy (Kirby, 2001; Melchior, 1999). Of 250 prevention programs evaluated, "service-learning programs have the strongest evidence of any intervention that they reduce actual teen pregnancy rates while the youth are participating in the program." While no one is sure why this is, plausible causes suggested by the authors include the following: Participants develop relationships with program facilitators, gain autonomy and competence, feel empowered by making a difference in the lives of others, and do their service during hours when they might engage in risky behaviors (Kirby, 2001).

Service-learning also helps students become active, positive contributors to society (Melchior, 1999; Billig & Conrad, 1997; Scales & Blyth, 1997). They vote more often than peers 15 years after participation in programs (Yates, McClellan, & Youniss, 1997). They also increase their political attentiveness, political knowledge, and become more politically active (Morgan & Streb, 2001).

Perhaps most importantly, service-learning improves academic learning and school engagement. It yields moderate to strong gains in language arts and reading, homework completion, and engagement in school (Weiler, LaGoy, Crane, & Rovner, 1998; Melchior, 1999; Loesch-Griffin, Petrides, & Pratt, 1995). It is associated with higher test scores on state basic skills tests (Santmire, Giraud, & Grosskopf, 1999) and with higher grades (Shumer 1994; Follman 1998); it also reduces dropping out of school (Supik, 1996; Rolzinski, 1990).

Service-learning influences personal and social development (Conrad & Hedin, 1981) by helping young people become aware of and achieve a higher sense of responsibility (Leming, 1998) and become more socially competent (Scales & Blyth, 1997; O'Bannon, 1999). By its very nature, service-learning simply requires students to have many personal interactions with a variety of people who may be older or younger and of different ethnic and racial groups.

While certainly not a panacea for all that ails schools, service-learning does have all the essential elements to engage students in meaningful learning that has both public and personal benefits. Positive outcomes are associated with good practice. It would be folly to suggest that all service-learning programs achieve all the outcomes all the time. Quality of conception and implementation matter.

What constitutes high-quality practice? Several factors have been identified that, when implemented, lead to excellent programs with positive outcomes. A simple outline, *The Seven Elements of High Quality Service Learning* lists seven key components: integrated learning, high-quality service, collaboration, student voice, civic responsibility, reflection, and evaluation.

A comparison of service-learning with 28 educational reform strategies describes the important elements that are highly compatible or compatible with good service-learning practice (Pearson, 2002):

Highly Compatible

- Teachers use a variety of learning materials other than textbooks.
- Opportunities are provided for students to apply their knowledge and skills to real-life situations and problems.

- Alternative assessments such as portfolios, presentations, and rubrics are used.
- Time is provided for student reflection in journal entries and classroom dialog.

Compatible

- Instructional methods include alternative strategies such as project-based learning and applied learning.
- Schedules (e.g., block schedules) allow flexible use of time.
- Interdisciplinary team teaching and/or experiential learning methods are used.
- The curriculum addresses specific local community needs.
- Students play a role in planning curricular activities.

Additional elements of successful service and experiential learning initiatives involve these dimensions (Shumer, 1997):

- Intensity and duration matter: Short-term projects, with a limited amount of time spent each week, don't have much impact. Initiatives that spend a significant amount of time each week, over the course of a semester and/or year, produce better and more long-lasting outcomes.
- Reflective practice is essential to learning from doing; projects must integrate reflective activities that connect the community-based learning with the academic program.
- The central organizing learning component in community-based service-learning is the task: How tasks are established, accomplished, and processed is important.
- Service-learning is fun. Students from elementary to secondary school define fun in many ways; in all cases, they derive some personal pleasure and satisfaction from the activities and the environment.

Program Examples

Given these elements required for effective practice, what do some successful programs actually look like? There are many examples of service-learning done well. Here, we highlight a few programs designed to address the issues of students who are potential dropouts or at risk of doing poorly in school.

In a project conducted at Dubuque (Iowa) Central High School, students took on the task of converting a nearby vacant lot into a city park. Students are assigned to Central because of low attendance, behavior problems, or special physical needs. What they are able to accomplish as a result of their service-learning projects is transformative; many of the risk factors disappear because the challenges of motivating, engaging, and educating such students make them into happier, more thoughtful, more skilled, and more caring individuals.

In the project, students learned about the history and design of parks. They applied principles of geometry and trigonometry as they plotted and graphed all the relevant angles involved in tree sun lines—knowledge necessary for selecting the plants. They read literature of nature writers and reflected in ongoing journals about their reading, their interactions with the community, and their work planning the park. Students improved their written and speaking skills and interacted more and more with the adult community. They worked with neighbors to help design the park, doing all the data collection and design work necessary to make the park reflective of community values and perspectives. They garnered neighborhood support and then took on the City Park Commission. They successfully presented their design to the Commission and won their support. The result of their service-learning project was not only the production of a new city park, but the successful transformation of a group of alternative school students into a knowledgeable civic force in their community (Cousins & Mednick, 1999).

Leaving Iowa, we find examples of service-learning initiatives in other communities. In Los Angeles, the Valley Alternative School initiated a service/experiential learning program in collaboration with UCLA called Community-Based Learning (Shumer, 1994). In this program, students spent two full days each week working on community projects either individually or in small groups. The community settings ranged from Veterans Administration hospitals to local schools for special needs students. In each case, students developed an individual learning plan based on their community work and their academic courses in the school. College students from UCLA worked with small groups of students to ensure that their academic agendas were being carried out in their community projects.

Results of the program were highly effective. Student attendance increased significantly. Students reported that the community connection kept them in school and helped them to see the value of academic learning applied in community settings. They also said it was the college tutors who helped them to learn the most; individual help is extremely valuable to students who have struggled with school in the past. The personal connections among the students, their college tutors, and community sponsors made the program personally satisfying—and meaningful.

Students' grades increased significantly. Their attitude toward school changed as they saw how learning was useful. The application of knowledge helped to ground their understanding—and made the academic component relevant and challenging.

While these examples came from the high school level, service-learning can be applied equally well in any setting, from elementary through high school. In fact, service-learning is particularly effective for adolescents in middle school; one could say that as a strategy for this age group, it's a perfect match.

Children in the middle grades are at a crossroads—beginning the journey towards adulthood, ready to take one road or another. Their teachers have an incredible opportunity to make a huge difference, for better or for worse. Well-designed service-learning experiences not only enhance the learning of middle-school students, but help to meet their developmental needs.

What are some of these needs? How does service-learning provide the perfect match?

- **The search for meaning.** Children become engaged in their learning as they find meaning in their service activity and see the need for the knowledge that supports it.

- **The need to belong.** Students work as a team with classmates and older adults to solve real community problems.

- **Becoming an adult.** Students are empowered by the responsibilities given them as they design and implement service projects. Adults take them seriously and listen to their ideas for dealing with situations that emerge from real-life experience.

- **Adult role models.** Exposure to positive adult role models, both in the community and in school, gives these children new visions of their own future roles.

- **Self-esteem and self-efficacy.** Their self-esteem and self-efficacy increase as they realize, through reflection, that they are able to make a difference in the lives of others.

- **Abundance of energy.** Students can direct their vast supply of energy towards projects that desperately need this kind of power.

Measuring Effective Strategies

Given these examples, how do we measure effective service-learning programs? The same way we measure any educational program—by the outcome. Outcomes associated with effective service-learning programs usually include:

- **Attendance and behavior.** Demonstrable changes occur as students take ownership of their learning. Maturity rises as responsibility is increased.

- **Academic achievement.** Academic performance—as measured by assessments such as portfolios, standardized tests, competency tests, and specific knowledge tests—is strengthened by the application of academic knowledge to a real-life situation and by the greater engagement of the learner.

- **Civic commitment.** Participants show an increase in the desire and skill necessary to get involved in addressing community issues. Many projects provide students with actual experience in engaging public agencies and government—all in the name of improving the community.

- **Love of learning.** Students show a desire to stay in school and continue learning. Students can see the fruits of their efforts and their increased knowledge.

- **Self-development.** Participants gain the ability to see themselves as fully functioning individuals, believing that people can grow intellectually and personally throughout a lifetime. Students' skills and the outcomes of their efforts provide the evidence for improved feelings about self and their ability to understand their own personal strengths and desires.

- **Interpersonal development.** As students interact effectively with other people in intimate and public environments, they are required to work more in groups and to work with adults in different roles.

- **Moral development.** Students gain the ability to make decisions based on principles and values. With guided reflection on important issues related to the service experience, they begin to develop a moral compass based on their study and their appreciation of the past.

Recommendations for Using the Service-Learning Strategy

Good service-learning practice can be adapted to efforts in any context, for any purpose. Engaging students in age-appropriate activities; including them in the development of the curriculum, the evaluation, and the implementation; doing meaningful work; and arranging tasks so they meet the programmatic goals of the initiative—all engender a high likelihood that objectives and goals will be met.

These principles apply in urban, suburban, and rural settings. All environments have issues or problems waiting to be addressed at multiple levels. When we ask young people to apply knowledge to an issue—when we view them not as the source of problems, but as part of the solution—we unleash a new resource. In fact, service-learning, especially at the high school level, has been shown to have especially important impacts on rural settings (Miller, 1997). It mobilizes resources and engages rural problems in ways few other strategies can address.

Conclusion

Service-learning has the potential to transform the culture of our schools—places which are uninviting, uninteresting, and uninspiring for young people. Instead, we envision schools as communities where students are eager to come each day to participate in engaging and important service-learning activities of their own making. Schools will become places of active learning, connected to people and programs in the community, inviting young people to become excited about the possibilities of helping others while helping themselves at the same time. Such schools will not only help students stay in school, they will hopefully make the stay worthwhile for everyone.

References

Billig, S., & Conrad, J. (1997). *An evaluation of the New Hampshire service-learning and educational reform project.* Denver: RMC Research.

Celebrese, R., & Schumer, H. (1986). The effects of service activities on adolescent alienation. *Adolescence, 21* 675–687.

Conrad, D., & Hedin, D. (1981, Fall). National assessment of experiential education: Summary and implications. *Journal of Experiential Education, 4*(2), 6–20.

Cousins, E., & Mednick, A. (Eds.) (1999). *Service at the heart of learning.* New York: Expeditionary Learning Outward Bound, Inc.

Doland, E. (2001). *Give yourself the gift of a degree.* Employment Policy Foundation. Retrieved May 28, 2002, from http://www.epf.org/media/newsreleases/2001/nr20011219.htm.

Follman, J. (1998). *Florida Learn and Serve: 1996–97 outcomes and correlations with 1994–1995 and 1995–1996.* Tallahassee, FL: Center for Civic Education and Service, Florida State University.

Harlow, C. W. (2003, January). *Education and correctional populations. Bureau of Justice Statistics Special Report.* Washington, DC: U.S. Department of Justice.

Kirby, D. (2001, May). *Emerging answers: Research finding on programs to reduce teen pregnancy.* Washington, DC: National Campaign to Prevent Teen Pregnancy.

Leming, J. (Autumn, 1998). *Adding value to service-learning projects.* Insights on Global Ethics.

Loesch-Griffin, D., Petrides, L. A., & Pratt, C. (1995). *A comprehensive study of Project YES—rethinking classrooms and community: Service-learning as educational reform.* San Francisco: East Bay Conservation Corps.

Melchior, A. (1999). *Summary report: National evaluation of Learn and Serve America.* Waltham, MA: Center for Human Resources, Brandeis University.

Miller, B. (1997). Service-learning in support of rural community development. In A. Waterman (Ed.). *Service-learning: Applications from the research.* Mahwah, NJ: Lawrence Earlbaum Associates, Inc.

Morgan, W., & Streb, M. (2001, March). Building citizenship: How student voice in service-learning develops civic values. *Social Science Quarterly, 82*(1), 155–169.

National Center for Educational Statistics. (2002). *Dropout rates in the United States: 2000.* Washington, DC: Author. Retrieved November 28, 2001, from ttp://nces.ed.gov/pubsearch/pubsinfo.asp?pubid=2002114.

National Service-Learning Cooperative. (1998). *Essential elements of service-learning.* St. Paul, MN: National Youth Leadership Council.

National Study of School Evaluation. (1997). *Executive summary: Presentation report for the NSSE opinion inventories.* Schaumburg, IL: Author.

O'Bannon, F. (1999). Service-learning benefits our schools. *State Education Leader 17, 3.*

Pearson, S. (2002). *Finding common ground: Service-learning and educational reform.* Washington, DC: American Youth Policy Forum.

Rolzinski, C. A. (1990). *The adventure of adolescence: Middle school students and community service.* Washington, DC: Youth Service America.

Santmire, T., Giraud, K., & Grosskopf, K. (1999, April). *Furthering attainment of academic standards through service-learning.* Paper presented at the National Service-Learning Conference, San Jose, CA.

Scales, P., & Blyth, D. (1997, Winter). Effects of service-learning on youth: What we know and what we need to know. *The Generator,* 6–9.

Scales, P., Blyth, D., Berkas, T., & Kielsmeier, J. (2000). The effects of service-learning on middle school students' social responsibility and academic success. *Journal of Early Adolescence, 20,* 332–358.

Seven elements of high quality service learning. (n.d.) Retrieved December 9, 2003, from http://www.yscal.org/resources/assets/HighQualitySL.doc.

Shumer, R. (1994). Community-based learning: Humanizing education. *Journal of Adolescence, 17*(4), 357–367.

Shumer, R. (1997). Learning from qualitative research. In A. Waterman (Ed.). *Service-learning: Applications from the research.* Mahwah, NJ: Lawrence Earlbaum Associates, Inc.

Shumer, R. (2000). *Shumer's self assessment for service-learning.* St. Paul, MN: University of Minnesota, College of Education.

Supik, J. (1996). *Valued youth partnerships: Programs in caring.* San Antonio: Intercultural Development Research Association.

U.S. Department of Education. (1990). *National Education Longitudinal Study of 1988 First Followup Study.* Washington, DC: National Center for Education Statistics.

Weiler, D., LaGoy, A., Crane, E., & Rovner, A. (1998). *An evaluation of service-learning in California: Phase II final report.* Emeryville, CA: Research Policy Practice International.

Yates, M., McClellan, J., & Youniss, J. (1997). What we know about engendering civic identity. *American Behaviorial Scientist, 40,* 620–631.

Yates, M., & Youniss, J. (1996). A developmental perspective on community service in adolescence. *Social Development, 5,* 85–111.

12

Alternative Schooling

Terry Cash

From a very broad perspective, the term *alternative education* refers to all educational programs that fall outside the traditional K–12 school system, including home schooling and special programs for gifted children. As an at-risk intervention strategy, however, the concept is more narrowly defined. For the purposes of this chapter, we consider an alternative school to be a school for students who have exhibited academic and discipline problems, as well as those having difficulty adjusting to the traditional school routine for a myriad of reasons. It could be a separate facility where students are transferred when they are suspended or expelled, or it could be a school-within-a-school. Either way, the program is specifically designed to reach students who are at risk of academic failure and dropping out of school.

Alternative schools are prevalent in virtually every school district in America and recently have begun to develop a significant presence in Europe. Although alternative schools have proliferated in the past decade, not only in numbers but also in school mission and philosophy, there is no reliable information on the number and kinds of alternative schools in existence today. Individual alternative schools develop their own schedule, their own organizational structure, and their own standards and criteria for success. Only recently have alternative schools been compelled to provide standards-related information on the students they serve, such as attendance, academic gain, number of dropouts, number of students returned to a regular school program, recidivism rates, discipline statistics. A systematic and reliable process is needed on the state and national levels to secure these data for further review and dissemination.

This chapter offers a brief review of the types of services and activities that make alternative schools different from traditional schools and summarizes what the research tells us are the best practices in alternative education.

Alternative Schools Are Different

Morley (1991) provides a broad definition of alternative education. He states: "Alternative education is a perspective, not a procedure or program. It is based upon the belief that there are many ways to become educated, as well as many types of environments and structures within which this may occur" (p. 8). An important factor in alternative education is that all personnel recognize that all children do not learn in the same way, so varied instructional methods and innovative curriculums are necessary. A supportive school climate is vital to student success and is achieved by teachers, parents, students, and community members demonstrating positive attitudes. Alternative programs require administrators and teachers to reexamine their teaching strategy for every student, based on the student's individual needs. This requires continual evaluation and adjustment that must be done through patience, insight, care and concern, professional maturity, and the willingness to take risks that may very well result in failure. These attributes and competencies are developed and achieved via a solid philosophical program design that develops in students a feeling of trust, security, and self-confidence.

An alternative school is no place for staff members shown to be incompetent in traditional settings, or for young, inexperienced teachers and administrators, even though they exhibit significant enthusiasm and zeal for teaching. Rather, it is a place for seasoned professionals with a multitude of "tricks up their sleeves" who truly want to be involved with the most demanding students. Teaching is a very rigorous profession and alternative school teaching is doubly so.

A selected review of alternative school programs by Schargel and Smink (2001) found a wide variety of organizational structures:

◆ *School-within-a-school:* designed for students needing a separate location within the traditional school, usually a separate wing with different staff, for their academic or social behavior programs.

◆ *Schools without walls:* designed for students requiring educational and training programs delivered from various locations within the community, usually requires flexible student schedules.

◆ *Residential schools:* designed for special case students, usually placed by the courts or the family, with special counseling and educational programs.

- *Separate alternative learning centers:* designed for students needing a special curriculum, such as parenting skills or special job skills, and a separate location from the traditional school, many times located in business environments, churches, or remodeled retail centers with excellent transportation services.

- *College-based alternative schools:* designed for students needing high school credits, and operated by public school staff; but using a college facility to enhance the student's self-esteem and offer other services that would benefit the student's growth.

- *Summer schools:* designed to be either remedial for academic credits or to enhance a student's special interests, perhaps in science, computers, and so forth.

- *Magnet schools:* designed to focus on selected curriculum areas with specialized teachers and with student attendance usually by choice.

- *Second-chance schools:* designed for students who are judged to be troubled and placed in the school by the courts or the school district as a last chance before being expelled or incarcerated.

- *Charter schools:* designed as an autonomous educational entity operating under a contract negotiated between the state agency and the local school sponsors (pp. 115–116).

For those wishing to do follow-up research on model alternative schools, the National Dropout Prevention Center has developed a database of successful dropout prevention programs that can be accessed via the Internet at www.dropoutprevention.org. The Model Programs Database contains descriptions of a multiplicity of alternative schools located throughout the nation.

To further address the specific needs of students within a particular organizational structure, a multitude of delivery models have been developed. These models—ranging from punitive to therapeutic—include academic and vocational intervention strategies that address students' frustration with traditional methods of learning and attempt to make school more meaningful by preparing students for the workforce. In essence, the programs and models designed to meet the needs of at-risk students are as diverse as the students themselves.

Alternative Schools and Students with Disabilities

In 2001, the University of Minnesota received a three-year federal grant from the Office of Special Education Programs (USDE) to conduct an alternative schools research project that looks at alternative programs across the nation and the students they serve, with particular emphasis on how alternative schools serve students with disabilities. Some of the critical issues that are being examined under the direction of Dr. Cammy Lehr include:

- defining today's alternative schools,
- capturing current policy and practices across the nation,
- describing characteristics of alternative schools and students who attend them, and
- understanding outcomes for students attending alternative schools.

Studying the impact of alternative schools on the education of students with disabilities is an important consideration. On average, students with disabilities are at a greater risk of dropping out than their nondisabled counterparts. Early research conducted by the Enrollment Options Project in the 1990s at the University of Minnesota found students with emotional/behavioral disabilities were attending alternative schools in much higher proportions than in traditional schools (Gorney & Ysseldyke, 1993), and subsequent research suggests alternative settings may be offering an option that successfully engages students with disabilities in learning. Alternative schools are also being used as Interim Alternative Education Settings for students with disabilities who are suspended or expelled as a result of amendments to *IDEA* (Individuals with Disabilities Education Act) put into place in 1997. Considering the unique nature of alternative schools to address individual needs for all students, it makes sense that an increasing number of students with disabilities are assigned to them. However, questions remain about the policies, processes and procedures that are often in place in many alternative schools that may serve to diminish the capacity of the school to provide appropriate services pertinent to a student's disability. Some would even argue that an alternative school could never be the least restrictive environment for students with disabilities.

Alternative Schools Make a Difference

The value of alternative schools as an effective dropout prevention strategy has been documented through research and anecdotal records going back to the early 1980s. Significant amounts of local and state effectiveness data suggest that alternative schools indeed make a difference in the lives of students struggling in traditional schools. Alternative schools have been shown to be successful with potential dropouts by reducing truancy, helping them accumulate high school credits, helping them to improve attitudes toward school, and reducing behavior problems.

Meeting the needs of individual students is the foundation from which a solid and effective alternative school program should be developed. Having the capacity and flexibility to adjust to differing needs is an essential component that sets alternative schools and conventional schools apart. In 1983, a major study assessed how well 14 alternative schools and 11 conventional schools in 10 states were meeting the needs of their students. The results showed alternative schools were clearly superior in meeting student's needs in three of four areas: social competence, self-esteem, and self-actualization. Only security was rated higher for conventional schools, and the differences in this area were not statistically significant (Gregory & Smith, 1983). The authors conclude that factors such as free choice and smaller school size contribute to the superior climate of alternative schools. Although two decades old, the results of the study have remained constant over time.

A more recent study arrived at the same conclusion, that alternative schools are effective models for student intervention, even in different countries and cultures. A review of alternative secondary school models in Hungary showed that alternative schools provide useful lessons for improving the educational attainment in Hungary, as well as in other countries in the region (World Bank & Soros Foundation, 2002). The researchers conclude that many of the ingredients of success identified in the study, including involving parents, supporting students outside the classroom and incorporating multicultural approaches to education "have the potential to improve the quality and inclusiveness of education systems as a whole, to the benefit of the entire population" (p. 30).

Ironically, the issues of attitude and behavior management are perhaps the easiest domains for alternative schools to improve when addressing the needs of students. As noted in the last section, effective alternative schools are philosophically designed to develop in their students a feeling of trust, security and self-confidence. The more difficult task is academic improvement, because the majority of students arrive at alternative schools with significant academic deficiencies.

The data reveal that alternative schools have yielded mixed results in improving student academic performance. A comparative study of alternative schools and regular K–12 school performance in North Carolina showed that alternative schools made the "Expected Growth" goal at almost twice the rate of the regular schools (Brewer, Feifs, & Kaase, 2001). A recent study of Indiana's alternative schools showed that well over 80 percent of the students enrolled either attain or make satisfactory progress toward meeting their goals each year (Lucas, Steiger, & Gamble, 2002). Teachers report that most of their students would have dropped out, had it not been for the opportunity to participate in an alternative program. Teachers also indicate that they expect 94 percent of their students to complete high school because of these programs.

Additionally, a report that examined whether students at risk for academic failure achieve success in Kentucky's alternative schools showed that 91 percent of students responding to a survey had improved grades while in the alternative program (Terpin & Hinton, 2000). However, a more recent evaluation of Kentucky's alternative school programs by Swarts (2002) revealed a difference of approximately 30 percent between the academic performance (e.g., language arts, mathematics, science, social studies, practical living, arts/humanities) of regular schools and that of alternative education programs. Other nonacademic data include attendance, dropout, retention, and transition to adult life. The approximate difference between alternative schools and regular schools was 20 percent for attendance, 23 percent for dropout rates, 9 percent for retention rates, and 4 percent for rate of transition to adult life. According to Swarts, "these findings reveal that the academic performance and nonacademic performance of alternative education programs (in Kentucky) is significantly poorer than regular schools" (p. 3).

Overall, these findings show that alternative schools have been successful in fostering an environment that is more favorable than typically found in regular schools. Countless anecdotal records and statements by teachers, parents, and former students validate the value and need for alternative education programs, but more hard evaluation data are needed as we move from the affective domain into an era of greater accountability for alternative schools.

Starting An Alternative School

Starting an alternative school requires serious thought and commitment on the part of those selected to define its mission and bring about its implementation. It is not a task for those unwilling to make a significant contribution of their personal time and energy. Every effort should be made to ensure broad-based community involvement by planning team members. It is wise to start the planning process at least one year ahead of the start-up date for the opening of the school.

Perhaps the first and most important decision of the planning team is to develop a philosophical construct and mission for the school. This step is absolutely essential to the successful implementation of any model. All other decisions, from program design and operation, to selecting staff members and designing the curriculum should be developed around the philosophy and mission statements. Some additional areas that should be considered include these:

- ◆ Ensure adequate funding to develop, implement, and sustain the school.
- ◆ Include financial incentives for faculty and staff members.

- Recruit faculty and staff based on their desire to work with students at-risk, their experience level, enthusiasm, and demonstrated competency.

- Ensure that the principal or director of the school has sufficient autonomy to adjust the school schedule and/or curriculum to meet the varying needs of the students.

- Publicize and promote the school as an important continuum of services for students with varying needs, not as a school for "troubled youth."

- Start small and expand the program after it has proven to be working well. Expect problems to crop up early. Adjust to them, make improvements, and move on.

Measuring Alternative School Effectiveness

The determination of an effective alternative school must be considered within the overall mission and objectives of the school. A school that operates from an alternative model that is rigid and disciplinary in nature has much different criteria for success than a school that is student-centered and focuses on the long-term rehabilitative process. However, there does appear to be a consistent profile of characteristics common to the most successful alternative schools, no matter what its mission happens to be. Schargel and Smink (2001) found that a successful alternative school had the following characteristics:

- total commitment to have each student be a success,
- maximum teacher/student ratio of 1:10,
- small student base not exceeding 250 students,
- clearly stated mission and discipline code,
- caring faculty with continual staff development pertaining to students at-risk,
- school staff that has high expectations for student achievement,
- learning program that is specific to the student's expectations and learning style, and
- flexible school schedule with community involvement and support.

A number of other researchers in the field have identified similar characteristics of successful alternative education programs (Buchart, 1986; Kadel, 1994; Kellmayer, 1995; Public Schools of North Carolina, 2000; Raywid, 1994). Synthesizing the research, a successful alternative school will incorporate the following elements:

- a strong mission and sense of purpose,
- a belief that all students can succeed,
- a low teacher/student ratio allowing individual attention,
- total enrollment that does not exceed 250 students,
- individualized learning programs to meet the needs of students,
- varied instructional strategies with an emphasis on active learning,
- high academic standards,
- holistic services to meet the emotional, physical, and academic needs of students,
- strong family involvement,
- caring and committed staff who want to work with youth difficult students,
- flexible scheduling,
- community involvement and support,
- a non-punitive philosophy, and
- state-of-the-art technology that is integrated into instructional practices.

A continuum of services is also important for students at risk. Although the dropout rate is highest in the ninth and tenth grades, the problem begins to manifest itself at the elementary and middle levels. Early intervention strategies that focus on academics, with an emphasis on reading and writing, are essential to eliminating at-risk behaviors before they become ingrained. Structured mentoring programs and parental involvement help students develop a daily plan for success. Assigned case managers also foster communication among the school, the student, and the family (Lloyd, 1997).

A discussion on the characteristics of effective alternative schools would not be complete without a brief review of the importance of good leadership. As noted above, alternative schools are not for the weak and weary. A healthy ego, a love for children, enthusiasm for problem solving, and the ability to do more with less are but a few of the prerequisites for an effective alternative school leader. Although the vast majority of alternative school principals are men (Lehr, C. A., & Lange, C. M., 2003), gender appears to have little or no bearing on the capacity of the school leader to get the job done. A classic example is the alternative school program in Lynchburg, Virginia, directed by Charlene Watson. Her leadership capacity, strength of conviction, and vision have developed the Lynchburg alternative program into one of the most comprehensive and effective K–12 programs in the nation. Watson embodies the research-based characteristics of effective leadership specifically directed at students most at risk of dropping out of school. She has proven that unorthodox and seemingly unconventional practices and policies can work very well alongside traditionally structured educational venues.

In the Lynchburg alternative school program, learning takes place in a safe, orderly environment where students are expected to behave according to established, fairly executed rules of conduct. Yet within the structure lies a fundamental philosophy that all children can learn if they receive the support, encouragement, and resources that match their learning style and situation in life. All of this adds up to a school climate that is conducive to learning—a place where students and staff want to belong and are expected to succeed. In the final analysis, the school leadership function is perhaps the most important variable in determining the success or failure of an alternative school program.

Program Evaluation

Alternative educators often cite the need for an evaluation instrument that adequately and reliably documents what their programs do. Established programs should be monitored regularly for strengths and weaknesses. This requires some formalized system of data collection. What to measure and how to measure it have been stumbling blocks for program managers responding to those seeking greater accountability for alternative schools. Historically, many alternative schools have not kept accurate records regarding attendance, discipline referrals, academic grades, recidivism rates, school completion rates, and so forth. Reports of program success are typically based on anecdotal evidence rather than hard data.

Alternative Schools: Best Practices for Development and Evaluation (Reimer & Cash, 2003), recently published by the National Dropout Prevention Center/Network, addresses alternative school evaluation issues in more depth, outlining a model evaluation instrument that helps to quantify pertinent data in specific categories. The instrument rates the school and staff on 121 best-practice indicators (identified through literature reviews of research-based initiatives for at-risk program development) in ten categories:

- ◆ student accountability measures,
- ◆ administrative structure and policies,
- ◆ curriculum and instruction,
- ◆ faculty and staff,
- ◆ facilities and grounds,
- ◆ school leadership,
- ◆ student support services,
- ◆ learning community (staff, students, parents, and community),

- program funding, and
- school climate.

The instrument described above is primarily a *Level One Analysis*. For alternative school leaders and program directors who seek a *Level Two* in-depth analysis from an outside evaluator, the National Dropout Prevention Center/Network has developed a Program Assessment and Review (PAR) process that has served well in a wide variety of applications and locales across the nation. Moving beyond simple data collection, the PAR process combines research-based strategies and solutions with professional assistance. The PAR process—analysis of local data, site interviews, and observations—is managed by local action teams consisting of representatives from the local school and community.

Data analysis aims to create meaning; the information gathered must be organized and presented in a way that helps people understand it and use it for program improvement. Numbers can be interpreted in many different ways; most often, they need to be placed in context or triangulated with other data sources. For instance: An attendance rate of 90 percent may not be considered very effective for a "regular" school, but it may be outstanding for an evening alternative school program. Qualitative data likewise need analysis and interpretation. Analyzing and bringing meaning to those indicators of alternative school effectiveness helps evaluation consumers place activities, methods, and program highlights into the context of program outcome measures. Finally, communicating and disseminating evaluation results maximizes the return on a program's investment in the project.

Conclusion

Alternative schools have been shown to be very effective at keeping more students in school until graduation. According to Knutson (2000), today's high schools should look at successful alternative schools for a model that better meets the needs of today's youth. Careful planning, adequate funding, sound program development and regular evaluation will help to ensure program success.

References

Brewer, D., Feifs, H., & Kaase, K. (2001). *Accountability policy for North Carolina's alternative schools, year one results.* (ERIC Document Reproduction Service No: ED453271).

Buchart, R. E. (1986). *Dropout prevention through alternative high schools: A study of the national experience.* (ERIC Document Reproduction Service No: ED273872).

Gorney, D., & Ysseldyke, J. (1992). *Students with disabilities use of various options to access alternative schools and area learning centers.* Research Report No. 3. Enrollment Options for Students with Disabilities. (ERIC Document Reproduction Service No. ED343363).

Gregory, T., & Smith, G. (1983). *Differences between alternative and conventional schools in meeting students' needs.* (ERIC Document Reproduction Service No. ED232257).

Kadel, S. (1994). *Reengineering high schools for student access.* Hot topics: Usable research. Palatha, FL: Southeastern Regional Vision for Education. (ERIC Document Reproduction Service No. 366076).

Kellmayer, J. (1995). *How to establish an alternative school.* Thousand Oaks, CA: Corwin Press, Inc.

Knutson, G. G. (2000). *Alternative high schools: Models for the future?* [Horizon Site: http://horizon,unc.edu/projects/HSJ/Knutson.asp]. Carrol College.

Lehr, C. A., & Lange, C. M. (2003). Alternative schools and the students they serve: Perceptions of state directors of special education. Policy Research Brief, 14(1). Research and Training. Center on Community Living, University of Minnesota, Institute on Community Integration (UCEDD), Minneapolis, MN.

Lehr, C., Lanners, E., & Ysseldyke, J. (2002). *Alternative programs across the nation and students they serve: Perceptions of state directors of special education.* (Available from C. Lehr, Institute on Community Integration, College of Education and Human Development University of Minnesota, 102 Pattee Hall, 150 Pillsbury Drive SE, Minneapolis, MN 55455).

Lloyd, D. L. (1997). Alternative education: Stepping stone to success. *Schools in the Middle, 6*(3), 36–39.

Lucas, B., Steiger, T. & Gamble, H. (2002). *Making a difference: Alternative education in Indiana.* Report presented by Indiana Department of Education, Division of Alternative Education and Learning Opportunities. Published by Indiana State University.

Morley, R. E. (1991). *Alternative education.* Clemson, SC: Clemson University, National Dropout Prevention Center.

Public Schools of North Carolina, State Board of Education, Department of Public Instruction Office of Instructional and Accountability Services, Division of Accountability Services, Evaluation Section. (2001, March). *Case studies of best practices. Alternative schools and programs: 1998–99.* Raleigh, NC: Author. Retrieved July 11, 2002, from http://www.ncpublicschool.org/accountability/alternative/case9899.pdf.

Raywid, M. (1994). Alternative schools: The state of the art. *Educational Leadership, 52*(1), 26–31.

Reimer, M., & Cash, T. (2003). *Alternative schools: Best practices for development and evaluation.* National Dropout Prevention Center. College of Health, Education, and Human Development, Clemson University.

Schargel, F. P., & Smink, J. (2001). *Strategies to help solve our school dropout problem.* Larchmont, NY: Eye on Education.

Swarts, L. (2002). *An investigation of alternative education programs in Kentucky.* Report published by Kentucky Department of Education, July 2002.

Turpin, R., & Hinton, H. (2000). *Academic success of at-risk students in an alternative school setting. An examination of students' academic success out of the mainstream school environment.* (ERIC Document Reproduction Service No. 440814).

World Bank & Soros Foundation (2002). Alternative schools and Roma education: A review of alternative secondary school models for the education of Roma children in

Hungary. World Bank Regional Office Hungary NGO Studies No. 3. [On-line: available at www.worldbank.hu/4roma.html #Alternative schools and Roma education.]

13

After-School Opportunities: A Time and a Tool to Reduce Dropouts

Terry K. Peterson and Bryan Fox

We need a chance for a life, too.

> James, a middle-school student in South Carolina, voicing his disappointment when the state legislature eliminated funding for his school's after-school program.

After-school programs can be important tools in the growing effort to increase the high school graduation rate. They are well suited to address the factors that predispose or influence kids to drop out of school. Furthermore, under the No Child Left Behind legislation, many students will need more time and adjunctive learning opportunities to meet tougher academic standards for promotion and graduation.

In this chapter we will examine three key points: the need to fill the dangerous "gap time" after school; the way after-school programs help equip students to meet future challenges; and the critical components of programs that keep at-risk students on the path to promotion and graduation.

Gap-Time Issues

Public/Private Ventures, an organization that provides a comprehensive community approach to positive youth development, found that "gap activities" respond to the basic needs of youth (Watson, 2002).

The increasing trend toward single-parent households and households where both parents work outside the home has put more than 8 million latch-key children on their own after school each day. Recent findings from an organization called Fight Crime: Invest in Kids (1999) indicated that the hours from 3 to 7 PM had the highest crime rate during the school week. This unsupervised time provides many opportunities for kids to involve themselves in criminal activity, drug use, and sexual activity. Other children and young adolescents not directly involved in criminal behavior tend to go home and simply "zone out." In either case, this daily block of unproductive time has the potential to sidetrack children and youth from the path toward graduation.

In today's world of technological advances and rapidly increasing educational demands, to allow these young people to fall through the cracks is both unacceptable and immoral. John Ervin III, project coordinator for the Modesto City Schools 21st Century Afterschool Learning Program states the importance of after-school programs very clearly: "Whenever a mom tells me how her daughter or son is bringing home report cards that have As where there used to be Fs, I reflect on my years growing up in South Central Los Angeles, trying to dodge the influences of gangs, drugs, and crime. I have been on both sides of the road, seeing effects of both the absence and presence of after-school programs. Only by providing a quality after-school program in every school will all children have the same safe, nurturing, enriching, and character-building opportunity, which will ensure that no child is left behind!" ("Life Before After-School Programs," 2002, p. 9).

The Afterschool Alliance (2003) cites examples of the impact of after-school programs:

♦ In Bedford-Stuyvesant, New York, the Blossom Program targets girls who are at-risk for gang activity. The program offers a safe, supportive environment of supervised activities, including community service projects, computer labs, physical fitness, and other activities that interest youth. One participant: "I was bad. I was always in trouble—fighting, talking back to teachers…I didn't intend to finish school, but my guidance counselor introduced me to Isis [creator of Blossom], and I came to Blossom."

♦ In Vancouver, Washington, the after-school program in the local Boys & Girls Club has seen juvenile crime in a local apartment complex drop by 45 percent.

♦ In Plainview, Arkansas, an after-school program contained an abstinence component. The graduating class of 2000 had no teen pregnancies, compared to six in 1998 (Afterschool Alliance, 2002).

An evaluation by Beth Miller (2001), senior research advisor for the National Institute on Out-of-School Time, confirms the power of after-school programs: "The most impressive research on the results of after-school programs links participation to significantly lower involvement in risky behaviors, including a lower incidence of drinking, smoking, using drugs, having sex, and becoming involved in violence…"(p. 7).

Support for Success

After-school programs do more than just keep kids out of trouble. Hundreds of thousands of students drift through high school without a clear path. For students like these, well-designed programs offer hope, opportunities and academic support.

Providing Hope

Students at risk of dropping out of school often fail to recognize their own potential. They cannot envision themselves attending college, working at interesting careers, or making a difference as active citizens. In many cases, the traditional classroom setting doesn't work for them. These students need an engaging atmosphere where they can make connections with caring adults and new opportunities. After-school and summer programs can provide such an environment.

Data from The Quantum Opportunities Program (QOP) illustrate this point quite clearly. This year-round service program provided academic and developmental services—after-school tutoring, homework assistance, life skills, future planning—for disadvantaged youth in five communities. Caring adults worked with them for four years. At the end of the four years, the results were compared with outcomes for youth in five other communities. QOP students graduated from high school more often (63 percent versus 42 percent), dropped out of school less often (23 percent versus 50 percent), became teen parents less often (24 percent versus 38 percent), and went on to postsecondary education more often (42 percent versus 16 percent) (Hahn, 1994).

Followup studies demonstrated the continued influence of the Quantum Opportunities Program. QOP students were three times as likely to continue their education and to receive an award or honor at graduation. Students not involved in QOP were twice as likely to drop out of school (Newman, Fox, Flynn, & Christeson, 2000).

In Hamilton County, Tennessee, the after-school and summer programs called Lights On! have seen dramatic effects on student achievement in both rural and urban settings. The program operates in the ten most economically stressed schools in the county, providing a wide range of services (from basic tutoring to cultural activities and the arts) until 7 p.m. According to Hamilton County School Board member Janice Boydston, "...children are doing better due to the extended and more intimate time the program allows them to meet with staff outside the school day, so they see that somebody cares and takes and interest, which can keep a kid from falling through the cracks" (Ashby, 2001).

Research supports the idea that utilizing out-of-school time activities to build student-adult relationships has a positive impact on student motivation and achievement (Mahoney, 2000; Jordan & Nettles, 1999). When students have hope, they see possibilities. And when they see possibilities, they are more motivated to learn. Quality after-school programs and other extended learning programs have the power to help provide hope to at-risk students.

Providing Opportunities

Children who are at risk of dropping out of school not only fail to see the doors their education can open, but also have fewer opportunities. These students would benefit greatly from a broad range of educational offerings that tap into their specific interests and aptitudes. Such an array, however, requires substantial funding and community partnerships—resources their communities and school systems too often lack.

This is particularly important for low-income rural and inner city students. Poshner and Vandell (1994) found that low-income children were deprived of experiences in the arts such as music and dance, and often had no involvement in team sports unless they were able to participate in an after-school program. A followup study also found that low-income students who participated in after-school programs had experiences similar to those of students from middle-class backgrounds with access to a broad array of enrichment opportunities (Poshner & Vandell, 1999). Other research has shown that affording students a wider choice of learning activities and opportunities has a positive effect on their motivation and commitment to school (Mahoney & Cairns, 1997).

The rise in educational standards presents another challenge, because it adds to the tasks of the regular school day. When accomplishing these tasks requires strict adherence to a structured format, engaging and enriching educational opportunities may fall by the wayside. After-school programs can fill the breach.

Providing Academic Support

Expecting children and young adolescents to master more material and tougher standards within the same traditional school day or year can lead to difficulties. To address this issue, former U.S. Secretary of Education Dick Riley (2003) recommended that "we design and operate schools as community learning centers to be open later and longer…to address the fact that children's minds don't stop learning at 3:30 PM when the typical school closes."

After-school academic support can help students stay on grade level with their peers—a vital goal for the at-risk student who is falling behind academically, because retention in grade is such a strong predictor of dropping out altogether. Tutoring and homework assistance can make the difference, but they should not take the form of stultifying "drill and kill" sessions.

A relatively new trend in after-school education is "credit recovery"—allowing students to use out-of-school time to retake courses for credit so that they remain on pace (or ahead of pace) for graduation. Such offerings have attracted high school students—often less likely than younger students to join after-school programs. At Park High School in Racine, Wisconsin, the after-school program draws 900 students, primarily due to their "reteach–retest" offering. This allows students to be retaught lessons they may have missed or not fully understood and then retake tests to improve their grade.

Central Components of Effective Programs

After-school programs, though not a "magic bullet" to keep students in school, can certainly address many of the risk factors associated with dropping out. Policy makers and practitioners interested in identifying the key components of effective programs can turn to studies of large-scale programs around the country, such as California's After-school Learning and Safe Neighborhoods Partnerships Program (ASLSNPP) (University of California–Irvine, 2001); LA's Best (Better Educated Students for Tomorrow) (Huang et al., 2000); The AfterSchool Corporation (TASC) (Policy Studies Associates, Inc., 2000); Foundations, Inc. (Foundations, Inc., 2003; Peterson, 2003), and the Extended Services Schools (ESS) Initiative (Grossman et al., 2002).

In effective after-school programs:

- ◆ **Academic offerings** include homework assistance, tutoring, literacy, and hands-on learning experiences meant to supplement the regular school day—often through four-to-five-week projects.

- **Enrichment and accelerated learning** involves introduction to visual and performing arts, field trips to community resources, character education/problem solving skills, learning about other cultures and languages, and using technology to learn (Peterson, 2003).
- **Supervised recreation** includes organized sports as well as sports education to inspire teamwork and cooperation, teach positive leisure time activities, and even promote emotional intelligence.
- **Community service** provides students with a connection to the community (and often to younger students) and instills a sense of "giving back."

These components work best when they are synchronized within a comprehensive program that operates from the end of the school day until 5:30 or 6 PM, four or five days a week.

Also, most of the effective programs surveyed connect to community and cultural resources. Such collaboration and partnerships allow students and their families to benefit from the broader community connections and resources. Furthermore, collaboration is critical for survivability in today's economy. States and the federal government are notoriously fickle when it comes to funding long-term after-school and summer programs. However, they periodically provide seed money for local initiatives that then must find the resources to become self-sufficient (Peterson, 2002).

Another key component is active involvement of parents. Parents not only support the program and promote attendance, but may also receive direct educational services themselves. As parents' educational level increases, so do their children's expectations and motivation to succeed in school (Peterson, 2003).

After-school programs for adolescents need to be more active, dynamic, engaging, comprehensive and probably even offered in multiple settings. For example, the local YMCA/YWCA could offer basketball, homework help, and career awareness on Wednesday and Friday, while the high school stays open after school on Monday, Tuesday, and Thursday at the high school for interest clubs, community service projects, tutoring and mentoring, credit recovery courses, and six-week art, music, and drama offerings.

The school district in rural Timmonsville, South Carolina resolved transportation problems by consolidating this mix of activities and providers at the middle school. Through a 21st Century Community Learning grant, the after-school program combines the regular middle school sports and band program, a Boys and Girls Club program, a Community in Schools program, a self-paced technology center, homework help, basic skills tutoring, and additional art and music classes. The program runs for two to three hours almost every day, with transportation provided, and almost 65 percent of the students participate regularly (Peterson, 2003).

Conclusion

Well-designed and effectively implemented after-school programs add to the chances that at-risk students will stay out of trouble, stay in school, and stay engaged with their education.

Programs that fill the afternoon "gap time" with constructive and engaging activities help to mitigate the risk factors associated with dropping out of school. Additionally, after-school programs provide hope, opportunities, and academic support to students who might fall through the cracks in the traditional educational setting. Students who make healthy connections with caring adults, are involved in engaging, alternative learning experiences, and are provided with tutoring and homework assistance are more likely to graduate successfully and continue their education beyond high school.

Communities, school districts, and local, state, and federal policy makers must realize that after-school programs are not a superfluous luxury. After-school programs should not be afterthought programs. We must use this powerful resource effectively to extend the regular school day and support positive youth development, especially for students at risk.

References

Afterschool Alliance. (2003, May). *Afterschool keeps kids safe* (Issue Brief No.7). Washington, DC: Author. Available at http://www.afterschoolalliance.org/issue_safe.doc.

Afterschool Alliance. (2002, July). *Afterschool and pregnancy prevention* (Issue Brief No. 11). Washington, DC: Author. Available at http://www.afterschool alliance.org/issue_safe.doc.

Ashby, N. (2001, July/August). Lights On! With their doors open after hours, schools serve as 'Lighthouses' in Hamilton County, Tenn. As cited in U.S. Department of Education. *Community Update, 98*, 4–8.

Foundations, Inc. (2003). *Improvements in math and reading scores of students who did and did not participate in the Foundations after-school enrichment program during the 2001–2002 school year.* Available at http://www.foundationsinc.org/ExtendedDayFolder/conclusions.asp.

Grossman, J. B., Price, M. L., Fellerath, V., Jucovy, L. Z., Kotloff, L. J., Raley, R., & Walker, K. E. (2002). *Multiple choices after school: Findings from the Extended Service Schools Initiative* [On-Line]. Available at http://www.ppv.org/content/reports/ess-multi-full.html.

Hahn, A. (1994, October). *Promoting youth development in urban communities: Unprecedented success for the Quantum Opportunities Program.* (A Forum Brief.) Available at http://www.aypf.org/forumbriefs/1994/fb102894.htm.

Huang, D., Gribbons, B., Kim, K. S., Lee, C., & Baker, E. L. (2000). *A Decade of results: The impact of the LA's BEST after-school enrichment program on subsequent student achievement and performance.* Los Angeles: UCLA Center for the Study of Evaluation (CSE).

Jordan, W, & Nettles, S. (1999). *How students invest their time out of school: Effects on school engagement, perceptions of life chances, and achievement.* (Report No. 29). Baltimore: Center for Research on the Education of Students Placed At Risk. (ERIC Document Reproduction Service No. ED 428 174).

Life before after-school programs. (2002, July/August). U.S. Department of Education *Community Update, 98,* 9.

Mahoney, J. (2000). School extracurricular activity participation as a moderator in the development of antisocial patterns. *Child Development, 71*(2), 502–516.

Mahoney, J., & Cairns, R. (1997). Do extracurricular activities protect against early school drop-out? *Developmental Psychology, 33*(2), 241–253.

Miller, B.M. (2001). The promise of after-school programs. *Educational Leadership, 58*(7), 6–12.

Newman, S., Fox, J. A., Flynn, E. A., & Christeson, W. (2000). *America's after-school choice: The prime time for juvenile crime, or youth enrichment and achievement.* Washington, DC: Fight Crime: Invest in Kids.

Peterson, T. K. (2002). *Survivor's test for successful after-school initiatives.* National After-school and Community Learning Resource Network: Columbia, South Carolina.

Peterson, T. K. (2003). *Boosting student success—The potential of after-school and what local school leaders can do about it.* Presentation made to the South Carolina School Board Association Meeting, Hilton Head, SC.

Policy Studies Associates, Inc. (2000). *Increasing and improving after-school opportunities: Evaluation results from the TASC After-School Program's first year, Executive summary.* New York: Author.

Poshner, J. K., & Vandell, D. L. (1994). Low-income children's after-school care: Are there beneficial effects of after-school programs? *Child Development, 65*(2), 440–456.

Poshner, J. K, & Vandell, D. L. (1999). After-school activities and the development of low-income urban children: A longitudinal study. *Developmental Psychology, 35*(3), 868–879.

Riley, R. (2003). *Building and designing schools as community learning centers.* Presentation at the Getty Symposium on Better Schools/Better Neighborhoods, Los Angeles, May 29, 2003.

University of California at Irvine, Department of Education. (2001). *Evaluation of California's After-school Learning and Safe Neighborhoods Partnerships Program: 1999–2000 preliminary report.* Irvine, CA: Author.

Watson, B. (2002). *Community Change for Youth Development: Ten lessons from the CCYD Initiative.* Philadelphia, PA: Public/Private Ventures.

Making the Most of Instruction

14

Professional Development

Mary Reimer

According to the National Center for Education Statistics (1999), 99 percent of teachers receive some professional development each year, but the quality of this professional development is often uneven. Some of this unevenness may be attributed to state requirements. Although professional development is mandated in 35 states, there are few standards regarding the quality and content of the offerings (Hirsch, Koppich, & Knapp, 2001). Most states are more concerned with "clock hours" and allow almost any kind of formal learning experience even if it is not relevant to teaching practice. "More often than not, staff development for teachers is fragmented and incoherent, lacks intellectual rigor, fails to build on existing knowledge and skills, and does little to assist them with the day-to-day challenges of improving student learning" (Sparks, 2002, p. 9–1). Although this is often the norm, staff development does not have to be this way. There are methods for creating a relevant, comprehensive, and challenging professional development program that can impact student learning and the high school graduation rate.

Professional Development Is Critical for Keeping Students in School

Having quality teachers in the classroom is the goal of every school. Teachers constantly need to learn new skills and teaching methods to keep abreast of changes. A strong case can be made for the importance of powerful professional learning to help teachers keep up-to-date. First, research shows that quality teaching makes a significant difference in student learning, particularly for those students who struggle to succeed in the classroom. Second, the professional learning of teachers and principals is a major factor in determining the quality of teaching. Third, district culture and structures that surround the school have a major impact on the quality of the professional learning (Sparks, 2002).

The No Child Left Behind Act (NCLB) defines highly qualified teachers as those who, at a minimum, must hold a bachelor's degree from a four-year institution, hold full state certification, and demonstrate competence in their subject area. Having a qualified, high quality teacher in every classroom is a challenge that is very difficult to meet. Research shows that highly qualified teachers are a rarity in classrooms.

According to the National Board for Professional Teaching Standards (1999), high quality teachers have the following characteristics: they know the subjects they teach and how to teach those subjects to students; they manage and monitor student learning; they think systematically about their practice and learn from experience; and they are members of learning communities. These characteristics are all supported and enhanced through quality professional development.

According to the U.S. Department of Education (2003), only 54 percent of our nation's secondary teachers were highly qualified during the 1999–2000 school year. The percentage of highly qualified teachers ranged from 47 percent of mathematics teachers to 55 percent of science and social science teachers. High-poverty districts were more likely to employ teachers on waivers than affluent districts, averaging 8 percent in the 2001–2002 school year compared with 5 percent in other districts (p. 7). The percentage of teachers on waivers with content expertise in high-poverty districts is an astounding 63 percent (p. 19).

Professional development can bridge some, but not all, of the gaps in education for classroom teachers. These statistics indicate the need for a comprehensive, well-planned professional development program for every school and district, but especially for low-performing schools, which are more likely to have a large population of students at risk of school failure.

Teachers who work with at-risk youth especially need an avenue by which they can continue to develop skills and techniques and learn about innovative strategies. Typical teacher education programs do not include methods for coping with at-risk students who often have severe discipline or therapeutic issues. Standard professional development activities rarely focus on the special needs of students in at-risk situations. Teachers often have to seek out alternative education conferences and state and regional meetings in order to receive pertinent training.

The National Dropout Prevention Center/Network, through its Program Assessment and Review (PAR) process, has found some commonalities in professional development topics requested by teachers who want to be able to facilitate learning for all of their students, but especially those who are least successful in the classroom:

- Teachers need to know more about learning styles and how to vary their teaching methods to reach everyone in their class.

- Active learning methods have proven to be more successful in motivating low-performing students than the typical skill and drill method.

- Many teachers are interested in learning more about classroom management.

- Teachers now have classrooms with students from all over the world, many who speak English as a second language. The teachers have recognized the need to understand the cultural differences of their students.

- Teachers desire to be part of a team, instead of being a loner in the classroom. Educators want to be members of a learning community and use team and interdisciplinary teaching. They want to support and be supported in their efforts to help their students achieve.

Impact on Student Learning

Recent research suggests that the quality of a teacher is the most important predictor of student success. A Tennessee study (Haycock, 1998) discovered that low-achieving students increased their achievement level by as much as 53 percent when taught by a highly effective teacher. The sequence of teachers to which students were assigned also seemed to have an effect. Darling-Hamond (1998) makes a strong argument for quality professional development by stating that each dollar spent on improving teachers' qualifications nets greater gains in student learning than any other use of an education dollar.

Wenglinsky (2000) found that certain types of professional development may have an impact on student achievement.

Students whose teachers receive professional development in working with different student populations are 107 percent of a grade level ahead of their peers in math. Students whose teachers receive professional development in higher-order thinking skills are 40 percent of a grade level ahead of students whose teachers lack such training in mathematics. Students whose teachers receive professional development in laboratory skills are 44 percent of a grade level ahead of those whose teachers lack such training in science (p. 26).

Research shows the effectiveness of certain methods of professional development, but they are not commonly used. It seems obvious that effective methods would be especially valuable when working with new teachers, and those who teach struggling students who are most apt to drop out of school, but this is not the case. Professional development must overcome the institutional barriers of time and money, and also teachers' personal barriers. "Educators' beliefs about students' capacities to learn, teachers' capacities to teach, and the requirements of individual and collective change are critical barriers to significant improvement" (Sparks, 2002, p. 13–14). Mental models such as only some students can achieve at high levels and teachers are born, not made, can be very difficult to change.

Research Base for Professional Development

Several national reports have emphasized the importance of professional development (National Staff Development Council, 2001). These reports found that the most effective programs use active teacher learning strategies such as study groups; collaboratives, networks, or committees; mentoring; internships; coaching; learning communities; and resource centers. Teachers were more likely to integrate new strategies into their classrooms when exposed to this type of professional development.

A number of studies suggest that the duration of professional development is a major factor in effective teacher change (Garet, Porter, Desimone, Birman, & Kwang, 2001). Professional development should be sustained, rather than a one-shot effort. Teachers need the opportunity to internalize and practice what they learn. Learning communities provide opportunities for discussion and support; while coaching and mentoring offer guidance and feedback as teachers hone their new skills. The opportunity to put into practice the new skills they have learned is vital to effecting change in the classroom.

School administrators play a major role in the type and quality of professional development in their school and district. Those who value their own professional development will ensure that their teachers have relevant professional development programs. Principals are often the ones who establish a school culture that promotes quality teaching and standards-based instruction. The National Association for Elementary School Principals (2001) recommends that principals take a key role in professional development by supporting teacher learning, tying school learning goals to professional development, providing opportunities for teachers to work collaboratively, and improving their own professional practice.

One report found that 56 percent of superintendents and 54 percent of principals viewed professional development as an effective way of improving school leadership (Farkas, Johnson, Duffett, & Foleno, 2001). The role of the principal is changing from being a building manager to an instructional leader, so professional development is important in developing the skills necessary to move into this new role. Effective staff development for administrators is the same as that for teachers: long-term, job-embedded, focused on student achievement, and providing opportunities to work collaboratively with peers. Coaching and visits to other schools are also important facets of leadership development. Sparks (2002) warns:

> The development of principals cannot continue to be the neglected stepchild of state and district professional development efforts. It must be standards-focused, sustained, intellectually rigorous, and embedded in the principal's workday. Nothing less will lead to high levels of learning and performance by all students and teachers (p. 8–5).

Relationship to the Other Effective Strategies

Professional development may be considered the foundation for the other 14 effective strategies for dropout prevention. The other strategies require making a change or acquiring a new skill. For faculty and staff, professional development is the way they learn new skills and how to make changes. Almost all school districts have some type of professional development for their teachers. The problem is that very few of these activities are effective in changing teaching practices or the school system. Most professional development is fragmented and short-term, known as "sit and git," and rarely focused on curriculum for students. Only 30 percent of teachers participated in professional development activities that required in-depth study of a specific field (Hirsch, Koppich, & Knapp, 1998).

Best Practices

There are schools that have developed award-winning professional development programs, and some of these have been low-performing schools. The National Awards Program for Model Professional Development was developed in 1995 to recognize schools and districts for comprehensive efforts to increase teacher and student learning through professional development. What makes these schools award winners is their spirit of efficacy, responsibility, and accountability. They are diverse, showing that more than one kind of school in one particular setting can achieve results. Although the schools are diverse, there are some similar patterns:

- Frequent analyses of multiple types of data keep schools focused on their results.
- The principal plays a significant role in establishing a productive learning environment.
- Teachers engage in diverse and extensive learning experiences.
- Change is not easy (Killion, 1999, p. 16–17).

One of the award-winning schools is H. D. Hilley Elementary School in El Paso, Texas. The majority of their students are poor and Latino. Through the use of professional development, student assessment scores have skyrocketed, and Hilley was named a Texas Successful School in 1997.

Immigrants and English language learners who speak 37 different languages populate the International High School at LaGuardia Community College, Long Island, New York. They have increased students' attendance, high school completion, and college acceptance rates.

Montview Elementary School in Aurora, Colorado, has a transiency rate of 126 percent. Professional development has helped the staff eliminate the performance gap between white and nonwhite students and raise math and reading scores from below the district average to the top of the district range.

Frenship Independent School District, Wolfforth, Texas, has made a district-wide commitment to professional development (Duttweiler & Madden, 2001). The district supports this effort, but site-based committees assess the needs of their school and plan the activities, which usually focus on curriculum and instruction. There is an emphasis on active learning instructional techniques and the integration of technology. Staff are encouraged to attend conferences and workshops and to visit other schools.

Frenship ISD has been able to virtually eliminate the achievement gap between Anglo and Hispanic students. From 1996 to 2000, the district raised the average Texas Assessment of Academic Skills (TAAS) scores of its economically disadvantaged students to about 90 percent in reading, mathematics, and writing (Duttweiler & Madden, 2001). For their efforts, they received a state rating of Exemplary.

Although these schools use formal professional-development activities, opportunities for informal professional development abound. Informal professional activities, often called followup activities, are practical and relevant to the classroom. Some examples are mentoring, peer observation, expert coaching, study groups, team teaching, and examining student work. Collaboration and collegiality result when teachers work together. Schools become communities of learning instead of isolated teachers in classrooms.

Designing good professional development is a challenge. Relevant content and a strong decision making and organizational process are vital to an effective program. The North Central Regional Educational Laboratory (Hassel, 1999) suggests the following steps:

- Include participants and organizers in the professional design process.
- Make a clear plan.
- Share the plan with the school community.

It is important to include critical stakeholders in the professional development plan and decision-making process. These stakeholders may include students, teachers, other staff, parents, principals, district professional development staff, district management, community members, and expert resources such as professors or consultants (Hassel, p. 9). Once the stakeholders have been identified, a decision must be made about what kind of input each person has.

Planning is time consuming, but important. Educational and professional development goals should align at all levels. Student learning goals drive the instructional team's educational goals, which set the school's educational goals, which determine the district's educational goals. Needs assessment measures both student and staff learning needs. Data sources can help determine student learning gaps and teacher competence. Some examples of student learning data sources are standardized tests, portfolios, and student, teacher, and parent surveys. Teacher competency sources include supervisor observation, peer review, and portfolios.

Time is a major barrier to successful professional development and should be addressed during the planning stage. Finding enough time for professional development during the regular workweek can be difficult. Expanding the workweek and using the extra time for professional development is effective, but requires additional funding. Another avenue that requires additional funding is to have a list of regular and excellent substitutes. Individual teacher planning time can be changed to team planning, grading, and problem solving. Staff meetings that are already scheduled can become opportunities for professional development. Some schools have eliminated faculty meetings and use newsletters or email to communicate routine information. Class scheduling can be changed to include a short time for professional development every day. Some schools schedule music, art, physical education, and computer instruction in a block so that teachers have some uninterrupted time to work with other grade-level teachers.

Sustaining a professional development program takes creativity and commitment. Allocating longer blocks of time for professional development requires even more creative planning. Scheduling activities on weekends may be one possibility. In order to encourage staff to attend, the school could offer babysitting, provide snacks and meals, and make the opportunity voluntary. It may be possible to create a half-day in students' weekly schedules and use the rest of the day for professional development. Staff may be willing to voluntarily lengthen the school day by ten minutes. The minutes can then be consolidated into longer blocks of time. One school was able to add four days per year using this method.

Effectiveness of Professional Development

A study by Lee, Smith, and Croninger (1995) of 820 secondary schools found that schools with learning communities evinced greater student academic gains in science, math, history, and reading than those in traditionally-organized schools. Another study (Garet, Porter, Desimone, Birman, & Kwang, 2001) found that professional development activities had significant, positive effects on teachers' self-reported increases in knowledge and skills and changes in classroom practice. Setting goals for improved student learning, particularly for academically challenged students, is an important part of professional development. Changes in teachers' attitudes do occur when there is discernible improvement in student learning. Some studies (Cohen & Hill, 1998) have found that student achievement improves when professional development focuses on specific subject content and how students learn that content. The most significant rewards of professional development are the teachers' increased self-efficacy and evidence of their students' achievement.

Professional development is a valuable tool in improving staff competency and student achievement, but it cannot stand alone. It is most effective when used in conjunction with the other 14 effective strategies described in this book. The best practices of professional development are embedded in the teacher's workday, are of sufficient length for teachers to internalize and practice what they learn, use active teacher learning strategies, establish learning communities for discussion and support, and are tied to student achievement and school improvement goals. Individual differences in teachers and high-risk students will never disappear, but these differences can be reduced through the use of powerful instructional systems and effective

forms of professional development so that every student has a highly qualified teacher and no child is left behind (U.S. Department of Education, 2003).

References

Cohen, D. K., & Kill, H. C. (1998*). State policy and classroom performance: Mathematics reform in California* (CPRE Policy Brief No. RB-27). Philadelphia: Consortium for Policy Research in Education, University of Pennsylvania.

Darling-Hammond, L. (1998). *Investing in quality teaching: State-level strategies, 1999.*
Denver: Education Commission of the States.

Duttweiler, P. C., & Madden M. (2001, Winter). *The district that does what's best for kids:
Frenship ISD.* (Special report on standards, assessment, accountability, and inter-
ventions for the Edna McConnell Clark Foundation, 5). Clemson, SC: National
Dropout Prevention Center.

Farkas, S., Johnson, J., Duffett, A., & Foleno, T. (2001). *Trying to stay ahead of the game: Superintendents and principals talk about school leadership.* Retrieved May 28, 2003, from
http://www.publicagendaorg/specials/leadership/leadership.htm.

Garet, M. S., Porter, A. C., Desimone, L., Birman, B. F., & Kwang, S. Y. (2001, Winter).
What makes professional development effective? Results from a national sample of
teachers. *American Educational Research Journal, 38*(4), 915–945.

Hassel, E. (1999). *Professional development: Learning from the best: A toolkit for schools and
districts based on the national awards program for model professional development.* Retrieved May 7, 2002, from http://www.ncrel.org/pd/toolkit.htm.

Haycock, K. (1998). *Good teaching matters.* Washington, DC: Education Trust.

Hirsch, E., Koppich, J. E., & Knapp, M.S. (2001). *Revisiting what states are doing to improve
the quality of teaching: An update on current patterns and trends.* Retrieved May 28,
2003, from http://depts.washington.edu/ctpmail/PDFs/States-HKK-
02-2001.pdf.

Killion, J. (1999, October). Islands of hope in a sea of dreams: A research report on the
eight schools that received the National Award for Model Professional Development. Retrieved June 21, 2002, from http://www.wested.org/wested/pubs/on-
line/Pdawards/07contex.shtml.

Lee, V., Smith, J., & Croninger, R. (1995, Fall). *Another look at high school restructuring. Issues in restructuring schools.* Retrieved May 30, 2003, from http://www.
wcer.wisc.edu/archives/completed/cors/Issues_in_Restructuring_
Schools/ISSUES_No_9_FALL_1995.pdf.

National Association for Elementary School Principals. (2001). *Leadership for student
learning: Reinventing the principalship: A report of the task force on the principalship.*
Washington, DC: Author.

National Board for Professional Teaching Standards. (1999). *What teachers should know
and be able to do.* Retrieved June 6, 2002, from http://www.nbpts.org/pdf/
coreprops.pdf.

National Center for Education Statistics. (1999). *Teacher quality: A report on the preparation and qualifications of public school teachers.* Washington, DC: U.S. Government
Printing Office.

National Staff Development Council. (2001). *Standards for staff development* (Revised). Retrieved June 3, 2003, from http://www.nsdc.org/library/Standards_RevEd.pdf.

Sparks, D. (2002). *Designing powerful professional development for teachers and principals.* Retrieved June 7, 2002, from http://www.nsdc.org/sparksbook.html.

U.S. Department of Education. (2003). *Meeting the highly qualified teachers challenge: The Secretary's second annual report on teacher quality.* Retrieved July 17, 2003, from http://www.ed.gov/offices/OPE/News/teacherprep/Title-II-Report.pdf.

Wenglinsky, H. (2000). *How teaching matters: Bringing the classroom back into discussions of teacher quality.* Retrieved May 30, 2003, from http://www.ets.org/research/pic/teamat/pdf.

15

Active Learning

Donna H. Foster and Linda J. Shirley

Active learning is a catchall phrase used to describe teaching and learning strategies that engage and involve students in the learning process. It is an effective dropout prevention tool because it provides students with a variety of opportunities to succeed in the classroom, thus increasing the chance that they will stay in school until graduation.

Active learning teaching strategies include (but are not limited to) *cooperative learning, learning styles theory, multiple intelligences theory*, and *project-based learning*. Active learning and teaching strategies allow students not only to listen, but also to speak, write, construct, and reflect as they solve problems, work in teams, perform new skills, and demonstrate procedures. Thus, the engaged and involved students create bonds with school through their interactions with the curriculum, with faculty, and with fellow students. They become more accountable and responsible for their role in the education process. Through active learning, students receive immediate opportunities to apply and associate new knowledge, making the curriculum more relevant, challenging, and rigorous.

At-risk youth benefit from academic situations that provide opportunities for interesting, engaging academic course work and help them develop trusting, positive relationships with their peers and teachers (Black, 2002; Sanders & Sanders, 1998). Numerous research studies conducted by David and Roger Johnson and Robert Slavin tout the value of active learning as a tool to increase student achievement, student psychological health, and student retention, with lowest-achieving students and minorities benefitting the most (Kagan, 1994).

- ◆ One example is Union City Public Schools in Union City, New Jersey. Administrators, teachers, parents, and students embraced active learning strategies and turned their failing school system into a successful system. Attendance increased, dropout and absentee rates decreased, and 80 percent of the students met state standards, up from 30 percent.

- ◆ Another program making a difference is *Success for All*. The program started in Baltimore, Maryland, and targets preschool through fifth grade students with reading difficulties. The program combines one-on-one tutoring and cooperative learning with frequent assessment and family support services. The program is now offered in 1,500 schools in 500 districts in 48 states and other countries.

While active learning strategies are not limited to the strategies mentioned here, this chapter explores these strategies, their application, and the benefits for troubled students.

Cooperative Learning

One active learning strategy effective with students in high-risk situations is cooperative learning. Cooperative learning is defined as *students working together to achieve a common goal*. It differs from group work in that it is carefully structured to ensure that teamwork takes place. Cooperative learning is effective because it provides students with peer interactions designed to build caring relationships, thus minimizing social isolation as a dropout factor. Two models of cooperative learning are Spencer Kagan's model (1994) and David and Roger Johnson's model (1992). Kagan's model is structured around four basic principles:

- ◆ positive interdependence,
- ◆ individual accountability,
- ◆ equal participation, and
- ◆ simultaneous interaction.

According to David and Roger Johnson of the University of Minnesota, a cooperative learning lesson should contain five basic elements:

- ◆ positive interdependence,
- ◆ individual accountability,
- ◆ social skills,

- face-to-face interaction, and
- team processing.

Whether one uses Kagan's four principles or the Johnsons' five basic elements, it is the structure that distinguishes cooperative learning teams from group work. These elements provide at-risk students the structure for positive learner-to-learner interaction, active academic engagement, the possibility of higher academic achievement, and individual reflection.

A deeper look into these two models' structures and principles is discussed in the following text.

Positive Interdependence

Positive interdependence is the "glue" that holds the team together. Spencer Kagan and David and Roger Johnson agree on the importance of this element when structuring cooperative strategies. Without positive interdependence, cooperative teamwork deteriorates into group work or even individual work. There are nine ways to structure positive interdependence: goal, task, reward, role, fantasy, resource, outside enemy, duty, and identity (Johnson, Johnson, & Holubec, 1992).

1. *Goal interdependence.* All cooperative learning activities should contain goal interdependence. A clear, shared goal ties the learning of the individual student to the learning of his or her teammates. Students believe they can only achieve their learning goals if and *only if* their teammates reach their goals (Kagan, 1994). This structure is important for students with problems in traditional learning situations because it establishes an atmosphere of trust and caring within the team, traits often lacking in many troubled youth. Goal interdependence can be communicated to students by asking each of them to "learn the assigned material and make sure everyone on their team learns the material."

2. *Task interdependence.* Task interdependence involves dividing the assignment into individual duties requiring each team member to complete his or her task in order to produce the completed assignment. The use of task interdependence teaches responsibility and accountability to students.

3. *Reward interdependence.* Reward interdependence is used to reward each team member when the team achieves its goals. Rewarding positive behavior or performance helps troubled youth feel successful and build self-esteem. Some ways to structure reward interdependence include awarding bonus points or "excused from homework" passes.

4. *Role interdependence.* In role interdependence, team members are assigned roles to perform that help the team complete an assignment. Some common roles are recorder, supplier, reader, encourager, and checker. Students who feel a sense of belonging and commitment to others stay in school.

5. *Fantasy interdependence.* Fantasy interdependence involves having teams imagine that they are in a make-believe situation, such as stranded on a deserted island. In these situations, students often need to use problem-solving skills and apply concepts in new ways. Students who perceive the curriculum as challenging rather than routine may remain in school (Black, 2002).

6. *Resource interdependence.* Resource interdependence involves sharing the resources needed to complete an activity. The shared resources can be information (only one textbook), materials (only one handout), or equipment (one computer or pair of scissors). One teaching strategy designed around resource interdependence is the jigsaw method, based on the concept of piecing the puzzle of information together so as to complete the whole.

7. *Outside enemy interdependence.* An example of outside enemy interdependence is the use of friendly competition in the classroom. Healthy classroom competition among students can generate enthusiasm and motivate students to become involved in the learning process.

8. *Duty interdependence.* A relay in physical education is a good visual example of duty interdependence. A division of labor, requiring the actions of one team member to be completed before the work of another can begin, is duty interdependence. An example of a task requiring a division of labor is writing a team paper. One student is responsible for researching a topic, another for writing the document, another for word processing the document, and another for editing the document. An example in the mathematics classroom is a math relay. Each teammate is given a problem to solve that requires substituting the answer to another teammate's problem into the problem before it can be solved. This activity generates friendly competition in the classroom.

9. *Identity interdependence.* Often when students work in teams for an extended period of time, they are allowed to name their team or choose a place for team meetings. This is an example of identity interdependence. Naming the team, designing team logos, and placing them on visors, T-shirts, or place cards creates a sense of owner-

ship and belonging for students, especially those in situations of high risk.

Individual Accountability

The saying "what gets graded gets valued" is still true in education today. Individual accountability ensures that all students understand how their academic performance will be measured either during the activity or through a more formal assessment at another time (Johnson, Johnson, & Holubec, 1992). In addition to an academic assessment, team members should expect to be evaluated on their contributions to the team. Social loafing is not allowed. Students learn that cooperative learning is not group work; in cooperative learning, no one hides or is allowed a free ride. All students are accountable for teamwork and academic progress. This element helps youth who are considering leaving school see the value of their contribution to the team and of responsibility to self.

Social Skills

Another critical element for cooperative learning is social skills. In order to perform as a highly effective functioning team, students need to get to know each other, exhibit trust and respect for each other, communicate effectively, and resolve differences. Placing students in teams and asking them to be nice to one another will not guarantee success. One must teach and model social skills before placing students in working teams and evaluating their behavior. Reviewing desired social skills before placing students in teams communicates clear expectations to students.

One way to teach social skills is by using a T-chart that lists a desired team behavior. A T is drawn under the behavioral word. Expressions demonstrating what the skill looks like are written on one side of the crossbar and expressions demonstrating what the skill sounds like are written on the other side. Posting the chart in the classroom allows the teams to reference it as needed.

It is recommended that classroom teachers concentrate on a small number of skills and focus on those skills repeatedly each time teams are used until the students automatically demonstrate the skills. During the teaming process, the teacher monitors the teams and records appropriate and inappropriate team behaviors. These observations are shared with the whole class, individual teams, or students during the team-processing stage. A student can also serve as the team monitor. It is often effective to allow a student with weak social skills to serve as monitor. While monitoring the team, the student observes the rewards of appropriate behavior and the consequences of inappropriate behavior (Johnson, Johnson, & Holubec, 1992).

Team Environment

Another factor that influences team success is team environment, the fourth element of a cooperative learning activity. This involves environmental team design that promotes effective communication and successful academic achievement. All team members need to be able to see and hear each other and to speak to work effectively. Teams should be evenly spaced about a classroom. It is a good idea to illustrate appropriate team arrangements before allowing teams to assemble. Careful consideration of team arrangement will prevent team splintering or member isolation. Students with low self-esteem or limited academic success may tend to drift from the team because of their lack of trust, academic preparation, or sense of belonging.

Team size is also a factor in effective communication and teamwork. Teams should be large enough to accomplish the task but small enough so that everyone can participate and contribute ideas. Student participation correlates with student success; those who participate are more likely to enjoy the process and make academic gains (Kagan, 1994). When teams aren't working, consider decreasing the team size and strengthening the positive interdependence (Johnson, Johnson, & Holubec, 1992). By designing effective team environments and considering team size, the need for separation can be eliminated and social support developed.

Group Processing

Group processing distinguishes cooperative learning teams from group work. Teams need to be given time at the conclusion of a team session or activity to reflect on their team and individual performance. The purpose of processing is to refine and improve the effectiveness of the team and its members in achieving the goals of the team (Johnson, Johnson, & Holubec, 1992). Group processing allows students to consider what actions were helpful and harmful to the team, make decisions on which actions to continue or change next time, and reflect on the performance of each team member as well as their own.

During the group processing time, teachers supportively communicate their observations to the class and/or individual teams, celebrate team success, and set goals for future work. Class celebrations provide students with feelings of joint success and appreciation of others, develop a commitment to learning, promote enthusiasm for teamwork, and build self-esteem. By celebrating team social development and academic success, the teacher demonstrates care for students. Research conducted by Stuart Yager indicates that students in cooperative learning teams with group processing achieved higher on daily academic work, unit assessments, and retention than students who completed work in groups or as individuals only (Yager, Johnson, & Johnson, 1985).

The Benefits of Cooperative Learning

The four principles or five elements must be present for group work to be cooperative. In cooperative learning, team members promote each other's learning and success, hold each other accountable to do their fair share, demonstrate interpersonal skills needed in the workplace, and process team effectiveness. Cooperative learning, when implemented correctly, can make a difference in a student's decision to stay in school.

The use of carefully structured and monitored cooperative learning strategies in the classroom can lead to some exciting outcomes for students. By comparing the goal structures of competitive and individualistic learning with cooperative learning, researchers provide evidence that the use of cooperative learning strategies in the classroom results in higher academic achievement by all students, positive interpersonal relationships that value diversity, and mental well-being and social development (Johnson, Johnson, & Holubec, 1992; Slavin, 1983). Students gain valuable experience in teaming skills such as trustworthiness, dependability, and communication for the future workplace. Cooperative learning is a positive response to the transformations occurring in today's society: the social void left by the erosion of the family, television, and lack of family communication (Kagan, 1994). Youth in high-risk situations who are given opportunities to build trusting relationships with peers and teachers and who view the curriculum as challenging, relevant, and engaging may choose to remain in school.

Learning Styles Theory

Learning styles theory is the research that refers to how people concentrate, practice, internalize, and retain new and difficult information. Its focus is on *identifying individual preferences in terms of environmental conditions and thinking processes.*

The traditional education system focuses on and rewards the abstract learner, leaving many students with the choice of adapting for survival or leaving school. It is teacher-dominated; instruction focuses on memorization, and assessment involves quantitative data. Today's schools are much more diverse than those traditional models. More than ever, schools are recognizing and valuing diversity—not just diversity in terms of ethnicity, but also diversity of teaching and learning styles. Effective schools realize that not all students learn in the same way; they provide instruction and extracurricular activities that address the needs and interests of all students.

After examining learning styles, some teachers have changed the way they judge student ability and how they define problem students (Ojure & Sherman, 2001). Students gain an increased awareness of their learning styles through interest inventories or surveys and can select and use study habits that address learning preferences. Teachers administer learning style inventories to gain information about student preferences for learning. Using the inventory results, lessons are designed to provide all learners with opportunities to achieve, based on the strengths they bring to the classroom. Learning is easiest when material is presented through a student's strongest modality (Boyles & Contadino, 1997).

Students who experience difficulty learning in verbal and logical settings benefit from learning experiences that address their strengths as learners. When teachers gear instruction to learning styles, more students will master the content. Outside the classroom, interest inventories help administrators plan extracurricular programs and activities to support a diverse student population.

There are many approaches to learning styles theory. A well-known approach is the Myers-Briggs Type Indicator, designed to test Carl Jung's theory of psychological types. It measures the relative preferences of two opposite functions. The preferences are classified along four continuums: Extravert–Introvert, Sensitive–Intuitive, Thinking–Feeling, and Judging–Perceiving.

A second approach, based on the research of Dr. Anthony F. Gregorc (1982), considers how information is perceived and understood. According to this model, information is perceived concretely or abstractly and ordered sequentially or randomly. The pairing of how information is perceived and ordered generates four possible learning styles: Concrete Sequential, Abstract Sequential, Abstract Random, and Concrete Random.

The work of Rita Dunn and Shirley Griggs (1998) is yet another approach that concentrates on environmental preferences for learning. These preferences can be characterized into five strands: Environmental, Emotional, Sociological, Physical, and Psychological. These strands then break down into 21 elements that teachers and students can address in order to accommodate personal preferences. These preferential elements and their categories are:

- *Environmental*: sound, light, temperature, design,
- *Emotional*: motivation, persistence, responsibility, structure,
- *Sociological*: self, pair, peers, team, adult, varied,
- *Physical*: perceptual, intake, time of day, mobility,
- *Psychological:* global/analytical, hemisphericity, impulsive/reflective.

Additional learning theorists include Walter Barbe and Raymond Swassing, whose work focuses on auditory, visual, and kinesthetic learning modalities, and Herman Witkin, whose work with Navy pilots addresses information processing (Tobias, 1994). Richard Felder and Barbara Soloman of

North Carolina State University have developed the Index of Learning Styles, an inventory of learner preferences which are categorized into four main quadrants of learners: Active/Reflective; Sensing/Intuitive; Visual/Verbal; and Sequential/Global.

The Theory of Multiple Intelligences

One brain-based educational theory highlighting diversity is what Howard Gardner (1983) of Harvard University called the Theory of Multiple Intelligences. According to Gardner, intelligence is the ability to solve problems, to create problems to solve, and to contribute to one's society. Gardner believes intelligence evolves over one's lifetime, an idea quite different from the traditional definition of intelligence. He has identified the following eight intelligences:

- *verbal/linguistic*—the ability to use both oral and written language fluently to communicate effectively;
- *logical/mathematical*—the ability to use abstract thought, precision, deductive/inductive reasoning, counting, organization, and logical structure to solve abstract problems and complex relationships found in mathematics and in the scientific process;
- *musical/rhythmic*—the sensitivity to pitch, rhythm, timbre, tone, color, and emotional power of music and the sounds of one's environment to perceive, discriminate, and express all aspects of music and environmental sounds;
- *visual/spatial*—the capacity to perceive the world in mental images, that is, to see form, color, shape, and texture in the mind's eye;
- *bodily/kinesthetic*—reliance on the whole body to express ideas and feelings and the hands to produce or transform things; components are balance, dexterity, strength, flexibility, and speed;
- *intrapersonal*—the ability to assess one's own feelings: self-awareness;
- *interpersonal*—the ability to know oneself and to act adaptively to accurately assess personal strengths/weaknesses, perceive inner moods, motivations, temperaments, and desires;
- *naturalist*—the ability to recognize and classify plants, animals, and nature by their differences, patterns, configurations, and so forth.

Each of these eight intelligences can be developed, and many ways of being smart exist within each. This theory aids in identifying the learning strengths and weaknesses of students and in designing active learning instruction around both the strengths (to advance academic progress) and the weaknesses (to improve that area's level of competency).

According to Thomas Armstrong (1993), author of *Seven Kinds of Smart*, based upon this theory, schools should be asking *how are you* smart, not how smart are you.

Currently, Gardner is considering a ninth intelligence, existential intelligence, which he defines as the ability to pose and think about questions about life, death, and ultimate realities (Reese, 2002). By his definition of intelligence, still more intelligences may be named.

Benefits of the Theory of Multiple Intelligences

The Theory of Multiple Intelligences celebrates and values diversity. In an educational setting, this leads to an appreciation of differences. When students not only see but also value the differences in their classmates, they see and value their own differences in a positive, self-promoting way. Additionally, by identifying strengths and weaknesses, students take a more responsible role in the learning process. Teachers, too, can help students improve in their weaker areas by encouraging them to try ways that take them out of their comfort level and expand their capabilities. Once individual strengths are determined, teachers can use active learning strategies to help students learn.

Many educators who use active learning strategies are designing lessons addressing the eight intelligences without formally studying the Theory of Multiple Intelligences. Keeping a list of the intelligences helps teachers focus on student strengths during the planning process. Another helpful tool is a graphic organizer called a *mindmap* (Figure 15.1 on the following page).

A skill, concept, unit, or theme is placed at the center of the map. The teacher then selects activities that address each intelligence to place around the skill. Once the mindmap is complete, the teacher may present the skill through all eight activities or a select few. Not all skills need to be taught in eight ways, as it is often easy to integrate one or more of the intelligences into one activity (Schargel & Smink, 2001).

Incorporating Multiple Intelligences Theory into Classroom Practice

The Key School, opened in 1987 in Indianapolis, Indiana, became the first multiple intelligences school in the United States. The school has expanded from an elementary school to include a middle and high school. Through multiple intelligences theory and other active learning strategies, teachers and students become partners in the teaching and learning process. Students are rewarded and celebrated for special achievements, given opportunities to strengthen skills and abilities, and provided with rich learning experiences that are effective for all ages.

Figure 15.1. Mindmap

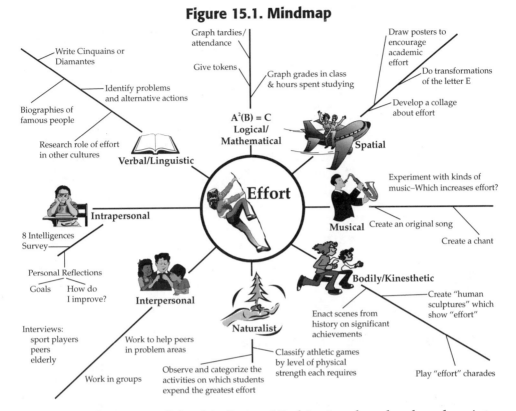

Lakes Elementary School in Lacey, Washington, has developed an integrated curriculum with emphasis on the naturalist intelligence. Students use the school grounds to develop observation skills and mentor to other students.

Project-Based Learning

The final active learning strategy addressed in this chapter is project-based learning. This strategy emphasizes learning activities that last several class periods or longer. Project-based activities are student-centered rather than teacher-centered, often interdisciplinary, address real-world problems, and often incorporate the use of technology. Students are motivated to learn because they are engaged in the learning process from start to finish, designing their own process for obtaining the necessary knowledge needed to complete the project. During the learning process students develop many of the skills desired by today's employers, including interpersonal skills, effective decision making, and taking initiative. There is an increase in teacher-to-student and student-to-student interaction as teachers become coaches, facilitators, and co-learners.

Project-based learning provides opportunities to build community relationships, as community members are involved as consultants and evaluators during project work and project presentation. One example of community and school integration is The School of Environmental Studies, known as the Zoo School, located at the Minnesota Zoo. At this school, students explore areas of interest through in-depth projects related to environmental studies.

Some troubled youth are burdened with family problems, live in unsafe environments, or have after-school employment (Clauss, 2001). Project-based learning can ease the stress these outside factors place on students. Learning becomes relevant and challenging and often takes place in environments that differ from traditional school settings.

The Seven Key Components of a Project-Based Learning Activity

According to the Challenge 2000 Multimedia Project conducted by the San Mateo County School District (Simpkins, 2003) in Redwood, California, there are seven key components for communicating, assessing, and planning project-based learning activities:

- **Content:** Interdisciplinary projects address curriculum standards.
- **Technology:** Use of various technologies should be included in the planning, development, and presentation of the projects.
- **Facilitation:** Projects need to be well structured with frequent feedback, maximizing student decision making and initiative.
- **Collaborative skills:** Students should be given opportunities to learn teaming skills.
- **Connections:** Real-world connections can be accomplished by encouraging communication with community professionals, by exploring information via the Internet, and by the issues raised in the project.
- **Time:** Adequate time should be assigned to allow for planning, revision, and reflection of student learning.
- **Assessment:** Ongoing, authentic teacher evaluations, peer evaluations, and self-evaluations are well communicated to students.

Benefits of Project-Based Learning

Project-based learning is an effective active learning strategy that engages students in the learning process and allows opportunities for them to explore their own interests. It supports and models lifelong learning. According to elementary and middle school teachers in Ross Valley School District in California, project-based learning promotes enthusiasm for learning, decreases off-task time, builds student confidence, which carries over to other activities, increases respect and understanding of others' viewpoints, and generates a feeling of connection to the community. Students from the same school district felt they benefited because no one is left out; everyone is needed. These students felt they could make a difference in their school and community after participating in project-based learning activities. Students recognized that they were using skills that would be needed in the workplace (Ridley University, 2003).

Like all active learning strategies, project-based learning has drawbacks. It can be seen as taking time that could be used to deliver curriculum standards. The use of project-based learning is hindered in some classrooms by the lack of adequate technology (Marx, Blumenfield, Krajcik, & Soloway, 1997). Even given these risks and barriers, project-based strategies can make a difference. Some schools have overcome the technology barrier; for example, Mott Hall School in New York's Community School District Six, a fourth through eighth grade magnet school, was one of the first schools to provide laptops to all students and teachers. Mott Hall uses the laptop technology to address project-based learning. Grants such as the one received by Mountlake Terrace High School in Edmonds, Washington, through the Bill and Melinda Gates Foundation, allow some schools to implement project-based learning on a smaller scale. In project-based learning situations, students and teachers are allowed to focus on in-depth, realistic, personally relevant content that engages everyone in the classroom in the learning process.

Conclusion

Schools and teachers are exploring and adapting a variety of active learning strategies to address the needs of all students. Whether a teacher chooses cooperative learning, multiple intelligence theory, project-based learning, or one of many other active learning strategies, students benefit. Academically, students interact with the content material sooner, tailor their studies to their own interests and learning preferences, and experience greater academic achievement. Socially, they build positive relationships that value diversity, develop learning partnerships, and model workplace skills. Schools using these methods have seen increases in student achievement and decreases in dropout and attendance problems. Better school performance today will lead to better citizens and employees in years to come.

References

Armstrong, T. (1993). *Seven kinds of smart*. New York: Penguin Books.

Black, S. (2002). Keeping kids in school. *American School Board Journal, 189*(12), 50–52.

Boyles, N., & Contadino, D. (1997). *The learning differences sourcebook*. Los Angeles: Lowell House.

Clauss, C. (2001). Barriers to education: Kids voice serious concerns. *On the Move With School-Based Mental Health, 5*(3), 5.

Dunn, R., & Griggs, S. (1998). *Multiculturalism and learning style: Teaching and counseling adolescents*. Westport, CT: Praeger Westport.

Felder, R. (1993). Reaching the second tier: learning and teaching styles in college science education. *J. College Science Teaching, 23*(5), 286–290.

Felder, R., & Soloman, B. (n.d.). *Index of learning styles (ILS)*. Retrieved July 10, 2002 from http://www2.ncsu.edu/unity/lockers/users/f/felder/public/ILSdir/ILS-a.htm.

Gardner, H. (1983). *Frames of mind: The theory of multiple intelligences*. New York: Basic Books.

Goodwin, L. (2000). Honoring ways of knowing. *WEEA Digest on Education Assessment*.

Gregorc, A. D. (1982). *An adult's guide to style*. Columbia, CT: Gregorc Associates.

Johnson, R., Johnson, D., & Holubec, E. (1992). *Advanced cooperative learning*. Edina, MN: Interaction Book Company.

Kagan, S. (1994). *Cooperative learning*. San Clemente, CA: Kagan Cooperative Learning.

Kroeger, O., & Thuesen, J. M. (1988). *Type talk*. New York: Delacorte Press.

Marx, R. W., Blumenfield, P. C., Krajcik, J. S., & Soloway, E. (1997). Enacting project-based science. *Elementary School Journal, 97*(4), 341–358.

Ojure, L., & Sherman, T. (2001, November 28) Learning styles: Why teachers love a concept research has yet to embrace. *Education Week, 21*(13), 33.

Reese, S. (2002). Understanding our differences. *Techniques, 77*(1), 20–23.

Ridley University. (2003). *Project-based learning benefits*. Retrieved August 17, 2003, from The Chandran Institute for Excellence and Innovation in Teaching Website: http://ridley.on.ca/departments/chandran/PBLOverview/Files/benefits.html.

Sanders, J., & Sanders, R. (1998). Anti-dropout interventions. *The Education Digest, 64*(4), 33–34.

Schargel, F., & Smink, J. (Eds.). (2001). *Strategies to help solve our school dropout problem*. Larchmont, NY: Eye on Education.

Simpkins, M. (2003). Project-based learning with multimedia: An overview. Retrieved August 15, 2003, from The Challenge 2000 Multimedia Project Website: http://pblmm.k12.ca.us/overview/25800/index.html.

Slavin, E. R. (1983). When does cooperative learning increase student achievement? *Psychological Bulletin, 94*, 429–445.

Tobias, C. (1994). *The way they learn*. Wheaton, IL: Tyndale House Publishers.

Yager, S., Johnson, D., & Johnson, R. (1985). Oral discussion, group to individual transfer, and achievement in cooperative learning groups. *Journal of Educational Psychology, 77*(1), 60–66.

16

Educational Technology: Why and How it Counts for Students At Risk

Ted Wesley

I am always ready to learn, but I do not always like being taught.

Sir Winston Churchill

The Secret of Education Lies in Respecting the Pupil.

Ralph Waldo Emerson

Appropriate use of contemporary technologies in education can powerfully promote student engagement in learning and thereby enhance academic performance and motivation for all students. Students who are academically at risk can benefit especially from technology-supported learning experiences. Recently, interrelated advances in technology capabilities, learning theories, and teaching methods have expanded the potential benefits of educational technologies for students who don't succeed, or find interest, in traditional learning experiences. Emerging values and methods of technology use, which differ substantially from earlier applications of educational technology, now present unprecedented potentialities for enhancing student interest and engagement in learning experiences and supporting improved academic performance.

Technology Benefits and Assumptions

Benefits of technology in K–12 education have been argued on grounds of both long-term and near-term advantages. Proposed long-term consequences include equipping students with computer skills and other practical and academic abilities that will be useful in later post-secondary education and/or career employment. More immediate benefits for educational effectiveness and productivity have also been claimed. Boe (1989) offers an illustrative summary of reasons why schools have traditionally invested in educational technology:

- ◆ to improve student content mastery,
- ◆ to improve student thinking skills,
- ◆ to increase individualized instruction opportunities,
- ◆ to improve student attitudes toward learning,
- ◆ to prepare students for a technology-oriented world,
- ◆ to increase teachers' job satisfaction, and
- ◆ to increase the cost-effectiveness of instruction (p. 39).

These purposes and the expectations associated with them assume persistent and engaged learners will participate in and benefit from educational technology. Fully realizing these proposed near-term and long-term effects requires that K–12 students participate actively in schooling and persist through completion of their educational program by earning a high school diploma. However, the assumption of an engaged and persistent learner is not a sound one when dealing with students academically at risk. Typically, high-risk students are effectively disengaged from education even if still attending school. For such students, the first purposes of any educational methods, including those involving technologies, must be to encourage their active and persistent involvement in school and promote academic success so they can and will graduate.

Interpreting the value of contemporary educational technology use for academically high-risk students requires consideration of their learning dilemma. Student failure and academic disengagement leading to dropout have these typical characteristics:

- ◆ Failure usually begins in early grades.
- ◆ At-risk students do not participate actively and productively in learning experiences.

- At-risk students often demonstrate less capability in the intelligences and learning styles commonly emphasized by traditional teaching methods than in others (e.g., linguistic and mathematical vs. spatial or kinesthetic intelligences, respectively (Gardner, 1993a, 1993b).

- At-risk students experience repeated failure and become increasingly discouraged about and disengaged from learning activities over time.

- At-risk students become increasingly alienated from school as they move from earlier to later grade levels, especially as they transition to middle and high school.

The following discussion focuses on ways in which technology use in education can support student engagement, persistence, and success. The discussion will address educational effectiveness of technology use as well as acceptance and employment of technologies by teachers and school leaders. A central point here is that the increasing capabilities of contemporary educational technologies, combined with advances in educational theory and practice based on expanded understanding of human learning processes, greatly amplify the potential for addressing learning needs and characteristics of high-risk students.

Trends and Discoveries: Lessons from the Field

Though the process has been halting and uneven, in the past decade enough American schools have installed a critical mass of contemporary technologies, trained a sufficient proportion of teachers, and enabled enough technology-based initiatives for some of the positive effects of technology use on at-risk students to be observed. Contemporary educational technologies widely available in schools include computers with powerful, cost-effective, and user-friendly telecommunications and multimedia capabilities; ancillary devices such as digital still and video cameras, text and image scanners, and other information manipulation tools; interactive computer-based learning software; and access to various forms of online information resources.

Experience in many schools is confirming that these technologies can play a crucial role in engaging the interest and active participation of at-risk students in learning, motivating achievement, and countering the decision to drop out. Teachers and school leaders are discovering, often serendipitously, that computer-based learning activities can change students who never begin, much less finish, conventional assignments into students who not only complete assignments but, after projects are finished, wish to continue polishing and perfecting their work. Teachers are learning that assignments that involve engaging technology-related tasks differ from the same assignments without the technology component in that, in the words of one middle school teacher, "...with the technologies, there is no groaning." Educators frequently find that students who have never wanted to do writing assignments in or out of class will write willingly and to a high level of technical correctness on a computer. Previously unmotivated students will come to school early and stay late to work on assignments (if allowed), knowing that the products of their work will be reviewed by peers, or even available to the entire world, over the Internet.

The apparently magical power of contemporary technology to have these effects on high-risk students relates to relatively recent co-evolutions in technology capabilities, teaching methods, and educational thinking that views learning as a constructive endeavor by students rather than a presentational practice by teachers or machines (Papert, 1980, 1993; Januszewski, 2001; LeBaron & Collier, 2001; Zucker & Kozma, 2003). As practicing educators acquire experience using current technologies and observe positive effects on high-risk students, they develop an appreciation of alternative ways of presenting learning activities to these students. Educators' attitudes change not only toward using technologies in their teaching, but toward what constitutes valid instructional methodology and toward the potential for learning in all students regardless of individual differences in learner characteristics.

For a variety of reasons, teacher resistance to fundamental changes in teaching associated with technology innovations has been a legendary fixture of the educational scene for decades (Cuban, 1986; Cohen, 1987; Kerr, 1990; Hodas, 1993). However, the positive developments discussed above signify substantive changes in teachers' attitudes toward technologies in recent years and in their instructional practices with technologies. How is it that contemporary technologies and what they offer students differ from preceding innovations? How is it that many teachers, whether they have approached technology with reluctance and doubt or with enthusiasm and determination, after successfully employing contemporary technologies in their work for a time, assert that they would never willingly return to their previous ways of teaching? A brief review of the evolving principles and changing applications of educational technologies will illuminate the issues of teacher acceptance and student benefit. For this, it is useful to contrast the predominant metaphors reflecting capabilities, values, and purposes of traditional vs. contemporary educational technologies. The capabilities of contemporary computing and communication technologies, coupled with changes in educational methods and theory, have led in recent years to a profound shift in the predominant metaphors of educational technology with significant implications for the education of high-risk students.

Changing Metaphors
of Educational Technology

Automation and Instrumentation–Metaphors of Teaching Technologies

Throughout most of the 20th century, the prevailing metaphor that defined applications of educational technology was *automation*. The automation metaphor, appropriated by education from industrial management and practice, was based primarily on these principles:

- Machines can perform the work of humans, including teachers, and can do it better, cheaper, and more efficiently.

- Machines can automatically process information and materials to produce products.

- Machines can be programmed for their tasks based on scientific analysis of targeted activities and results.

Automation-focused uses of technology in education have typically been grounded in values associated with efficiency of cost and effort coupled with tenets of behaviorist learning theory. These principles have guided a series of educational technologies including automated testing and programmed learning machines in the mid-20th century and much computer-assisted instructional software. In its starkest form, the automation metaphor led to efforts to partially or completely replace teachers with machines with learning content and presentation determined by experts outside of the classroom. A more finessed form of the automation metaphor, which could be called the *instrumentation* metaphor, applies technology as a set of tools whereby teachers develop their own automated presentations of materials and assessments, thereby, at least partially, replacing themselves in traditional teaching activities (see Note 1, p. 222).

Some automation-oriented technologies have attempted to address humane concerns for the personal experience of students in learning, often with a particular focus on needs and characteristics of high-risk students. These efforts sought to support psychological comfort in learning through:

- individualization of instruction,

- non-judgmental assessment,

- clear and simple criteria for learning success,

- easily assimilated lesson segments, and

- "failure-proof" learning experiences.

Although substantial enthusiasm by proponents has accompanied technology innovations based on automation and instrumentation principles, these applications have not been widely welcomed, extensively adopted, or consistently used by educators. Neither have they fundamentally altered the overall landscape of educational practice (Cuban, 1986) or improved learning among at-risk students sufficiently to diminish academic failure or reduce school dropout generally.

If technologies built on principles of teacher replacement and augmentation, instructional effectiveness and efficiency, learning reward contingencies, and psychological ease and comfort of learning have proven limited in their capacity to motivate and benefit at-risk students, then what experience-grounded claims can be made for technology's value for these students?

Emerging Metaphors—Technologies for Learning

In contemporary uses of technology, the automation and instrumentation principles are being displaced by two new metaphors of great relevance to learning activities of all students, especially those at risk. These new technology metaphors are *exploration and discovery*, and *construction and creation*. The new metaphors are based on quite different principles of technology:

Exploration and discovery:

◆ Technology can be an adaptable medium for information access and communication by students.

◆ Technology can be an instrument for student research.

Construction and creation:

◆ Technology can be used in the cognitive construction of knowledge by students.

◆ Technology can be used in the active creation of learning products by students.

In practice, these emerging educational technology metaphors reflect engaging and effective learning experiences with great promise for teaching and learning of high-risk students. They capitalize on individual learners' full range of capacities to experience lesson content, to manipulate information, to construct knowledge and understanding of targeted material, and to creatively produce learning products.

The more dynamic and participatory implications of these new metaphors signify a shift from an emphasis on teachers as presenters of knowledge to students as builders of their own knowledge. Teachers are not replaced by technologies under the new metaphors, but play the essential role of developing, providing, and supporting substantive learning experiences involving exploratory and creative activities through students' use of technologies.

The implications of these new metaphors are especially significant for students who do not perform well in traditional learning situations. The new metaphors of educational technology reflect cognitive and constructivist philosophies of learning that take account of individual variation among learners in sensory and cognitive strengths. To maximize learning opportunities for all students, teachers' repertoires of instructional methods can and do grow to encompass a range of approaches activating a broad spectrum of students' capabilities. Contemporary technologies offer teachers a variety of tools to employ in this effort.

Educational Technologies and Learning Alternatives for At-Risk Learners

Employing technologies to provide alternative learning experiences that support enhanced sensory and cognitive access to course content and motivate participation in learning activities involves the following focuses: multiple learning options, active manipulation of information, and interactive and collaborative learning.

Alternatives and Multiples: Options = Opportunities

Educational approaches that accommodate individual learning characteristics are effective in teaching at-risk students. Many students fail at education not because they lack capacity for learning in some pervasive and absolute sense, but because traditional learning experiences do not capitalize on their strongest learning capabilities. Differences in learning styles, sensory modality preferences, pace of learning, patterns of intelligence, and other factors place some students at a disadvantage in the traditional learning situations that are most familiar to and comfortable for their teachers. These students can learn more effectively when their particular learning strengths are engaged in technologically supported activities. When teachers incorporate computer multimedia technologies in learning experiences, for instance, lesson content can be enriched with visual, auditory, color, text, motion, and other sensory inputs in highly flexible ways to engage perception, promote interest, enhance comprehension, and enable active manipulation of learning materials and products by all students.

Active Engagement: Hands-On = Minds-On

Learning activities in which students actively pursue, discover, and manipulate information to solve problems or advance projects they find interesting are inherently motivating. Employing electronic information resources for this purpose involves a variety of sense modalities and intelligences and opens information manipulation to all students.

Student manipulation of lesson content using interactive multimedia technologies exploits individual patterns of sense modalities, intelligences, and performance abilities enabling all students to demonstrate learning and to experience success. Offering students multiple and flexible approaches to manipulating the material, image, auditory, and conceptual representations of lesson content augments their capacity to engage and explore the content, construct meaningful understanding, and create authentic and symbolic products that demonstrate learning.

Alone and Together:
Individual and Collaborative Learning

Online research technologies such as the Internet and other electronic resources can be utilized for both individual and group learning activities. Similarly, students working individually or collectively can use multimedia technologies to create products that reflect their learning. Teachers implementing technologies can blend individual and group activities to add variety of learning experiences to their lesson plans. The socializing benefits of group learning projects and production activities are considerable. Academically stronger students can help other students build their comprehension and skills in dealing with content. Technologically stronger students can provide peer support to expand their colleagues' technology capabilities in the context of content-rich learning experiences. Furthermore, of particular relevance to high-risk students, participation in group learning activities, where successes and failures are shared among group members, can create a psychologically safe environment for struggling students and counter the tendency to withdraw and disengage from schoolwork due to a sense of personal failure. Collaborative learning can supportively encourage the mentality that failures and errors in the learning activity process are acceptable as part of the creative dynamics of learning, leading ultimately to success in academic performance (see Note 2, p. 223).

Intended Benefits and Fringe Benefits:
Lessons from the Field

Successful implementation of technology applications based on the new metaphors fits a wide range of learner characteristics and leads to a consistent pattern of effects on learners. These effects are particularly important for high-risk students.

Success!—
Public Esteem and Self-Regard

Employing technologies in accord with the new metaphors is seen in practice to activate the interest of students in many ways and encourage participation in learning activities and in creating learning products. Students who are unsuccessful in traditional learning situations can find ways to be successful using diverse technologies. With success experiences, students' develop enhanced self-esteem in association with their learning activities. This process creates a self-reinforcing spiral of improved performance and learning over time.

Motivation and Interest—
Electronic Attraction

Interest in learning through technologically augmented experiences motivates students to seek access to technology resources outside of the usual class and lab times such as during free periods, lunch times, and before and after regular school hours. Educators have begun to accommodate this interest by arranging additional technology access time through informal and formal arrangements for individuals and groups of learners.

Role Reversal—
The Student Becomes the Master

A familiar consequence of technology implementation in schools is that students quickly surpass their teachers in technology competency. Many teachers have learned to use this to advantage and rely on technology competencies among their students as a resource for student peer teaching and support for technology use and for technical problem solving in classrooms and labs.

Outcomes—
Assessment and Performance

The ultimate test of technology use in education is to increase student performance on formal measures. This is the universal obsession of the accountability movement. For at-risk students, it is essential to keep in mind that technology use is first of all aimed at engaging students in the processes of research, exploration, discovery, knowledge construction, and learning product creation, and for all of these processes to motivate interest and involvement in learning and persistence in school. If these results occur, the benefits can be substantial for at-risk students. These processes, if successful, should result in increased ability for students to demonstrate learning on formal assessments. Learning experiences can and should be designed by teachers to ensure that this happens.

Nonetheless, if standard measures of learning rely excessively on sensory and cognitive abilities other than those that are strongest for at-risk students, a performance gap can be expected between what a student knows and what he or she can demonstrate knowing. Just as alternative learning methods are necessary for at-risk students, so alternative assessments that capitalize on students' dominant capabilities for expression of knowledge should also be available and creditable.

What Teachers Know and Do:
Lessons from the Field

Teaching Kids to Use Technology—
Forget about It!

Teaching today's students to use the new computer and telecommunication technologies is about as challenging as teaching ducks to swim. A brief introduction to the operation of software, digital cameras, minicams, and the like is usually sufficient if followed by hands-on practice. Hands-on practice is especially effective in the context of learning experiences that are about more than merely learning to use technology. Students who are at a disadvantage in traditional learning situations often demonstrate surprising advancement and capability when learning to use technologies that engage a wide range of abilities and intelligences. Students who perform less well academically often become experts and can be of great value as peer instructors of technology use. Capability for effective technology use spreads rapidly among students in groups if they are allowed to communicate with and support each other. Teachers who take advantage of student expertise and encourage peer teaching and technical support can relieve themselves of much of the burden of technology teaching and apply more of their attention to course content instruction.

The Other Way Around—
Integrating the Curriculum into Technology

Phrases such as "integrating technology into the curriculum" or "integrating technology into teaching" are commonplaces in current educational technology discourse. Such expressions refer, often with admonitory intent, to fitting technology-related activities into instructional sequences. The phraseology also intentionally seeks to emphasize that technology use and knowledge are subordinate to and should be in the service of actual course content learning. Teachers and technology promoters alike have expressed concern that learning to use technology should not outweigh emphasis on addressing academic content and related objectives and standards.

This section's heading, "Integrating the Curriculum into Technology," is not intended to imply that technology learning should predominate over curricular content learning. It is intended to reflect an effective approach to technology use. Teachers new to integrating technology into learning often conceive the task as imbedding occasional isolated technology activities here and there throughout a course sequence as "enrichment" or even as a reward to students. A fuller understanding of the power of contemporary technologies views the "integration" process as embedding curricular content within technology-based activities that serve as pathways to the content and shape students' access to and processing of the material. Wrapping an engaging technology-supported activity around course content materials especially amplifies such access by nontraditional learners.

As an example of this practice, a social studies teacher used the approach in teaching a unit on the American Civil War. Her students were assigned to produce a multimedia project involving digital photography and video. The teacher organized the project's learning criteria around state curriculum standards for the unit content. She arranged for her class to attend a Civil War battle reenactment where, working in small groups, students gathered visual, audio, and textual information firsthand. While processing their original materials and creating multimedia products, students were also involved in related lectures, reading assignments, and other non-technological learning experiences. At the end, student groups presented their multimedia projects to classmates as lessons and were graded, primarily, on the substantive content of their projects. This activity motivated a high level of task involvement among all students, capitalized on the benefits of collaboration, and offered all learners multiple avenues to experience, process, and learn the course content.

Creating Context— Reasons for Learning

A perennial challenge by unsuccessful students appears generally as the question, "Why should I learn about [history, geometry, algebra...]? What use is it?" Such questions are typically answered by reference to long-term, eventual values of the knowledge that appear irrelevant or inconsequential to disengaged students. Activities such as the Civil War history project described above provide a more immediate contextual purpose for learning course content. Meeting informational needs of a project that students find interesting creates a meaningful context in which course material is immediately relevant and useful.

Redistribution of Authority— Power to the Pupil

Teachers who effectively employ contemporary technologies in their teaching find that issues of power and control undergo modification in the classroom. Technology offers an opportunity for students who readily acquire technological ability to become more active agents in the learning environment. Furthermore, project-oriented learning activities that capitalize on technology's ability to engage all students depend on students' increased self-control over learning activities to be effective. These factors require teachers to extend empowerment to students, giving up some measure of top-down control of the learning environment.

Teachers have reported on not only their own unreadiness to relinquish close control over learning activities to students, but also the unpreparedness of students to take on such self-management of learning activities. Some teachers have found it good practice to organize the transition from teacher-controlled learning experiences to student-centered activities through a progressive process over time. Throughout a school term, teachers can systematically and progressively shift the responsibility for directly managing learning projects over to students as they work individually and/or in groups. Eventually, however, the need for such transitional processes may diminish as students of all abilities come to be involved in project-oriented, problem-based learning activities employing the capabilities of contemporary technologies throughout their school years and become adept at and socialized to student-managed learning activities.

Conclusion

Until recently, the predominant approaches to educational technology use, shaped by restricted concepts of learning and the modest operational capabilities of available technologies, have had limited power to extend effective learning experiences to students at risk. Now, burgeoning technological capacity, usability, and reliability; improving cost/capability ratios; expanding concepts of learning and growth; emerging conceptions of the organization and functioning of educational institutions; increasing experience by educators of the potentialities of technology; and advancing understanding of the complexities of intelligence and learning abilities are flowing together to provide rich, active, substantive, and engaging learning experiences that motivate effort and academic accomplishment among all students.

Notes

Note 1: Automation metaphor technology applications focus on productivity and efficiency in teaching and on control and predictability of learning experiences. They typically involve:

- lesson material presented in small, discrete segments,
- programmability of learning experiences,
- technical control over the pace and sequence of instructional procedures,
- immediate feedback of performance results,
- discrete positive reinforcements precisely correlated with discrete correct performance responses, and

- automatic presentation of remedial procedures and supplemental materials in response to deficient performance responses.

Note 2. Notably, such group activities present a stark contrast to automation-based models in which students typically worked in isolation, in some instances with the specific intention of keeping their performance struggles and failures unknown to others.

References

Boe, T. (1989). The next step for educators and the technology industry: Investing in teachers. *Educational Technology 29*(3), 39–44.

Cohen, D. K. (1987). Educational technology, policy, and practice. *Educational evaluation and policy analysis. 9*(2), 153–170.

Cuban, L. (1986). *Teachers and machines: The classroom use of technology since 1920.* New York: Teachers College Press.

Gardner, H. (1993a). *Multiple intelligences: The theory in practice.* New York: Basic Books.

Gardner, H. (1993b). *Frames of mind: The theory of multiple intelligences.* New York: Basic Books.

Hodas, S. (1993). Technology refusal and the organizational culture of schools. *Educational Policy Analysis Archives* [On-line serial] *1*(10). Available by e-mail: LISTSERV @ASUACAD.BITNET Message: GET HODAS V1N10 F=MAIL.

Januszewski, A. (2001). *Educational technology: The development of a concept.* Englewood, CO: Libraries Unlimited, Inc.

Kerr, S. T. (1990). Technology: education: justice: care or thoughts on reading Carol Gilligan. *Educational Technology 30*(11), 7–12.

LeBaron, J., & Collier, C. (Eds). (2001). *Successful technology infusion in schools.* San Francisco: Jossey-Bass.

Papert, S. (1980). *Mindstorms: Children, computers, and powerful ideas.* New York: Basic Books.

Papert, S. (1993). *The children's machine.* New York: Basic Books.

Zucker, A., & Kozma, R. (2003). *The Virtual high school: Teaching generation V.* New York: Teachers College Press.

17

Individualized Instruction

Deborah M. Switzer

Every person has a diverse set of experiences on which to build knowledge. Each has a set of values, instilled by family and culture. Each has special interests. Because of this uniqueness, each child needs different things from an instructional setting. When the teacher adjusts instruction for each student according to his or her needs, this is called individualized instruction.

Individualized instruction has been shown to be an effective teaching strategy for at-risk students (Hamby, 1989). From Socrates recitation to Vygotsky scaffolding, educators have used many flavors of individualized instruction to reach each child. Individualized instruction can be broken down into two major components: learning and motivation. To individualize learning means to recognize and build upon each child's unique past experiences and prior knowledge. To individualize motivation means to recognize and use the keys to a child's interests, goals, and confidence. Effective individualized instruction considers both individualized learning and individualized motivation.

Individualized Learning

When a person is learning something for the first time, the most efficient and effective way to get that information into long-term memory is to find something already in memory to which to *hook*. Imagine a room full of floating, glowing globes. The globes are connected to each other with distinct rays of light. You walk into the room with a new globe in your hand. To get the globe to stay in the room, you must connect it to at least one of the existing globes. You find a likely candidate and spin your strand of light between the globes. It anchors. You have just taught that child something new. But notice that to do that you found something she already knew and helped her make the connection. That is teaching. During instruction, the teacher gives the new information *meaning* by getting it to *hook* to prior knowledge. To individualize learning means to recognize that each child's set of glowing globes (concepts) and rays of light (relationships between those concepts) are floating in unique orientations to each other in that room. Additionally, some of the globes and rays are one-of-a-kind, others are misunderstandings, and some globes and rays are missing entirely, all according to that child's personal set of life experiences. To individualize learning, a teacher must assess a child's unique existing knowledge and then hook to that knowledge.

Since the teacher cannot see into a child's head, prior knowledge must be inferred through information gathered from many sources. Initially the teacher must use pretesting, questioning, and observation to tease out the child's unique set of existing knowledge. Test scores and past reports can add valuable information. As the year progresses, close monitoring to guarantee that learning occurred before moving on to the next standard is critical.

But understanding the existing knowledge structure, the orientation and content of those glowing globes, is only the beginning of the job. The primary job is adding new globes, and spinning new and more complex connecting rays of light. The more connections made between a concept and existing knowledge, the more meaningful, and therefore the more useful, information will be. The instructional philosophy known as *constructivism* centers on the fact that the most effective teaching allows learners to give meaning to new learning in light of their unique prior knowledge (Keefe & Jenkings, 2000; Caine & Caine, 1991).

Constructivist teachers

♦ set up problems for the students to solve, allowing them to draw inferences and conclusions beginning with what they already know (Palincsar, 1986);

♦ recognize that prior knowledge is a major factor in comprehension of new material (Kujawa & Huske, 1995);

- connect curriculum content to what is familiar from culture and experiences (Beyer, 1991; Peshkin, 1992);
- include techniques like individual and group summarizing, brainstorming, Socratic dialogue, and problem-solving processes (Jones, Valdez, Nowakowski, & Rasmussen, 1994); and
- use class discussion and student-developed graphic organizers to activate and organize prior knowledge.

Resources for teachers offer a wealth of information on effective teaching strategies for at-risk youth that allow these students to construct knowledge. Central to all of these is active, experiential learning—creating a situation where the child is actively interacting with the new information, forging those new concepts and relationships (Caine & Caine, 1991; Cuban, 1989). Instructional strategies designed to encourage the learner to be the co-producer of knowledge, rather than simply a receiver of knowledge, include

- problem-based learning and reciprocal teaching (Palincsar, 1986),
- peer tutoring (Greenwood, Delquadri, & Hall, 1989),
- cooperative learning (Johnson & Johnson, 1990),
- hands-on learning,
- journaling,
- projects,
- role play,
- simulation, and
- inquiry.

The teacher facilitates learning by providing support, or scaffolding (Vygotsky, 1978), while the student is challenged. High achieving learning environments have proven effective for at-risk youth when the chosen activities are meaningful, authentic, and related to students' culture, experiences, and prior knowledge (Howard, 1990; Levin, 1988). The idea is to "involve students at all grade levels in real-life situations that force them to confront issues of personal living" (Hamby, 1989, p. 25).

To individualize instruction for at-risk students, the teacher needs to choose flexible strategies that allow for student differences. Effective instruction for at-risk youth must include opportunity for intensive one-on-one remediation when necessary, especially in reading (Slavin & Madden, 1989). Unfortunately, typical pull-out programs with at-risk students rarely use higher-order thinking, nor are they challenging, interesting, meaningful, or contextualized (Means & Knapp, 1991). By contrast, effective individualized instruction offers flexible time limits so that students can work at their own pace, opportunities for students to ask questions, one-on-one assistance, continual monitoring of student progress, and consistent feedback (Hamby, 1989).

Even if a teacher has activated the child's prior knowledge, and designed an instructional situation that allows each child to build on his or her unique existing knowledge, learning may not occur. Ultimately, learning occurs by the will of the student. The child must be motivated to learn.

Individualized Motivation

Our society, through law, requires that children go to school. We cannot assume that every child comes to school motivated to learn. To engender motivation, it is important to recognize the individual differences of each child and how these differences play into his or her motivations. We need to individualize motivation strategies.

A useful theory for understanding motivation is *VIE theory* (Green, 1992). VIE theory states that

Motivation = Valence **times** Instrumentality **times** Expectancy

In other words, the motivation to perform a specific behavior will be influenced by the value of the behavior and related goals (valence), multiplied by the perceived probability that the behavior will lead to the goals (instrumentality), multiplied by the perceived likelihood of successfully performing the behavior (expectancy). The fact that the elements are multiplied has two critical implications. First, if *any one* of the elements is zero, motivation will be zero (i.e., there will be no motivation for that behavior). Second, increasing any one of the elements enhances motivation. Teachers who understand and maximize each element can set the stage for motivated learning.

Goals

We choose behaviors in order to accomplish something, to advance toward a goal. We pull weeds so that the pretty or edible plants will have room to flourish. We go to a movie to have fun. We study for a test in order to make a good grade. To understand our motivation to perform a behavior, we must also consider the goal of that behavior. Sometimes the goal is simply the enjoyment or challenge of the behavior itself, for example, going to a movie. But much of the time the behavior has little intrinsic interest or value. In fact, it might be somewhat aversive (like studying for a test instead of going to that movie). But we choose to perform the behavior anyway, because of the associated goal (making a good grade).

Individualized motivation must consider goals. Academic behaviors such as doing homework, paying attention, or studying do not exist in a vacuum. They have a purpose, and that purpose should be clear to the student. The teacher must work with the student to develop clear goals, and then associate these goals with specific behaviors. In the next two sections it will become clear that these goals should be valuable to the student, as well as strongly connected to the corresponding behavior.

Valence: *V* I E

For motivation to exist, the behavior and/or the goal must have positive value, or valence. If you worked in a widget factory, either it would need to be fun making those widgets, or you would need to get some reward for making the widgets (satisfaction from how the widgets are used, or a paycheck). In other words, either the behavior has to have value (be fun or interesting or satisfying to perform), or the goal of the behavior has to have value (the consequences are important, fulfilling, or valuable).

How can teachers make classroom activities fun or interesting?

- Links to prior experience often spark student engagement (Maehr, 1984). An interest inventory can help the teacher gather ideas, especially when it includes questions delving into the cultural diversity in the classroom. A teacher might incorporate the students' names, hobbies, and other personal interests in the activities, or let students choose from a variety of topics and mediums.

- Using technology can make an activity more interesting (Means & Olson, 1995). At-risk children from low-income families are less likely to have home computers (Becker & Sterling, 1987); they may find it novel and interesting to do even simple skill practice on a computer.

- A sense of ownership—the student's perception that the activity was of his or her own conception and execution—can also add value to a behavior (Brophy, 1987).

Another way to make an activity satisfying is to incorporate social activity, such as tutoring, sharing ideas, and working with a team.

- Peer tutoring programs (keeping in mind that at-risk youth can serve as tutors themselves) give students an opportunity to learn from each other (Hamby, 1989).

- Using cooperative learning teams leads to higher achievement than competitive activities, with more engagement and more solutions to problems (Johnson and Johnson, 1990).

- Cooperative learning teams are a source of social support, leading to increases in confidence (Erikson, 1987).

The most effective recipe for at-risk students appears to be a combination of instruction in small groupings of students with similar skill level and instructional needs, progressing to student work teams that are heterogeneous, with mixed sexes, cultures, abilities, and socioeconomic backgrounds (Slavin

& Madden, 1989; Jones et al., 1994). The instructional groups receive information from the teacher at an appropriate level, and then the work teams master the material, with members supporting their peers, and all members sharing their ideas. A classroom community that values diversity and multiple perspectives will build upon the strengths of the members (Jones et al., 1994). At-risk students need to feel that their participation is meaningful (Benard, 1995). Assignments can be personalized within cooperative learning teams and peer tutoring sessions (Oakes, 1990).

If a behavior does not have positive value, then the value must come from the goals associated with that behavior. At-risk youth respond especially well to two types of goals: useful skill acquisition and rewards.

Educators have long recognized the value of usefulness—how a skill fits into the context of everyday life (Cuban, 1989). All students want to understand how new information and skills will benefit them. Math story problems, science labs, problem-solving and critical thinking—any activity that puts a skill into context—can add value to goals. So can authentic activities—real-world tasks that are challenging and integrate several subject areas (Means, Chelemer, & Knapp, 1991; Cuban, 1989). Using computers within an activity can add real-world practice in word processing, design and graphing software, spreadsheets, and databases (Means & Olson, 1995). Activities should be designed around the concept of engaged learning—challenging, authentic, problem-based tasks that continue for a sustained amount of time, in collaboration with peers and mentors (Jones et al., 1994). Authentic assessments allow students to perform in a real-life context. This type of assessment is especially valid for at-risk students, since the hands-on, realistic nature of the situation increases the perceived value of the activity, therefore increasing motivation.

But it is difficult to put all academic learning into valued, real-life contexts. In this case, adding a reward structure can be useful. Incentive systems are not new. Teachers who have students list on an index card the things they most like about school create a treasure chest of incentives. They can then choose activities from the list to reward completing assignments, turning in a week's worth of homework, or other target behaviors. Approval and praise, from the teacher, classmates, or parents, can be another strong incentive. Many teachers use a class store, where points are earned and cashed in for a variety of items such as pencils, memo pads, and key chains. A gentle reminder for those skeptics who question the use of incentives—how long would any of us work if we were not going to receive a paycheck, or accomplish something useful? In any case, it is important that the incentives are strongly associated with academic achievement (Newman, 1989), and are individualized—that there are a variety of incentives to choose from—so that each student can pick something that they value. For all students, but particularly at-risk students, it is important to remember to recognize not just high achievement, but incremental improvement (Hamby, 1989).

Instrumentality: V / E

Motivation to perform a behavior depends on the perception that the behavior will lead to the goal. If your paycheck depends on the number of widgets you produced but not their quality, why make quality widgets? If studying for hours does not lead to a better test grade, why study the next time? Students must make the connection that hard work leads to academic achievement (and therefore to rewards) (Newman, 1989).

Teachers must establish a very clear connection between behavior and consequences from the beginning, and then follow through fairly and consistently. A personal contract is a wonderful way to communicate to at-risk students the expected behaviors and associated goals. Spelling out behaviors and rewards in a written document creates clarity; having both the teacher and the student sign the contract generates a sense of commitment for both parties. Strong instrumentality thrives in a classroom grounded in mutual trust and respect, fairness, communication, and consistency.

Expectancy: V I *E*

The third component of motivation is expectancy—the perception that the behavior can be achieved with the skills and resources at hand. No matter what incentive the factory foreman offers to workers who turn out 1000 widgets a day, your motivation will be low if you know that parts are in short supply, or that the machinery breaks down at high speed, or that you haven't mastered one of the steps in the process.

Students must believe that they have all the resources they need to complete the activity, like materials, books, and opportunity for questions. Motivated students are confident. They feel they have the time, skill, and endurance necessary to successfully accomplish the task (Erickson, 1987). Frustration comes readily to those who perceive that they do not know or have what they need to succeed.

What can schools do to individualize and maximize expectancy for the at-risk child?

◆ Have high expectations of success and communicate this belief to each student (Benard, 1995).

◆ Create a caring environment, a social support that is not contingent upon academic success. At-risk students tend to perceive school as aversive and threatening (Hamby, 1989). To counteract, the environment has be safe and comfortable both physically and emotionally, allowing the students to feel that their skills and knowledge are valued.

- Give each child the time needed to finish the project.
- Provide prompt, specific feedback on activities.
- When the activity allows, be flexible in the form it takes. For example, if one student's learning preferences include quiet introspection, consider letting him go to the library or complete part of the activity at home. If another prefers movement, consider allowing her to perform a skit or dance to show what she has learned. A learning preference develops from strengths and past successes; allowing children an occasional activity aligned with their particular preferences will increase their expectancy for success.

Conclusion

At-risk students respond to individualized instruction. To be effective, individualized instruction must consider both learning and motivation. Effective individualized learning hooks new material to prior knowledge, recognizing the child's culture and experiences. It includes active interaction with the content in authentic activities. Remediation and flexible time limits are available, as well as frequent monitoring and feedback of progress.

To individualize motivation, the teacher must consider the child's valence, instrumentality, and expectancy (VIE) for the behavior. Either the activity or its associated goals must have valence. That means either the activity itself is fun or interesting, or the goal of the activity is a reward or useful skill acquisition. The child must be aware of the instrumentality, or the connection between the activity and its associated goals. And there must be high expectancy of successful completion of the activity. That means the child must perceive that he or she has the skills and resources needed, within a supportive environment of high expectations.

References

Becker, H. J., & Sterling, C. W. (1987). Equity in school computer use: National data and neglected considerations. *Journal of Educational Computing Research, 3*(3), 298–311.

Benard, B. (1995). Fostering resiliency in urban schools. In B. Williams (Ed.), *Closing the achievement gap: A vision to guide change in beliefs and practice.* Oak Brook, IL: Research for Better Schools and North Central Regional Education Laboratory.

Beyer, B. K. (1991). *Teaching thinking skills: A handbook for elementary school teachers.* Boston: Allyn and Bacon.

Brophy, J. (1987). Synthesis of research on strategies for motivating students to learn. *Educational Leadership, 45*(2), 40–48.

Caine, R. N., & Caine, G. (1991). *Making connections: Teaching and the human brain.* Alexandria, VA: Association for Supervision and Curriculum Development.

Cuban, L. (1989). At-risk students: What teachers and principals can do. *Educational Leadership, 46*(5), 29–32.

Erickson, F. A. (1987). Transformation and school success: The politics and culture of educational achievement. *Anthropology and Education Quarterly, 19*(3), 335–356.

Green, T. B. (1992). *Performance and Motivation for Today's Workforce: A Guide to Expectancy Theory Applications.* London: Quorum Books.

Greenwood, C., Delquadri, J. C., & Hall, V. R. (1989). Longitudinal effects of classwide peer tutoring. *Journal of Educational Psychology, 81*(3), 371–383.

Hamby, J. V. (1989). How to get an "A" on your dropout prevention report card. *Educational Leadership, 46*(5), 21–28.

Howard, J. (1990). *Getting smart: The social construction of intelligence.* Lexington, MA: The Efficacy Institute.

Johnson, D, & Johnson, R. (1990). *Learning together and alone.* New York: Prentice Hall.

Jones, B., Valdez, G., Nowakowski, J., & Rasmussen, C. (1994). *Designing learning and technology for educational reform.* Oak Brook, IL: North Central Regional Educational Laboratory.

Kajawa, S., & Huske, L. (1995). *The strategic teaching and reading project guidebook (rev. ed.).* Oak Brook, IL: North Central Regional Educational Laboratory.

Keefe, J. W., & Jenkings, J. M. (2000). *Personalized instruction: Changing classroom practice.* Larchmont, NY: Eye on Education.

Levin, H. (1988). Accelerated schools for disadvantaged students. *Educational Leadership, 44*(6), 19–21.

Maehr, M. L. (1984). Meaning and motivation: Toward a theory of personal investment. In R. E. Ames and C. Ames (Eds.), *Research on Motivation in Education, Vol. 1, Student Motivation.* Orlando, FL: Academic Press.

Means, B., Chelemer, C., & Knapp, M. S. (Eds.). (1991). *Teaching advanced skills to at-risk students: Views from research and practice.* San Francisco: Jossey-Bass.

Means, B., & Knapp, M. S. (1991). Models for teaching advanced skills to educationally disadvantaged children. In B. Means & M. S. Knapp (Eds.), *Teaching advanced skills to educationally disadvantaged students.* Washington, DC: U.S. Department of Education, Office of Planning, Budget and Evaluation.

Means, B., & Olson, K. (1995). *Technology and education reform: Technical research report, Volume 1: Findings and conclusions.* Menlo Park, CA: SRI International.

Newman, F. M. (1989). Student engagement and high school reform. *Educational Leadership, 46*(5), 34–36.

Oakes, J., Ormseth, T., Bell, R., & Camp, P. (1990). *Multiplying inequalities: The effects of race, social class, and tracking on opportunities to learning mathematics and science.* Santa Monica, CA: RAND Corporation.

Palincsar, A. S. (1986). Reciprocal teaching. In *Teaching reading as thinking.* Oak Brook, IL: North Central Regional Educational Laboratory.

Peshkin, A. (1992). The relationship between culture and curriculum: A many fitting thing. In P.W. Jackson (Ed.), *Handbook on research on curriculum* (248–267). New York: Macmillan.

Slavin, R. E, & Madden, N. A. (1989). What works for students at risk: A research synthesis? *Educational Leadership, 46*(5), 4–13.

Vygotsky, L. S. (1978). *Mind in society: The development of higher psychological processes.* Cambridge, MA: Harvard University Press.

18

Career and Technical Education: Increasing School Engagement

James R. Stone III

The value of career and technical education (CTE) in the overall high school experience for American youth has long been debated. In the wake of *No Child Left Behind*, the debate has sharpened to focus on how CTE supports the goals of increasing academic achievement and closing the achievement gap. Of particular interest is how basic literacy and math skills are developed in the context of CTE.

Before we can think about closing achievement gaps or improving academic achievement, we have to ensure that students are in schools to learn. It is evident that if students leave school prematurely, schools will not be able to help them master the skills thought to be necessary in the workplace or in future education.

In this chapter, we review recent evidence on the role of CTE in reducing dropouts. For this we rely on two sets of data: one from the class of 1992 and the other from youth who graduated, or should have graduated, in the late

1990s. Then we explore CTE-based strategies the evidence shows are connected to keeping youth in schools.

CTE and Dropouts: The Evidence

CTE has long been thought to have a role in reducing dropout rates
among high school students. Until recently, however, the data to support this
contention have been relatively sparse. In addition, CTE has undergone tremendous changes in the past decade due to reform-oriented federal legislation (the School-To-Work Opportunities Act, and Perkins II, and Perkins III).
Although more time will be needed to assess the real impact of this legislation on the American schools and students, there are already some interesting trends uncovered. For example, we found that CTE students are taking
more math and science and higher levels of math and science than their general track counterparts (Stone & Aliaga, 2002), which suggests that the reforms of the 1990s are beginning to have an impact on CTE students'
course-taking behavior.

But what is the impact of participating in CTE and the likelihood of dropping out of high school? And if CTE does help reduce dropout rates, what is it
within CTE that we can link to this outcome? For the purpose of this discussion, we will refer to CTE and CTE-related activities as including enrollment
in the CTE "major" or concentration, in a career pathway or career academy,
in tech prep and/or in any of the work-based learning activities (cooperative
education, job shadowing, mentoring, school-based enterprise, and
internship/apprenticeship).

Research on the relationship between participation in CTE and dropping
out of high school has yielded mixed results. Two different analyses of the
National Education Longitudinal Study of 1988—NELS:88 (U.S. Department of
Education, 2003) came to two different conclusions. The *National Assessment
of Vocational Education* (Silverberg, Warner, Goodwin, & Fong, 2002) found
there was no relationship between students classified as CTE concentrators
(those who took three or more labor market preparation courses in a sequence) and a reduced probability of dropping out of high school.

Plank's (2001) analyses of the NELS:88 examined CTE as a proportion of
the high school experience or as a ratio, and found that the greater the percentage of CTE in a youth's high school experience, the lower the probability
of youth dropping out. This was especially true for lower-ability youth. He
concluded that a balanced combination of CTE and academic courses may indeed reduce the possibility of dropping out. For lower-ability youth, a ratio of
slightly more than half of the total high school coursework invested in CTE
maximized the likelihood of staying in school. He then suggested that if a
middle-range mix of CTE and academic courses can lower the risk of drop-

ping out for some students, such a mix should be encouraged, even if it brings slight reductions of overall academic achievement. However, he warned, an overemphasis of career and technical education courses may increase the risk of dropping out. Much like Plank's (2001) suggestion of combining CTE with a solid academic background, Brown (1998) also proposes combining CTE with other programs that address the special conditions that place individuals at risk.

More recent data are available through a new study (the *National Longitudinal Survey of Youth 1997*, or NLSY97) sponsored by the Bureau of Labor Statistics (2003). This survey included youth who were 12 to 16 years old in 1997, or who would graduate in 1999 and beyond. Our findings based on this survey are similar to those from the NAVE; that is, there does not seem to be a CTE effect on dropout rates when youth are categorized into curriculum concentrations (CTE, academic, general, or dual). This may be construed as either good news: CTE does not increase the likelihood of dropping out of school—or bad news: CTE does not reduce the likelihood of dropping out of school. Unfortunately, the transcripts for all students in this survey are not available, so we cannot replicate Plank's approach.

Dropping Out in 1999

The NLSY97, with its present analytic limitations, does provide an up to date picture of who drops out of high school. Drop outs in this analysis are identified as those who have neither a high school diploma nor a GED, or who are working on a GED, or have obtained a GED as "drop outs" as they have not obtained a conventional high school credential (for an extended discussion of this approach, see Greene, 2001).

We found that 11.3 percent of this cohort left school before completing a high school degree. By comparison, the *Current Population Survey* of October 2000 (U.S. Census Bureau, 2003) reports dropout rates of between 5.8 percent for 16 and 17 year olds and 12.6 percent for 18 and 19 year olds. The findings from the NLSY97 are consistent with the Current Population Survey for the same age cohorts (for a copy of the tables containing data referred to in this report, please contact author).

However, we expect that the NLSY97 figure may understate the true dropout rate within this cohort. We suspect that when asked if they completed high school, many noncompleters will answer yes to avoid embarrassment. Also, the NLSY97 lost about 9 percent of its original sample in subsequent follow-ups (Bureau of Labor Statistics, 2003, p. 8). We suspect that many, if not most of these missing cases were dropouts.

Our analysis found that males drop out more than females; blacks drop out more than whites; and Hispanics drop out more often than non-Hispanics. Youth in urban areas and in the Southern United States drop out at a higher rate than other youth. Youth from poorer families drop out at higher rates than others. Parents' education is also related to the dropping out of high school but in a curious pattern. Youth whose parents' did not graduate from high school exhibited higher drop out rates with the rates declining with more educated parents. However, youth whose parents started a graduate degree saw an increase in the drop out trend over youth whose parents had attained a college degree. Youth who drop out of high school exhibit different course taking patterns before leaving school. Not surprisingly, youth who are more inclined to leave school take less math and science than those who do not.

Factors Predicting Who Drops Out of High School

From the descriptive analyses we move to identifying predictors of youth who drop out of high school. First, enrollment in the CTE concentration has a neutral effect on dropping out of high school. In other words, being in the CTE (and for this matter in the General or Dual concentration) does not have a significant impact on drop out behavior when we control for background characteristics. Only youth who are self-described as academic concentrators are significantly less likely to drop out of high school.

But our analyses did reveal that two CTE-related activities were also significantly related to a reduced probability of dropping out of high school. Youth who participated in a career major or career pathway were about half as likely to drop out of school as youth who did not participate in a career pathway. Youth who participated in any form of work-based learning (cooperative education, job shadowing, mentoring, school-based enterprise, or internship/apprenticeship) were about 30 percent less likely to drop out of high school than those youth who did not participate in work-based learning.

Thus, while students who self-identify as either a CTE concentrator or dual concentrator are neither more nor less likely to drop out of high school, youth who participated in career pathways or work-based learning were less likely to leave school before graduation.

CTE Practices that Reduce Dropout Rates

We now move the discussion from analyses of national data on youth and schools to examining the CTE-based practical techniques that engage students and minimize the chances of their leaving school before graduation.

Career Guidance

In addition to the research evidence supporting career pathways and work-based learning as important predictors in reducing dropouts, other studies have career guidance as an important factor as well. Hill and Bishop

(1993) found that students who decide to drop out of high school do not make academic plans to the same degree as other students, they choose a general track featuring survey courses, and work in jobs unrelated to their career goals. Woloszyk (1996) found that for vocational programs to be successful in retaining students, they must contain a comprehensive guidance program that helps students to identify and plan for postsecondary goals. Students must know that their ideas about their education are important so that they can feel some measure of control over their education and their futures.

In their study of career development strategies used by high schools, Dykeman, Herr, Ingram, Pehrsson, Wood, and Charles (2001) identified four basic types of career development interventions: advising interventions, introductory interventions, work-based interventions, and curriculum-based interventions. Their definitions indicate that the first two are closely related to the concept of career guidance.

In a 1995 study of twelve vocational sites, Hayward and Tallmadge (1995) identified counseling as a key component of successful efforts to reduce dropout rates. This counseling included not just guidance in identifying career and educational goals but also assistance in skills necessary for employment, such as interviewing and conflict resolution as well as life skills. Bragg (1997) found that of all the components of Tech Prep, assistance in school to work transitions rated second in importance. Also key were programs designed to improve decision-making skills, communication, and problem solving skills, all of which would fall within the area of guidance.

Using a guidance model including career interest inventories and job readiness training, one program was able to increase student retention in an at-risk population from below 50 percent to above 85 percent (Bauer & Michael, 1993). According to Imel (1993), students need help not only in applying for jobs, but also in such areas as following schedules and working with other people. Students may lack skills needed to understand their own emotions, making it difficult to work successfully with others.

While there is significant variation in the types of guidance systems provided in vocational programs successful at reducing dropout rates, it is clear that a guidance program is necessary. Some common components are as follows:

- **Academic planning counseling.** Students must feel that the high school activities they are engaged in are related to their goals.
- **Career counseling.** Whether they attend postsecondary education or move immediately to full-time employment, it is a primary goal of education to prepare students for career success.
- **Job location assistance.** Work-based learning is a key component of successful vocational programs, but for it to be successful in pre-

venting dropouts, students must be involved in work that is related to both their interests and their schoolwork.

♦ **College application assistance.** It is the high school's goal to prepare the student for whatever they will do after graduation, and for many students, this will be college.

Work-Based Learning

Work-based learning provides students with an opportunity to see the knowledge they have gained in the classroom put to use. Like comprehensive guidance systems, it is key to dropout prevention. Work-based learning is generally thought to include cooperative education, school-based enterprises, internships and apprenticeships, job shadowing, and mentoring. It is similar to the Dykeman et al. (2001) category of "work-based interventions," although the elements are defined more generally. Work-based learning works for some youth because it shows them how their school-based learning connects to the world outside of school. For other students, work-based learning may link to their career goals as well as their academic courses, and therefore, they see school as relevant to their lives (Woloszyk, 1996). For still others, especially those who may be planning for college, work-based education can allow them to become qualified for the jobs they would like to hold after graduation.

Cooperative education (coop ed) programs involve the cooperation of schools and businesses. Businesses work to train students for employment with the hope of eventually being able to hire the students as trained employees. Such programs ensure that students are adequately prepared for the workplace. Coop ed can be a cost-effective solution for both parties, with the companies training employees before they are hired and the schools receiving materials and instruction for which they do not have to pay. The emphasis on real-world skills and the possibility of using the coop ed experience as a transition to post–high school employment are both proven components of successful dropout prevention programs (Hayward & Tallmadge, 1995). About one million students each year spend part of their day at work and part in school as a cooperative effort, although this number includes fewer than 8 percent of adolescents (Stone, 1995).

School-based enterprises (SBE) are businesses that exist entirely within the school environment, although they may serve customers in the larger community. They may be located off school grounds, but they are school-owned. School-based enterprises may lack the real-life benefits of other forms of work-based learning, but they offer several distinct advantages. Because they occur within a school setting, all enterprise positions are available to students, rather than simply the entry-level ones. Students can move from job to job and experience all aspects of running a company. SBE programs have developed for a variety of reasons: to teach entrepreneurship, to provide application of classroom-developed skills, to enhance social and personal development, and to support economic development. SBEs may be more flexible about working with student needs and more closely linked to educational objectives. The protected environment is an ideal setting for students to learn employability skills (Stone & Madzar, 1993). This is a key component of dropout prevention programs

Internships and apprenticeships both occur within the community rather than the school. Students' interests are matched with the skills of community members. However, few students in the United States are offered that opportunity. Internships are more common and are frequently seen in both tech prep and career academy settings. Students receive school credit while working at jobs related to their educational goals. These programs are appropriate for older students who have identified a career focus and are willing to make a substantial time commitment (Stone & Mortimer, 1998). Having a clear career focus is a common trait of programs that reduce drop out rates (Crain et al., 1999).

Job shadowing is a practice that allows students to observe workplace activities. It is closely related to both internships and apprenticeships, but does not require the investment of time and resources of the previous programs. It is often used with younger students to help them identify their career interests and begin their career planning. Such an opportunity allows students to explore a variety of career options before focusing on one.

Mentoring as a work-based learning strategy is one of the critical components of a vocationally based dropout prevention plan, according to Hayward and Tallmadge (1995). In mentoring, a student is paired with an adult from the community who is involved in all aspects of their life. The adult not only serves as a career role model but also may help the student make academic and personal decisions. Mentoring is most effective when the mentor can relate to the student's experiences, although it serves primarily to provide the student with a supportive relationship with a caring adult.

While there are at least five types of work-based learning, in order to be effective, each must accomplish the following objectives.

- ◆ Link work-based learning directly to class activities. Students need to see the practical applications of their coursework.

- ◆ Link work-based learning directly to student goals. Students leave school because they do not see how it can help them achieve their goals.

- ◆ Prepare students for well-paying and attainable jobs. In order to succeed in the labor market, students must have skills that employers are seeking.

Career Pathways

Career pathways are one way of incorporating a vocational focus into a school. At the high school level, the curriculum in a career pathway is organized around a cluster of related careers. Sometimes referred to as a career major, this is closely related to the Career Academy model. Components of successful pathways or academies generally include, among other things, a strong link to area businesses and to life after high school in the world of work, in postsecondary education, or both. Career pathway programs work closely with local employers to provide students with internships and other forms of work-based learning that are directly related to their area of study. Career pathways are a recent addition to the educational options available and so have not yet been adequately evaluated (Castellano, Stringfield, & Stone, 2002). Until research on career pathways is available, we can best understand the programs by looking at their close relative, the Career Academy.

Career Academies are schools-within-schools formed around a specific career area. A subset of students and teachers are grouped together in the academy for a block of classes. This block of classes contains not only classes that would traditionally be seen as vocational, but also academic classes tailored to the focus of the academy. Career academies avoid the stigma of tracking by combining a strong academic program with a career focus in order to attract a wide range of students.

Because the career focus applies to all courses taught within the academies, there is a high degree of integration between the academic and vocational courses. Such integration helps students to see the courses as relevant to their goals, which is particularly important for at-risk youth who are less likely to recognize the value of school (Brown, 1998; Woloszyk, 1996). The high degree of integration inherent in the academy's common focus ensures that teachers can clearly elucidate the connections between schoolwork and career success.

In a study of a diverse group of career academies, Kemple and Snipes (2000) found that, for the students most at risk of dropping out, being enrolled in a career academy significantly decreased their chance of leaving before graduation. These same high-risk students also were absent less frequently and took more classes than their non-academy peers. Interestingly, the difference in course-taking was negligible in vocational areas. It was in academic areas that the career academy students showed a clear increase in course-taking. Kemple and Snipes attributed these differences not only to the strong career focus at the academies, but also to the close relationships developed between students and teachers.

Maxwell and Rubin (2001) found that students in career academies were 2.5 times less likely to drop out of high school than students with similar risk factors not enrolled in academies. Career academy students also had significantly higher GPAs. They concluded that the dropout reduction was due primarily to the improved GPAs of academy students, but were careful to state that this was due not to easier classes but rather to the strong emphasis on academics and the clear ties between the academic areas and the world of work.

Stern, Dayton, and Raby (2000) concluded that career academies combined several components key for success with at-risk students. The common focus of the academy provides students and teachers alike with a sense of belonging, while the strong academic focus encourages college-bound students who might otherwise not consider a program with a vocational emphasis to interact with students who do not consider themselves college bound.

It is clear that career academy programs, when properly implemented, engage students in school and may contribute to higher academic performance. Effective career academies share the following elements:

- School-within-a-school structure. Career academies must be separate from the larger school community.

- Joint planning time. A climate of cooperation and community among the teachers is key to an integrated curriculum.

- Strong academic program. It is through improved academic skills as well as vocational ones that students experience success.

- Comprehensive guidance system. Students at risk for dropping out of school need to see how the skills they learn in the academy can move them towards their goals.

Tech Prep

Similar to the career pathway model, the tech prep model has used what is known about vocational programs to create a system that combines strong academics with career training. Tech prep differs from other CTE programs in that it is directly connected to postsecondary education. The tech prep model generally assumes a four-year program, including the last two years of high school and two years of community college, although some programs may begin earlier in high school or be linked with a four-year college. Tech prep students are often able to get college credit for the classes that they take during high school, and the high school curriculum is developed with the goal of being an ideal preparation for the classes offered at the college level. Although tech prep programs generally lead to an associate's degree or a licensure, they do not preclude attending a four-year college. Students may move directly into a baccalaureate program after high school graduation or transfer to one after enrolling in a two-year program. Because tech prep programs generally begin in 11th grade and continue with at least two years of college, they are not as focused on dropout prevention as other programs. In addition, many tech prep programs have admission requirements, which insist on good attendance and so may not even accept those students most at risk for dropping out of high school. Nonetheless, tech prep's focus on integrating academics and vocational skills and its clear links to the world of work are both strategies common to successful dropout prevention programs.

Although there is some variety among tech prep programs, there are several essential components. In order to facilitate the college process, Bragg (2001) recommends that high school classes that are equivalent to ones offered at the college level classes should qualify for college credit. According to Bragg, students find the potential time and financial savings of tech prep programs appealing, but are often confused by the process and may not apply for college credits that they have legitimately earned in high school for fear that they are not adequately prepared. A streamlined articulation process would ensure that students received the credits they had earned and clarify the legitimacy of those credits.

It is important that the tech prep program is linked both in practice and in reputation with good jobs that pay well. If the program is seen as a stepping stone to a rewarding career, it will attract a wide range of students. The following practices are recommended when implementing a tech prep program:

- ◆ Preparation for a number of careers in one area of focus. This will allow program participants to prepare for a career that they find appealing.
- ◆ Alignment of the program with industry standards. After completion, graduates should be qualified for good jobs that pay well.
- ◆ Opportunities for students with varying skills and abilities. If tech prep is to serve as a dropout prevention technique, it must provide realistic opportunities for at-risk youth as well as for more successful students.

In conclusion, although the effects of Career and Technical Education on dropout rates are unclear, research has shown that certain aspects of CTE are effective in reducing dropout rates. Successful programs contain comprehensive guidance systems, work-based learning, and a career focus that leads to well-paying jobs. They must also remain free of the stigma that has historically been attached to vocational programs by offering strong academic components and preparing students for postsecondary education. These elements have made the career academy and tech prep models successful, and can be incorporated in other models for similar results.

References

Bauer, R., & Michael, R. (1993). *They're still in school: Results of an intervention program for at-risk high school students*. Paper presented at the annual meeting of the American Educational Research Association, Atlanta.

Bragg, D. D. (1997). *Educator, student, and employer priorities for Tech Prep student outcomes*. Berkeley, CA: National Center for Research in Vocational Education.

Bragg, D. D. (2001). *Promising outcomes for tech prep participants in eight local consortia: A summary of initial results*. Columbus, Ohio: National Dissemination Center for Career and Technical Education.

Brown, B. L. (1998). *Is vocational education working for high-risk populations? Myths and realities*. Retrieved June 9, 2003 from the ERIC Clearinghouse on Adult, Career, and Vocational Education web site: http://ericacve.org/docgen.asp?tbl=mr&ID=66.

Bureau of Labor Statistics (2003). *NLS Handbook, 2003*. Washington, DC: Author.

Castellano, M., Stringfield, S., & Stone, J. R., III. (2002). *Helping disadvantaged youth succeed in school: Second year findings from a longitudinal study of CTE-based whole-school reforms*. St. Paul, MN: National Research Center for Career and Technical Education.

Crain, R. L., Allen, A., Thaler, R., Sullivan, D., Zellman, G. L., Little, J. W., & Quigley, D. D. (1999). *The effects of academic career magnet education on high schools and their graduates*. Berkeley, CA: The National Center for Research in Vocational Education.

Dykeman, C., Herr, E. L., Ingram, M., Pehrsson, D., Wood, C., & Charles, S. (2001). *A taxonomy of career development interventions that occur in U.S. secondary schools*. Saint Paul, MN: National Research Center for Career and Technical Education.

Greene, J. P. (2001). *High school graduation rates in the United States* (Rev. ed.). New York: Black Alliance for Educational Options / Manhattan Institute.

Hayward, B. J., & Tallmadge, G. K. (1995). *Strategies for keeping kids in school: Evaluation of dropout prevention and reentry projects in Vocational Education*. Washington, DC: American Institutes for Research in the Behavioral Sciences / Research Triangle Institute / RMC Research Corp.

Hill, S. K., & Bishop, H. L. (1993). *A review of the literature regarding the impact of vocational education on student retention: A paper to support a research study regarding Georgia Secondary School Vocational instructors, Vocational Education supervisors, and principals*. (ERIC Document Reproduction Service No. ED 371 219)

Imel, S. (1993). *Vocational Education's role in dropout prevention*. Columbus, Ohio: ERIC Digest. (ERIC Document Reproduction Service No. ED355455).

Kemple, J. J., & Snipes, J. C. (2000). *Career academies: Impacts on students' engagement and performance in high school*. New York: Manpower Demonstration Research Corp.

Maxwell, N. L., & Rubin, V. (2001). *Career academy programs in California: Outcomes and implementation*. Berkeley, CA: California University, California Policy Research Center.

Plank, S. (2001). *Career and technical education in the balance: An analysis of high school persistence, academic achievement, and postsecondary destinations*. Saint Paul, MN: National Research Center for Career and Technical Education.

Silverberg, M., Warner, E., Goodwin, D., & Fong, M. (2002). *National Assessment of Vocational Education: Interim report to Congress*. Washington, DC: U.S. Department of Education.

Stern, D., Dayton, C., & Raby, M. (2000). *Career academies: Building blocks for reconstructing American high schools.* Berkeley, CA: California University, Berkeley Career Academy Support Network.

Stone, J. R. III. (1995). Cooperative vocational education in the urban school. *Journal of Education and Urban Studies, 27*(3), 313–327.

Stone, J. R., III, & Aliaga, O. A. (2002). *Career and Technical Education, career pathways, and work-based learning: Changes in participation 1997–1999.* Saint Paul, MN: National Research Center for Career and Technical Education.

Stone, J. R., III, & Madzar, S. (1993). School-owned and student operated enterprises. *Epsilon Pi Tau, 19*(2).

Stone, J. R. III, & Mortimer, J. T. (1998). The effect of adolescent employment on vocational development: Public and educational policy implications. *Journal of Vocational Behavior, 53,* 184–214.

U.S. Census Bureau (2003). *School enrollment—Social and economic characteristics of students: October 2000 (PPL-148).* Retrieved June 11, 2003 from the U.S. Census Bureau web site: http://landview.census.gov/population/socdemo/school/ppl-148/tab01.xls.

U.S. Department of Education (2003). *National Education Longitudinal Study of 1988.* Retrieved June 10, 2003 from the National Center for Education Statistics web site: http://nces.ed.gov/surveys/nels88/.

Woloszyk, C. A. (1996). *Models for at risk youth: Final report* (p. 106). Kalamazoo, MI: Upjohn Institute for Employment Research.

Conclusion and Recommendations

19

A Prescription
for America

Franklin P. Schargel

*In the 21st century, the education and skills of the workforce [will]
end up being the dominant competitive weapon.*

Lester C. Thurow

Introduction

Schools hold within their walls tomorrow's adults. If adults are to be responsible citizens, they must have knowledge of history and government. If they are to cherish the world's cultural heritage, they must understand and appreciate art, music, and literature. If they are to contribute to society in a positive way, they must learn to resolve conflict peaceably. If they are to be productive workers, they must master a broad array of academic and technical skills. A child who is to thrive in the world tomorrow must thrive in school today.

No one can project a complete picture of the future, but we know that income is directly proportional to educational attainment. As a society, we cannot afford to let a significant number of students drop out of school. How can America prosper if we waste our human resources? Our schools must graduate young people who are ready for jobs—including jobs that haven't been invented yet, and careers in companies manufacturing products that haven't been imagined yet. Of course, schools don't exist just to train workers—but they do bear responsibility for ensuring that everyone is prepared for the workforce.

Maintaining global competitiveness may well require raising educational standards. However, simply raising standards is futile unless we provide the means for all students to reach them. Economists at Cornell University and the University of Michigan found that increasing the number of course credits required for graduation would increase the dropout rate between 3 percent and 7 percent a year. This would mean that an additional 26,000 to 65,000 students would drop out annually ("Findings," 2000). The potential results for those students include poorer job prospects and lower lifetime earnings (Olson, 2000).

Conversely, lowering standards only hurts those whom we claim to be helping. In the short run, it may seem that placing underachieving students in less demanding courses will build their self-esteem. In the long run, such courses leave students unprepared for higher education or future employment. True achievement is the only solid foundation for self-esteem.

America's schools spend huge amounts on remediation of students who fail. For most students, however, remediation simply means repeating a grade or attending summer school—returning to the same system that failed to educate them in the first place, tackling the same material in the same way. Not surprisingly, many give up and drop out.

America will face many challenges in the coming decade. There is no greater challenge than its dropout problem. As policy makers seek to improve our school systems—by raising standards, by setting national and state goals, by improving the quality of schools and teachers—they must not lose sight of the fact that too many young people leave school before graduation. Because the jobs once available to people with low skills and minimum education have shifted to foreign countries in recent years; high school dropouts become a burden on communities, states, and the nation. If we do not find a way to keep students in school, the costs—for welfare, for medical care, for incarceration—will continue to mount.

Furthermore, American workers now compete for jobs in a global economy. National borders no longer limit domestic and multinational producers of goods and services. Companies can, and do, look to schools worldwide for graduates with a broad range of specialized skills in foreign languages, computer literacy, and technical knowledge. In the foreseeable future, the wealth of nations will be more clearly linked to knowledge than to a nation's raw material.

If America is to flourish in the twenty-first century, we must do a better job of educating *all* our children. As a first step, we must reject the notions that some children can achieve and others cannot, that some young people should attend college and others should not, that some students deserve to graduate and others do not. Dropping out is nondiscriminatory; its problems don't start or stop at the city line, the poverty line, or the color line. As long as we accept the myth that dropouts are inevitable, students will fall by the wayside. We must replace this long-ingrained myth with the new conviction that dropping out is unacceptable—an insidious disease that affects not only students, but also parents, teachers, and communities—*and we must act on that conviction.*

In this chapter, we offer bold prescriptions for action. We demand changes in the way schools work and in the way we treat students. We propose higher expectations for parents, for teachers, and for those who train and support our teachers. We challenge local, state, and federal leaders to set new priorities to match new educational standards and goals. We call on the business community and the media to promote student achievement. All of us must do our part. America's children deserve no less.

Schools

Schools should be as customer-driven as any successful business. Outside the school, today's young people are active—engaged in sports, at the computer, at work and at play. Schools must be equally engaging, exciting, and intellectually stimulating. Children are naturally motivated to learn, and most start school as active learners. But often as they progress through the system the responsibility for learning shifts, until by high school it is the teacher who is the worker. Too many high schools resemble factories where knowledge is poured into students like coal into a furnace or molten steel into a mold. Schools must treat students not as passive recipients of content, but as active participants in their own learning.

First of all, we must face the dropout issue. We must insist that all states track students from kindergarten through high school graduation. We must ensure that all school districts understand the importance of keeping students in school until they graduate. We must provide schools with the resources to tackle this urgent problem—keeping in mind that the place to start is in the primary and middle schools. We must offer incentives, not sanctions; it makes little sense to aid the schools that are succeeding while punishing the schools that are not able to meet their goals.

There is no shortage of creative, innovative ideas for school reform. We must choose the programs that work; we must implement the strategies that have proven their effectiveness.

- *Early education is effective.* We must fund preschool programs fully and make them available to all.

- *Mentoring is effective.* We must offer students personal direction in structured and supportive relationships.

- *Alternative education is effective.* We must implement programs that are open to a diversity of learning styles.

- *Professional development is effective.* We must train our teachers in the techniques they need to promote student achievement at a high level.

- *Individualized instruction is effective.* We must provide flexible learning opportunities for those who learn at a different pace.

- *Instructional technology is effective.* We must find ways to weave technology seamlessly into the teaching and learning process.

- *Community collaboration is effective.* We must link schools with partners outside the classroom that support the learning process.

- *Safe learning environments are effective.* We must provide a safe, supportive and nurturing school environment. We must recognize that many students bring problems to school, and help them deal with those problems.

These strategies and others—service learning, out-of-school enhancement, and career education—are familiar from earlier chapters. Of course, there is ample room for other creative ideas. Why not pay senior citizens a stipend to teach young children to read, or serve as mentors to teens? Why not link their computers to those in students' homes for after-school help with homework? Why not establish high schools that are open into the evening hours, so that students who must hold down paying jobs can continue their education? This will allow students to work, if they must, and attend school as well. In short—why not find ways to make schools work for *all* students?

Students

Too often, we speak of at-risk children as if they were responsible for the problems they face. We assume that our time-honored teaching methods must be correct; therefore, the students these methods fail to reach must be at fault. Students who struggle against the constraints of "one size fits all" education are identified as "at risk," with the entire stigma the label implies.

But the educational system doesn't fit all students; it never did. This often comes as a surprise to people who were a good match for the system as students (many of whom return to the system as teachers). Now that we know better, however, we must change our approach to the students in our schools.

Students and student learning must be at the center of what happens in school. For any task involving students, we must ask, "Does this add value to student learning?" (Frequent classroom interruptions don't add value. Physical education classes in which instructors throw balls to the assembled masses don't add value. Teachers who daily hand out unexplained worksheets do not add value. Unsupervised, unstructured study halls—though they may serve the school's scheduling program—don't add value.) Tasks that don't add value to student learning have no place in schools.

Schools must use a variety of techniques to find out what students know and can do. Assessment of student work must be valid, authentic, and continuous.

Students should no longer compete for grades against their peers. Instead, each student's academic growth should be measured against meaningful and relevant standards.

Individual education plan (IEP) teams must maintain high expectations for students with disabilities. Schools must see to it that vocational education, service learning, community work experience, and other programs help these students develop workforce skills and adult living skills.

Students must have a voice in the decision-making processes that affect their education. Confining students for six hours a day in a place where they do not want to be is ultimately a prescription for failure.

We know that retention in grade doesn't work. Rather than holding students back because they fail a single standardized test, we must identify students who are at risk of failing the test and build safety nets to support them.

While no conclusive evidence links exit examinations and increased drop out rates, we do know that the exams impose additional burdens on students and schools—too often without offering additional resources. We must take steps to ensure that exit examinations do not present one hurdle too many for students who already struggle in school.

Parents

In most cases, parents are their children's first and most significant teachers. They bear the primary responsibility for nurturing and guiding their sons and daughters from infancy through adolescence. Although they entrust schools with the education of their children, parents can certainly make a difference—after all, children spend 91 percent of their time under the influence of their parents and only 9 percent in school. We must teach parents how to encourage and support the learning process.

Statistics indicate that parental involvement diminishes as a child progresses through the educational system. Just when students need more support to overcome peer pressure, gangs, drugs and the media, parents become less involved. We must draw parents back into the school setting—and not merely as spectators or fund raisers. In this effort, schools must recognize the constraints on a parent's time. It makes little sense, for example, to schedule parent-teacher meetings at a time when parents have to be at work or tend to younger siblings.

Because parents of special education students play such a critical role in assisting their children, schools must open their doors to these parents, offering additional assistance as they establish strategies and methods to aid their children in making the transition from school to adult life.

Teachers

In the twenty-first century, information, knowledge, and technology will rule. Teachers continue to be purveyors of information, but because the amount of existing information now doubles every five years, teachers must also become enablers, giving students the techniques and tools to find information for themselves and the power to transform that information into knowledge.

Teachers must impart to students the skills of investigation and analysis, writing, mathematical reasoning, problem solving, and conflict resolution. They must develop confident and independent learners who can work alone or in groups to gather information, order it, manipulate it and apply it. And they must do this throughout the school, not just in the classrooms of innovative educators.

Teachers must embrace new methods. In too many of today's classrooms, nobody sees a student's written work except the teacher. Why not present an excellent paper to the class as a model of quality work?

Too often, teachers are evaluated on their teaching styles and techniques, rather than what students have learned. Why not change the emphasis and direction to place greater value on improved learning?

Too often, we send untrained and inexperienced teachers into schools with a high percentage of at-risk students. In most professions, novices start at positions with less responsibility and work their way up. In education, the opposite is true. Teachers tend to begin their careers in the most difficult of schools, working with the most challenged young people, with limited resources, in schools that are in desperate need of repair.

We must learn to recognize the signs that a student is at risk of lagging behind or dropping out. We must develop training materials and programs specifically geared toward identifying at-risk students early and responding appropriately. We must find mechanisms and direct funds to place our most innovative and experienced teachers in the schools with a high at-risk population.

We must change the way we educate educators. Too often, academicians without any recent classroom experience—and some who have never been in an American public school at all—are teaching our future teachers. The deans of our schools of education must meet with those in our K–12 system and jointly design programs to help *all* children to learn. We must create a seamless educational system from pre-K through the university—a system that fosters lifelong learning.

Doctors, dentists and other professionals continually upgrade their skills. Teachers should do no less. The teaching profession suffers from the common misperception that teachers only work when they are in front of a class. A professional teacher's workday must include time to collaborate with colleagues and explore new teaching methods. We must value lifelong learning as much for teachers as for students.

We must train our teachers to reach *all* learners. This takes time and effort, but our schools must strive to educate every child—not just those who cooperate and master material easily.

As educators, we must show students the relevance of what they learn. We must stop teaching bits and piece of information and start teaching how facts are connected to each other to produce a coherent body of knowledge. We must stop teaching "what to think" and start teaching "how to think"—how to solve problems, how to think creatively and analytically, how to work on teams.

Finally, we must coordinate our efforts. Too often, teachers, schools, and community organizations operate in virtual isolation. Educators from pre-kindergarten to college must recognize that we all belong to the same educational system. We must learn to work together for the benefit of all our students.

Government Leaders

Today's American society is enraptured with novelty. In many cases, this leads to grasping at straws—untried, untested, and nonreplicable models to "fix" our educational system. Politicians look for expedient answers that won't cost additional money and will be measured only after they have left office, or settle for short-term "solutions" that arise from shortsighted thinking.

America's leaders must give education the high priority it deserves. This means spending money. We must stop trimming school funding from local, state, and federal budgets. Schools cannot be expected to achieve the same or better results with less funding; children should not have to compete with municipal services for scarce community resources. Our actions must match our rhetoric. To propose improvements without funding them may make for excellent sound bites, but it does little to improve schools.

Legislators at both the state and the federal level must receive adequate and accurate data regarding dropout statistics. They need coherent and standardized information if they are to set priorities accurately, budget properly and demand accountability fairly.

Education reform must move to the top of our national agenda—above prisons, above highways. The federal government should join states in setting goals, developing performance standards, evaluating existing programs and disseminating results from successful schools and replicable model programs. This too will cost money.

Within the next decade, schools across America will need to replace most of their teacher and administrative staff. If these schools are to hire qualified people, they must be able to pay them salaries commensurate with their responsibilities and their education. (Astonishingly, some communities pay their sanitation workers more than they pay their educators.)

Our nation's educational infrastructure—buildings and grounds, electrical systems, plumbing, heating—also demands attention. Many of our schools were built in the early part of the last century. Some have only recently converted from coal heating. Our government leaders must find the money to upgrade these systems before a tragedy involving the death of children and teachers forces them to do so.

Some states already spend more money on prisons than on education. Data indicate that more than three-quarters of those in prison dropped out of school. When a society has the resources to incarcerate its young people but not to educate them, something is wrong. Education is a one-time cost; ignorance is a lifetime expense. If we can find the money for prisons, we can find the money for schools.

The goals of the No Child Left Behind legislation are admirable and nonarguable. However, unless we supply adequate financial and administrative support mechanisms, we will only add to the cost of schools without changing the outcome. We already know which students tend to do poorly on standardized tests; these are the same students who tend to drop out of school. We must ensure that new requirements help these students rather than victimizing them.

We must seek a single standard for academic success. The No Child Left Behind Act allows each state to write its own rules for applying the law's regulations and sanctions. As a result, nationwide comparisons are impossible. A school may be labeled "in need of assistance" according to New York's standards but escape that label in Arkansas. How can parents compare the success of programs in their state and a neighboring state?

The Business Community

Schools and businesses share a deep common interest in keeping students in school until they graduate. Students who drop out of school will have difficulty getting a job or sustaining a career. Too often, their options shrink to two socially costly and unproductive choices—crime or welfare. Conversely, businesses need active and intelligent employees who achieve to their maximum ability. When students fail to master the skills the workplace demands, the options of American businesses are limited. They can move elsewhere—an expensive proposition. They can "dumb down" their activities. Or they can work to improve the schools.

The business community must assume a more active role in schools. Although many business leaders lament the quality of workers schools produce, most never work closely with schools to define the skills they seek. Closer consultation, perhaps coupled with long-term hiring relationships, could benefit both schools and businesses. Business managers could bring the world of work into the school, introducing students to real-world skills like writing a résumé or conducting a job interview.

Some businesspeople have concluded that there is little correlation between grades and success in the business world. Few businesses ask for school transcripts or consult school officials about a prospective employee's attendance, tardiness, or academic achievement. This must change.

Education will be the cornerstone of economic success in the twenty-first century. If American business is to thrive in the world marketplace, it must focus on creating a world-class public education system. Many foreign students compete to attend America's highly acclaimed colleges and universities. Few, if any, come to this country expressly to attend our public schools. Primary and secondary schools serve far more students than colleges and universities do, and spending money on the early grades is by far the most cost-effective way to raise student achievement levels. Yet businesses, foundations, and other organizations lavish funds on college and universities while ignoring the needs of the public schools that underpin our nation's educational system.

The business community has much to gain when public schools thrive. Too often, educators have one agenda, politicians another, and businesspeople yet a third. We challenge America's educational and business organizations—the National Education Association, the American Federation of Teachers, the American Society for Quality, the National Alliance for Business, the AFL/CIO, and the National Association of Manufacturing, to name a few—to form a coalition to address the essential task of strengthening public education.

The Media

Today's media largely promote values that are in many ways contrary to the values of families, schools, and society in general. Television, radio, Hollywood, the music industry, and the world of professional sports glorify instant gratification, material possessions, glamour, beauty, wealth, celebrity, entertainment, drugs, alcohol, and violence, while giving scant attention to education, community service, conflict resolution, respect for diversity, commitment, hard work, and responsibility. Against this vast and relentless current, schools must exert an enormous effort if they are to maintain the principles and values that support educational achievement for all. We call on the media to acknowledge a greater responsibility for forming the character of America's young people in a way that benefits our society. They must be as dedicated to this as they are to making a profit.

The Rest of Us

We must realize that education is not a science. What worked ten or twenty years ago may not work today. What works for one group of students may not work for all. We must be flexible in our teaching and learning techniques. We must encourage teachers and administrators to take risks, to challenge the philosophy that "this is how I learned; this is how I teach."

We must overcome complacency about our schools. Our own children may have good teachers; our own community may have good schools; our own state may have good standards and good accountability. But that is not enough. We must work to ensure that *all* our nation's children have good teachers, *all* communities have good schools, and *all* states have good standards and good accountability. We must insist that full education and high achievement are goals that *all* can reach.

If we as a nation are truly committed to leaving no child behind, we must encourage our representatives at the state and federal levels to increase school funding, put highly qualified individuals into classrooms and school administrative offices, and fully fund early childhood programs for all qualified children.

As we have seen, education is also an economic issue. We must measure our schools against the world's best. Our nation's workforce competes in a global marketplace. At the top of the scale, American businesses demand well trained, technologically prepared employees. If they cannot find them at home, they will look elsewhere. Likewise, the world is full of low-skilled, low-wage workers. The job market for young people who drop out of school today is limited at best. To maximize the potential of our nation's human resources, we must work to ensure that all our students stay in school—and all succeed.

Educational change is inevitable. We must not tolerate a public school system that does not function as it should. The question is not whether to reform our public schools, but how? And who will be the driving force behind this change? Parents, businesspeople, political leaders, and educators all have a stake in school reform. All of us must rise to the challenge.

One thing is abundantly clear: America will never reach its full potential unless its public school system does the same. Public education is the key to economic development. American society faces many problems—welfare, health costs, substance abuse, crime, poverty. As we work to solve each of these problems, we encounter the need for better education and dropout prevention. As we work to improve our educational system and keep students in school, we begin to address these pressing social concerns as well.

Education is America's great liberator. The ability of children to get a better education than their parents has always opened doors to upward mobility. Success in our economic system largely depends on success in our educational system. But the 2000 census data indicate that more and more Americans are slipping into poverty—nearly 1.7 million in the last year alone. Poverty rates are rising among African-Americans, Hispanics, rural residents, and the young. About 12.1 million children live in poverty. Their best hope—and our best hope for our communities—lies in a robust education.

If the nation's graduation rate does not improve, the economic consequences of an uneducated workforce will strain the economy of the United States. We–that is governors, mayors, school boards, superintendents, and schools of education, must do better.

Efforts to strengthen our schools and keep students at school until they graduate may seem a daunting task, even a burden. But we as a nation can bear this burden if we share it. All of us—educators at all levels, parents, businesspeople, politicians—have a stake in the outcome.

In this book, we have shown that solving the school dropout problem is an essential component of school reform. We have outlined fifteen effective strategies for dropout prevention, ranging from early education and family involvement, through professional development and individualized instruction, to community collaboration and career education. We have described individual programs that have implemented these strategies with noteworthy success. Each strategy can make a difference on its own; applied in a concerted effort; the fifteen strategies are a powerful force.

Explore these strategies; put them to work. Start somewhere, and start soon. America's future depends on each of us.

References

Olson, Lynn. (2000). Study links dropout rate with course requirements. *Education Week*, March 29, p. 6.

Findings. (2000, May). *Teacher Magazine*.

Thurow, L. C. (1992). *Head to head: The coming economic battle among Japan, Europe, and America*. New York: William Morrow and Company.

Meet the Contributing Authors

Terry Cash, assistant director of the National Dropout Prevention Center (NDPC), has significant experience working with special education programs at the elementary and secondary levels. Dr. Cash was principal of three alternative schools in North Carolina and South Carolina that served students with severe emotional disabilities. He developed a unique secondary after-school program designed to provide a less restricted environment for students with severe behavior and emotional disabilities. Before coming to the NDPC as assistant director, Dr. Cash served as director of volunteerism and mentoring at the South Carolina Department of Education, where he provided training and technical assistance to school districts across the state that were interested in developing mentoring and volunteer programs for behaviorally and emotionally disturbed students.

Sam F. Drew, Jr. has been the associate director of the National Dropout Prevention Center since 2002. His career in education spans 34 years, with positions at the local, state, and federal levels. He has been a teacher, school principal, and superintendent of a countywide school system in South Carolina. Dr. Drew worked as a special assistant in the United States Department of Education and as deputy director of education in the South Carolina Governor's Office. He served as state director of adult education in South Carolina for eight years before joining the Adult Literacy Media Alliance in New York as director of state partnership development. Dr. Drew holds a B.S. in psychology, an M.Ed. in elementary education, and a Ph.D. in educational administration from the University of South Carolina.

Marty Duckenfield is the public information director for the National Dropout Prevention Center in the College of Health, Education, and Human Development, Clemson University. In this role, she oversees all their publications: newsletters, books, and journals. Since 1993, she has coordinated all Center service-learning initiatives, including the Center's role as the regional partner in the former National Service-Learning Cooperative/Clearinghouse and the current National Service-Learning Exchange. She also serves on the board of directors for the International Center for Service-Learning in Teacher Education. She received her bachelor's degree in history from Bates College, her master's degree in nutritional science from Clemson University, and is a former classroom teacher.

Patricia Cloud Duttweiler served as assistant director of the National Dropout Prevention Center from 1992 until 2001. During this time she was the senior evaluator for the NDPC, overseeing third-party evaluations, conducting Program Assessment and Review (PAR) processes, and coordinating grants and research projects. Dr. Duttweiler has a B.A. in sociology, an M.Ed. in social science education, and an Ed.D. in adult education from the University of Georgia. Before joining the National Dropout Prevention Center, she was assistant director for research at the South Carolina Center for the Advancement of Teaching and School Leadership at Winthrop College in Rock Hill, South Carolina; a senior research associate with the Southwest Educational Development Laboratory (SEDL) in Austin, Texas; a training evaluation specialist with the University of Georgia Center for Continuing Education; and a classroom teacher.

Donna Foster currently serves as Developmental and Transitional Studies department chair at Piedmont Technical College in Greenwood, South Carolina. She joined Piedmont Technical College as developmental mathematics coordinator in 1992. Mrs. Foster earned a B.S. in science teaching, mathematics in 1983 and an M.Ed. in secondary education in 1985 from Clemson University. She has presented numerous workshops on active learning strategies and coauthored *Cooperation in the Classroom*. Her honors include selection as the 1996 South Carolina Governor's Professor of the Year in the two-year college division.

Bryan Fox is the senior research assistant at the National After-School Resource Network. He is currently pursuing a doctorate in motor development at the University of South Carolina. Before returning to school, Bryan ran an outpatient program targeting adolescents with substance abuse issues for eight years. Building on his clinical work, he continues to search for opportunities to help kids reach their potential.

Linda B. Gambrell is professor and director of the Eugene T. Moore School of Education at Clemson University. Before coming to Clemson University she was associate dean for research at the University of Maryland, where she taught graduate and undergraduate reading and language arts courses. Dr. Gambrell began her career as an elementary classroom teacher and reading specialist in Prince George's County, Maryland. She has written books on reading instruction and articles published in journals such as *Reading Research Quarterly, The Reading Teacher, Educational Psychologist,* and *Journal of Educational Research.* Her current interests are in the areas of reading comprehension strategy instruction, literacy motivation, and the role of discussion in teaching and learning.

Karen L. Mapp is the president of the Institute for Responsive Education (IRE). Dr. Mapp joined IRE in 1997 as project director for the Boston Community Partners for Students' Success initiative, which focused on the development of activities and programs to familiarize parents with the recently established Boston Citywide Learning

Standards. Dr. Mapp holds a doctorate and master's of education from Harvard University in administration, planning, and social policy, a master's in counselor education from Southern Connecticut State University, and a bachelor's degree in psychology from Trinity College in Hartford, Connecticut. She is the author of "Making the Connection between Families and Schools," published by the Harvard Education Letter (1997); *A New Wave Of Evidence: The Impact of School, Family and Community Connections on Student Achievement*, published by the Southwest Educational Development Laboratory and coauthored with Anne T. Henderson; and "Having Their Say: Parents Describe How and Why They Are Engaged in Their Children's Learning," in *The School Community Journal* (2003).

Terry Peterson is the only American who served as the chief education advisor for a governor and a United States Secretary of Education—in each case for eight years and in each case for Dick Riley. Always searching for "what works," he has visited almost 1,000 educational institutions covering almost every state and 15 countries. He has taught at all levels of education, from health (in Portuguese, in the jungles of Brazil) to high school chemistry in the first years of school integration and later, statistics at the university level. He has also been the executive director of a state business-education oversight committee and assistant to a university president. Dr. Peterson is currently the U.S.C. Educational Foundation Senior Fellow for Policy and Partnerships and holds a similar position at the College of Charleston. He recently won a million-dollar grant from the Mott Foundation to start a National After-School Resource Network.

Mary Reimer is the information resource consultant on the staff of the National Dropout Prevention Center at the College of Health, Education, and Human Development, Clemson University. Dr. Reimer holds a master's degree in library science from Kent State University and a Ph.D. in curriculum and instruction from Clemson University. A librarian for over 20 years, with an extensive background in social science educational literature research and school improvement strategies, she currently manages the NDPC/N web site.

Linda J. Shirley has been the special projects coordinator at the National Dropout Prevention Center since 1987. With a master's degree in industrial education and a B.A. in elementary education from Clemson University, she has been an educator for more than thirty years. She has conducted numerous staff development activities and is the author of several publications, including *The Pocket Guide to Multiple Intelligences* and *The Facilitator's Guide—Integrative Learning: An Active Approach to Learning*. She was the principal developer of a cooperative learning game titled MI Game, in which participants have an opportunity to apply the Theory of Multiple Intelligences to real classroom settings. She has worked with the South Carolina Advanced Technological Education Grant from the National Science Foundation to assist community college faculty from across the states of South Carolina and Texas in implementing multiple intelligences and active learning into the classroom. She serves as project director of a grant to expand the teaching skills of childcare providers in Pickens County, South Carolina.

Robert Shumer is the former director of field studies at the University of California, Los Angeles (UCLA) and former director of the National Service-Learning Clearinghouse and Research Center for Experiential Learning and Service-Learning at the University of Minnesota. He has taught courses on research, youth development, and experiential learning for 15 years. Dr. Shumer holds a B.A. in history from UCLA, an M.A. in educational psychology from California State University, and a Ph.D. in Education from UCLA. He is currently conducting research in Pennsylvania, Mississippi, Connecticut, and New York on youth programs that connect schools with communities. His current interest is in youth as evaluators.

Dolores (Dee) Stegelin is an associate professor of early childhood education in the Eugene T. Moore School of Education at Clemson University. Dr. Stegelin is facilitating the development of an expanded undergraduate and graduate early childhood teacher education program at Clemson. She is the author of four textbooks and numerous professional articles. Her research interests include early literacy, public policy, inclusion of children with disabilities, public school early childhood programs, the Reggio Emilia approach, and parent involvement. Dr. Stegelin is active in the National Association of Early Childhood Education, the National Association of Early Childhood Teacher Educators, the Association of Childhood Education International, and the American Educational Research Association, all at the national level. She is the public policy chair for the South Carolina Association for the Education of Young Children and is active in several state-level professional education organizations. She is also involved in the research and instructional dimensions of the *First Steps to School Readiness* early childhood program in South Carolina.

Ronald D. Stephens currently serves as executive director of the National School Safety Center. His past experience includes service as a teacher, assistant superintendent, and school board member. Administrative experience includes serving as a chief school business officer, with responsibilities for school safety and security, and as vice president of Pepperdine University. His undergraduate and graduate degrees are in the field of business management; he received his doctorate from the University of Southern California. Dr. Stephens holds the California teaching credential and administrative credential as well as the Certificate in School Business Management. Dr. Stephens has appeared on every major television network, including the *Today Show, Good Morning America, Jim Lehrer News Hour, Oprah,* and CNN. Dr. Stephens has conducted more than 1,000 school security and safety site assessments throughout the United States. Described by the Denver Post as "the nation's leading school crime prevention expert," he is the author of numerous articles on school safety as well as the author of *School Safety: A Handbook for Violence Prevention.*

James R. Stone III is the director of the National Research Center for Career and Technical Education at the University of Minnesota. An associate professor in the department of Work, Community and Family Education, Dr. Stone earned his B.S. and Ed.D. at Virginia Polytechnic Institute and State University and a master's in school administration at George Mason University; he also taught secondary marketing education in Virginia. Dr. Stone has directed or co-directed ten national CTE studies. Currently he is co-director of a study examining CTE-based, whole school reforms in schools serving disadvantaged youth. He has authored or coauthored more than 60 research reports, journal articles, and books and presented more than 150 papers, speeches, and workshops. He has served on the editorial board and as editor of the *Journal of Vocational Education Research*. Dr. Stone has worked with Oakland Public Schools (California) helping to implement a community-based school-to-work plan that included career academy development and school-based enterprise and with a Minneapolis high school developing a program for American Indian urban youth.

Deborah M. Switzer is an associate professor in the Eugene T. Moore School of Education, where she has taught since 1990. She received her undergraduate degree in mathematics from the University of Texas and her master's and doctorate in educational psychology from the University of Illinois. Her first teaching job was in a schoolwide program of individualized instruction, teaching secondary mathematics and computer science. Dr. Switzer has been named a distinguished professor by the South Carolina Commission on Higher Education and an outstanding faculty member in teaching in the School of Education. She was honored with the 2003 Prince Award for Innovation in Teaching. Her research expertise includes learning and instructional theory, assessment, and research design. She has collaborated with faculty in engineering, psychology, education, recreation, counseling, public health, and business.

Ted Wesley is a research associate with the National Dropout Prevention Center. He has performed educational research addressing program effectiveness, equity, and teachers' technology adoption in public schools. Dr. Wesley has served as a university administrator and as project officer for the Youth Opportunities Unlimited Alternative School project for the state of Mississippi. He has performed evaluation research in the fields of education, alternative schools, community mental health, and community economic development. Dr. Wesley has a Ph.D. in educational leadership with technology emphasis and an M.S. in industrial/organizational psychology. He has been involved in the use of technologies in teaching youth and adults since 1982. His primary interests in educational technology combine focuses on the psychology of teacher adoption of technology, self-organizing system dynamics in school organizational change with technology integration in education, and the use of advanced technologies for meeting diverse learning needs.